Good footpath
(sufficiently distinct to be followed in mist)

Intermittent footpath
(difficult to follow in mist)

Route recommended
    but no path
(if recommended one way only, arrow indicates direction)

Wall ∞∞∞∞∞∞∞   Broken wall ∘∘∘∘∘∘∘∘∘∘∘

Fence ++++++++++++   Broken fence ::::::::::::::

Marshy ground ⅄⅄⅄⅄⅄   Trees 🌳🌳🌳🌳

Crags 🪨🪨🪨   Boulders ∘∘∘∘∘

Stream or River
        (arrow indicates direction of flow)

Waterfall   Bridge

Buildings ▪▪▪   Unenclosed road ::::::::::::::

Contours (at 100' intervals)   1900
                                1800
                                1700

Summit-cairn ▲   Other (prominent) cairns △

Wainwright's TV Walks
Second Edition

Wainwright's TV Walks

BBC4/BBC2 *Wainwright Walks* – Series 1

Haystacks from Gatesgarth
Blencathra via Sharp Edge
Scafell Pike via Esk Hause
Castle Crag from Borrowdale

BBC4/BBC2 *Wainwright Walks* – Series 2

Helvellyn via Striding Edge
Catbells from Hawse End
High Street from Mardale Head
Bowfell via Crinkle Crags from Langdale
Helm Crag from Grasmere
Pillar from Black Sail

Granada Television *Wainwright Country*

Stybarrow Dodd from Sticks Pass
Thornthwaite Crag from Hartsop
Eagle Crag from Stonethwaite
Pike o' Blisco from Wrynose
Great Calva via Whitewater Dash
Knott Rigg and Ard Crags from Newlands Hause
Yewbarrow from Overbeck Bridge

ITV (1990s) *Wainwright's Remote Lakeland*

Stickle Pike from Broughton Mills

Wainwright's
TV Walks
Second Edition

Introduced
by Eric Robson

FRANCES LINCOLN

Frances Lincoln Limited, 4 Torriano Mews, Torriano Avenue, London NW5 2RZ
www.franceslincoln.com

The Pictorial Guides to the Lakeland Fells published by Frances Lincoln 2003
This anthology first published by Frances Lincoln 2007
Second edition of this anthology published by Frances Lincoln 2010

Publisher's Note
The fell pages in this book are taken from the Second Edition of A. Wainwright's
Pictorial Guides to the Lakeland Fells, comprehensively revised and updated by
Chris Jesty. For further information on the Second Edition of Wainwright's
Pictorial Guides see page 10.

Please bear in mind that fellwalking can be dangerous, especially in wet, windy,
foggy or icy conditions. Be sure to take sensible precautions when out on the fells.
As Wainwright himself frequently wrote: use your common sense and watch
where you are putting your feet.

Printed and bound in China

A CIP catalogue record is available for this book from the British Library.

ISBN 978 0 7112 3121 4

9 8 7 6 5 4 3 2 1

Contents

Preface

I'm not quite sure what suddenly made Alfred Wainwright television's flavour of the month. Maybe it was the fiftieth anniversary of the first publication of his Pictorial Guides to the Lakeland Fells. Maybe it was the centenary of his birth. Maybe it was public demand. But I doubt it. That cuts very little ice when television commissioning editors are deciding what we should watch on the box.

Whatever sparked the interest, television planners had managed very happily without the help of Mr Wainwright since the late 1980s. That was when I was involved in several BBC series with him – the first he'd ever agreed to do. The programmes introduced him to an audience beyond the fell walking fraternity. Showed a shy, thoughtful man – scarcely a household name – who had apparently, inexplicably, sold more than a million books. A television oddity. Even odder, the programmes pulled a big audience.

For anyone unacquainted with the man his fans know simply as A.W., Alfred Wainwright was born in Blackburn on January 17th, 1907. He loved his mother and his father was an alcoholic. He stuck in at school and got a job in the Borough Treasurer's office. His working life was, by most standards, humdrum although he didn't think of it that way. He loved the order to be found in a well-kept balance sheet. But hardly the stuff of prime-time television so far. His first marriage was unhappy and eventually he was divorced. It was a big deal for him and Ruth and his son but unremarkable to anyone else. It certainly didn't make him a must-have for tabloid TV.

But what made A. Wainwright different from the run of balance sheet clerks and elderly divorced men was a different sort of love affair that began on a day in 1930. That was when he first visited the Lake District. He walked out to a high point above Windermere and looked across at the mountains. It was a view that changed his life. He determined to explore every corner of that landscape. Shortly after that first visit, he got a job in Kendal as an accountancy assistant and eventually worked his way up to Borough Treasurer. Predictable and ordinary. How could you make a television programme from any of that? But by night Wainwright was making magic, sitting in his little office at home, writing and drawing the idiosyncratic books that would introduce many thousands of people to the Lakeland summits and the joys and challenges of fell walking. He produced seven Pictorial Guides which revolutionised the interpretation of the fells. He was awarded an MBE. He appeared on *Desert Island Discs* and he died in 1991. And then there was silence. Wainwright had apparently melted away to where he was always happiest. Into the heart of the lonely mountains.

And then suddenly he was back. Out of nowhere, BBC4 produced a biography programme and Julia Bradbury presented some of his favourite walks. The programmes were repeated on BBC2 and were so successful that a second series of walks was immediately commissioned. Granada decided to celebrate his life, too, in a series called *Wainwright Country*, presented by Fred Talbot. Thousands of people were introduced to Wainwright's work for the first time and they saw in it a message that chimed with very modern concepts of environmental awareness.

Suddenly, Wainwright wasn't so much of an oddity after all. People were saying what his dedicated fans had known for years, that he was ahead of his time. His message was of sustainability and personal responsibility and care for fragile landscapes long before those arguments were dominating the environmental agenda. For a big man he even had a very small carbon footprint (even though the phrase hadn't been invented at the time) because he made most of his visits to the mountains by public transport in the form of a Ribble bus.

Of course, there have been changes in the Lakeland landscape since Wainwright's time and they continue to happen, some subtle, some dramatic. They're not the damaging consequences for which some detractors blamed him after he died.

They said that his books were attracting too many people with too little soul; people who couldn't possibly appreciate Lakeland the way 'we' do. And, yes, there are more people venturing onto the hills these days, but not so many more, and there's still a lot of space out there on the mountain tops. When we're filming on and around even the most popular summits we still have very little trouble taking shots with no people in them.

The changes have come from other quarters. For many years it was said that the Lakeland tops were overgrazed. Initiatives such as the Environmentally Sensitive Areas Scheme dramatically reduced the number of sheep on the fells. Foot and mouth finished the job. The unintended result is that there are now tracts of fell where the grass is so strong the sheep will no longer eat it. It grows on and harbours the pioneer species that will eventually turn open moorland to scrub. Now, that may be a thoroughly good thing. Perhaps some of the tops should be allowed to return to a sort of scrubby wilderness. There's an environmental argument that such a landscape would be more species-rich, an improvement on what we have now – what some naturalists describe as a wet desert. But do the people who walk the fells in Wainwright's footsteps want that? Do they want the landscape to change in that way? Who knows. What I'm suggesting, as Wainwright the environmentalist suggested all those years ago, is that there ought to be a debate about how we manage these precious places, a debate involving all of us. There may well be good reasons for farming the bog asphodel rather than the Herdwick sheep but let's talk about it.

At the same time we should be debating not just 'how' but 'who' is going to manage these places on our behalf. At present most of it is managed by fell farmers, but upland farming is in decline. Wasdale and Eskdale are no longer, to use the European jargon, 'severely disadvantaged' or even 'less favoured areas' compared with bits of Romania. It's time we realised that the farmers of Lakeland do a valuable job on our behalf, a job that needs to be paid for. Landscape needs managing and management costs money. One word bedevils the argument – subsidy. Why is it that a million pounds of government money ploughed into a micro-chip plant that never opens its doors is 'investment', while a few thousands given to a farmer who manages a chunk of Borrowdale or Langdale is 'subsidy' with all its connotations of something for nothing and featherbedded farmers?

There are other changes happening, too, and they may be even harder to come to terms with and find answers to. I've no idea if we're seeing climate change or merely a cyclical weather pattern but in some places the Lake District is drying up. Mountain streams which were merrily gurgling becks in Wainwright's time are now half their size, bogs have turned to dust.

So television's renewed interest in Wainwright territory after a break of twenty years or so is timely. It gives us a chance to re-evaluate his ideas. Hopefully it will also encourage a wider audience to engage in a debate about how we want the world-class Lakeland landscapes he described to look in the eyes of another generation.

Wainwright's TV Walks SECOND EDITION

Wainwright's Pictorial Guides have been prized by walkers for half a century and more. But over the years since his books were devised countless changes have taken place on the fells. Paths have appeared or vanished; trees have been felled and planted; gates, stiles, walls, fences, signs and recommended routes have inevitably changed, in some cases drastically. This collection makes use of pages from the Second Edition of the Pictorial Guides which have been thoroughly and almost invisibly updated by Chris Jesty to take account of these changes. Thousands of revisions to the original text and maps have been incorporated and paths and routes have been picked out in red to make them easier to see. Wherever possible, car parking and campsite information has also been included.

Introduction

Somebody once sent me a videotape of a 'revolutionary' new walking programme. According to the notes on the sleeve it was the answer to all armchair fell walkers' prayers. It broke the mould of television as we'd hitherto known it. It captured the very essence of the exploration of the hills. No distractions, no irrelevant shots, no commentary and certainly no music.

I almost committed it to the grey repository of mould-breaking revolutionary concepts that sits under my desk but for some reason (perhaps that I was doing my VAT returns or some such) I put it in the video player instead. What appeared was a continuous shot from a home movie camera held to the walker's eye as he headed, I think, for Scafell. And it carried on that way for an hour and a half as the one-eyed walker stumbled his way ever upwards. I have to say it wasn't gripping. As I remember, the most exciting bits were occasional glimpses of toe ends and encounters with bemused Herdwick sheep whose expressions indicated that their attitudes to the shambling cameraman and mine were remarkably similar.

It was so bad it was compulsive viewing. I started to be drawn in to the hypnotic meanderings. Perhaps it was installation art. Turner with altitude. Maybe it was a surreal commentary on man's uncertain relationship with landscape. And, hey, just think how much I could be saving on camerawork and editing.

Into the bin it went.

I only mention this failed attempt at capturing the spirit of the mountains because, when you think of it, even well-produced walking programmes are a strange thing to make. The charm of hill walking is surely that it brings together a whole range of sensations and challenges – the feel and smell of the weather; the texture of the ground; scree shifting in the silence; knees and lungs protesting; the spirits of the generations that moulded the landscape who travel with you, quarrymen and miners and farmers. Pretty views, the stock in trade of fell walking programmes, are only part of it. And arguably not the most important part.

Of course the most serious fault of most walking programmes is the pretence that the presenter is out there on his or her own. Presenters actually have the easy end of it. All they have to carry to the top of the hill is a packet of sandwiches, a handful of research notes and a hair brush. Tramping up behind them is a cameraman carrying a 56-lb pack of equipment, a sound recordist with 20 or 30 lbs of electronics and probably a sherpa (rarely Nepalese these days) lugging the tripod which is a particularly numb piece of kit. As the years have gone on, I've stopped pretending the crew isn't there and their noises off have enlivened many a dreary trudge.

Before I talk myself out of a job, though, let me say that fell walking programmes are hugely popular. In recent years all the major television channels have made them and many of them have achieved record audiences. Some people watch to remind themselves of walks they once did, places they visited when they were younger and sprightlier. Others tune in to get ideas of new places to explore and to see how tough, how satisfying, the route's likely to be before they try it themselves. There's a fair bit of incipient sadism lurking in the audience, too. I can guarantee that the programmes which get the very best response are the ones where the presenter is being rain-lashed on some God-forsaken moor while at the same time stumbling face first into a peat hag. Gosh, that makes people laugh, egged on, of course, by a chortling crew.

When I made my first fell walking programmes in the 1980s they were rather more of a gamble. Television commissioning editors took some persuading that a chap wandering up a hill would be more exciting than the potter's wheel or the test card, come to that. The fact that most such editors operated out of the challenging landscapes of places like

London W12 meant that mountains were something of a mystery to them. The attitudes of the age of the picturesque seemed to persist. They'd read somewhere that the Lake District was 'beauty in the lap of *horreur*' and why would anybody in their right senses want to go wandering about in the accursed mountains? (At times you got the impression they were mixing up Lakeland with Albania.) It couldn't possibly be safe. There would be insurance issues. More to the point, even if I was mad as a ferret and chose to blunder about on Crinkle Crags, why would anybody else want to watch me do it?

Fortunately we had an ally that even the commissioning editor in far-away White City had heard of – A Wainwright.

* * *

Wainwright was a rare bird – a Borough Treasurer turned phenomenon. Born in back-to-back Blackburn, the son of an itinerant stonemason (more itinerant than stonemason as it turned out), he discovered the joy and release of fell walking in early expeditions into the low hills around Nelson and Darwen. But then, one day in 1930 at the age of twenty-three, he took the Ribble bus from Blackburn to Kendal. He walked out to Orrest Head above Windermere and was hooked.

'I had seen landscapes of rural beauty pictured in the local art gallery, but here was no painted canvas; this was real. This was truth. God was in his heaven that day and I a humble worshipper.'

In truth he never left the Lake District again, and when he was forty-five he started on the project that would make him Britain's best known fell walker by a mile. He gave himself thirteen years to finish the seven volumes of his Pictorial Guides to the Lakeland Fells. He finished them one week ahead of schedule – just before the end of the summer bus timetable in 1966. Wainwright never had benefit of a car until he married his second wife, Betty. She once told me, not entirely in jest, that it was the prospect of having a chauffeur that swung it.

Wainwright's first marriage had been claustrophobic and unhappy. Obsessive as he was about his books he must have been a joy to live with, spending every weekend in the hills and every evening writing up the results. But Betty brought a sparkle of adventure and happiness into his life. More than that, in her company he actually found a life away from his pen and his desk. Betty shared his love of the mountains and Wainwright now had time to savour them in her company, unshackled from the self-imposed deadlines that had driven the great project.

He died a happy man. I don't know if he got his wish – to be soaring on angel wings above Great Gable (they would have to be a fair set of wings because he was a big chap) – but the Wainwright legacy is beyond dispute. Yes, there had been guide books for ever more, ever since Wordsworth's time, but none like his. He read and reported the landscape better than anyone. He opened up the Lakeland mountains to people who, until then, had thought they were beyond them. He liberated tens of thousands of amateur explorers.

When he died, a few critics came out of the woodwork – generally people who hadn't been brave enough to give mouth while he was still alive. They said that Wainwright's real legacy was that he'd killed the goose that laid the golden eggs; that he'd encouraged too many people of the wrong sort to clutter up the Lakeland mountains. Well, leaving aside the fact that 'the wrong sort of people' is a profoundly worrying phrase because it could so easily be applied to you and me, there are a few people ahead of Wainwright in encouraging greater use of the high, wild places of Lakeland. I'll offer just two. There was Margaret Thatcher who blessed us with so much more leisure time by throwing thousands of people out of work. And there was the man who designed the M6 motorway and by doing so brought the conurbations of Lancashire within day trip distance of the Lake District.

Yes, the mountains are busier now than they were when A.W. set off on his solitary exploration. Yes, there are tourist honeypots, as there are in every world-class landscape. Everest isn't exactly deserted. But there's still plenty of space out there. On many of the filming days for the walks that feature in this book we saw hardly anyone. During the filming of *Wainwright's Remote Lakeland* we saw other walkers on just two out of the twelve filming days. We saw more visitors when we were filming the series with Wainwright himself in the 1980s, but I suspect that was because the bush telegraph was at work. In fish-and-chip shops across the north of England the word was out. 'Wainwright's going to be at Black Sail on Tuesday.'

* * *

When it came to the filming of the very first Wainwright programme it wasn't supposed to be me.

One way of sliding a difficult programme under the viewer's nose is to get a celebrity to present it. Some things never change. And fell walking being perceived as a difficult programme to sell to the audience, big names were suggested. 'Melvyn Bragg's your man, or Chris Bonington. They're both Lake District sort of chaps, aren't they? Should know their Bow Fell from their elbow,' sort of thing. Fortunately for me Mr Wainwright wasn't having any of it. He put his scuffed boot down at the suggestion he'd have to work with 'television types', the phrase spoken with more than a hint of Borough Treasurer's disgust.

The person who managed to persuade the solitary, obsessive A. Wainwright to abandon his principles and even consider supping with the devils of television was Richard Else, a talented young producer at BBC Newcastle who had a fondness for fell walking. How long it had taken him to bring A.W. round I don't know. Some years, I suspect, and the plan almost unravelled when Wainwright dug his heels in about the suggested walking companions.

'Oh no,' said Richard, doing some nifty footwork of his own, 'the person I was thinking of asking is actually a fell farmer from the Wasdale Valley called Eric Robson.' Wainwright had never heard of me, but a close association with Herdwick sheep obviously being preferable to a close association with celebrity, he agreed. In all the years we filmed together, Wainwright never came to my small-holding in Wasdale so he never found out how far from being a fell farmer I really was. Similarly, in all the years he worked with Richard Else I don't think A.W. ever knew how close he drove him to distraction.

But first things first. Wainwright had been tempted because he was trying to raise money for his animal rescue centre near Kendal and the BBC was offering a fee. I was tempted for similar reasons, although in my case they had nothing to do with stray dogs and cats. I was a freelance and freelances are always tempted by the offer of fees. The downside was that I'd heard of Wainwright and didn't much relish what I'd heard. Yes, he'd written those great Pictorial Guides to the Lakeland Fells which had sold a million copies, but rumour had it that he was misogynist, humourless, introverted and pernickety. Lovely way of spending four or five weeks. However good the scenery was going to be, it would have its work cut out making up for all that.

'It won't be as bad as you think,' said Richard, desperately trying to salvage something from the time he'd invested in the Wainwright project, 'at least I don't think it will be.'

Armed with that certainty I headed for a greasy spoon in Kendal to meet the great man. I chatted about Herdwick sheep. Wainwright grunted. His wife, Betty, said how much A.W. was looking forward to the project. Wainwright resisted the temptation to agree. In turn, I resisted asking why a slice of boiled ham had just disappeared off my plate into his pocket. 'Oh, that will be for Totty the cat. Loves boiled ham,' said Betty who'd also noticed. Wainwright smiled. We were making progress.

From such inauspicious beginnings fine programmes grow. The deal was done, the dates were set and, unknown to us, Wainwright set about writing the script. So did Richard and the scene was set for manuscripts at dawn.

Making a fell walking programme should be relatively simple because, by their very nature, walks have a beginning, a middle and an end. Assuming of course that you haven't been weathered off, lost the film crew in the mist or mistaken a sheep trod for a footpath and ended up in the wrong valley. On our first day on the hill with Wainwright we were spared all those problems because the weather was cracking on Pen-y gent, he knew the ground and from the off we could see the valley we were heading for. What we hadn't foreseen was that Wainwright had decided to treat television producers in rather the same way he'd dealt with publishers and type setters. He was going to keep control so we couldn't screw it up.

'I'll be sitting on the summit having a sandwich and you'll walk up and see that I've got a Wainwright book lying beside me. You won't know who I am, of course.'

'No, of course not,' said I, not having the faintest idea what he was talking about.

'And you'll ask if you can join me. It's important to be polite, even on the hill and some walkers just have no manners.' He looked me up and down, his suspicion that I probably fell into that category undisguised. 'And after a long pause – it's important to respect other walkers' silences – you'll say something like – "Oh, I see you use Wainwright, too." And I'll say "Yes, I knew him – slightly." And then we'll walk down to Horton in Ribblesdale. And when we get there somebody will come up to me in the car park and say to me "Hello, A.W., haven't seen you for ages" and you'll realise who I am and ask me to sign your Wainwright book.'

This was the longest statement Wainwright had ever made in my presence and when it finished there was a very long pause indeed. Richard Else filled it by turning pale. Eventually he managed a 'But … ' which Wainwright swept away by suggesting that if we sat around any longer we'd never get the walk finished and he needed to be home by half past six.

And so began a filming collaboration that lasted for more than four years and took us from Limestone country to Lakeland, the Highlands of Scotland to the Coast to Coast walk. Once Wainwright realised that our aim in the programmes was not to hang him out to dry, he mellowed. He allowed us to work to our own script. He continued to quibble about the music Richard chose and he curbed our worst excesses (which he identified as too much talking and not enough landscape) by coming out each filming day with a carefully rationed number of things he wanted to say. He never did grasp why the camera looked at him while he was talking rather than at the mountains he was describing. I suspect that if Wainwright had been let loose to make the programmes as he wished they'd have come out looking very much like the one-eyed stumbling version mentioned earlier. Except that A.W. would have struggled to switch on the camera. Practical he was not.

Some bits of Wainwright's life were non-negotiable. Film schedules always had to take into account the transmission time of *Coronation Street*, the need to listen to the Saturday football results (particularly those involving Blackburn Rovers) and the proximity of the worst café in any given district.

But while all this was going on, a remarkable thing happened. As he got used to the television interlopers in his ordered life he began to loosen. He smiled more and harrumphed less. He was kind and generous. When my young kids came out on filming days he sent them home with presents. We soon realised it was shyness, not bloody-mindedness that cast a shadow over much of what he did. I remember the cameraman saying to me with some surprise in the hotel bar one night that Wainwright wasn't the curmudgeonly old sod we'd all thought he was going to be. More than that, he was really quite impressed by him. I should explain that's positively hagiographic coming from a cameraman.

His influence crept over us all. It started, naturally enough, with admiration for his work. That combination of dedication, of solitary man hours and cartographic excellence. It occurred to me that he was rather like the man who devised the London Underground map. He took a three-dimensional image – in A.W.'s case a Lakeland mountain – then turned it into a two-dimensional image which, defying logic, made it more understandable. It was a spectacularly good idea that hasn't been rivalled, let alone improved on, in more than half a century.

Another appealing characteristic that dawned on us very early was the fact that this whiskery old chap in baggy trousers and a sweater unravelling round the tobacco burns engaged his considerable brain before opening his mouth. He was a merciful relief in the age of the cheery soundbite. But more than any of that was the fact that after he went home each day we would carry on talking about his ideas. His knowledge of the landscape of Lakeland was second only to that of the fell shepherds. But, in a way, he added an extra dimension to that knowledge. He was talking passionately about how to care for those wild and fragile places long before the word 'sustainability' became the misused, misunderstood mantra it is today. His interpretation of the mountains was underpinned by his appreciation of the almost spiritual bond between man and landscape. Of course, he wouldn't have put it like that.

On good days we were treated to glimpses of a younger, Jack-the-Lad Wainwright with a wickedly dry sense of humour. When that kicked in, he was even prepared to stray from his own script. I remember one very wet day in Borrowdale when the filming almost had to be abandoned because of the weather. He and I had taken shelter in the doorway of an old barn and I suggested it would make a good shot – us standing there with the rain pouring off the roof in front of us. Richard said he could do it as long as it was brief. The camera was wrapped in its waterproof cover and the crew huddled around it in the middle of the field in the rain. At which point Wainwright remembered all manner of interesting stories. How he was frightened of cows, which is why he never camped on the hill in case one should get into his tent; how he was never happier than spending a night chain smoking in the lee of a stone wall and waiting for the sunrise; how he was hefted to the Lakeland hills in very much the same way as the Herdwick sheep. He managed to fill twenty, unscripted minutes before saying he thought we should abandon filming for the day so we didn't get too wet. He waved cheerily to the dripping crew as Betty drove him away.

Wainwright wasn't easy to work with. Often he would arrive on location and deliver nothing more than the brief descriptions that were his quota for the day. I remember once, on a slope above Mardale on the climb out to Small Water, him treating us to about three sentences before fumbling for his pipe and suggesting to Betty that it really was time they went home. It was half past ten in the morning. Betty's wiser counsels prevailed but, although he chatted to us quite happily between takes, he said nothing while the camera was running for the rest of the day.

Occasionally we managed to hi-jack him. One rain-sodden afternoon we retreated to the lounge of the Haweswater hotel and dripped on their carpets. Richard set up the camera, more in hope than expectation, and I manfully tried to prise some conversation out of him that we could use to fill the gaps in the other programmes. There were certainly plenty of those. For half an hour we got nowhere but then I think boredom kicked in and A.W. treated us to an hour of reminiscence brim full of his love affair with the Lakeland mountains. He was in full, glorious flow – talking, I seem to remember about a day, many years before on Kentmere Pike – when out of nowhere he said 'Do you think they do fish and chips here?'

We obviously weren't going to get any more but Richard still looked the happiest he'd been in weeks. He had a series.

I think he would have punched the air had Wainwright not still been in the room.

We made two more series after that and started on a fourth but A.W. didn't live to see it finished. He was taken ill during the filming of a programme about his early life in Blackburn and died in January 1991. His ashes were scattered, as he wanted, by Innominate Tarn on Haystacks.

When the first series went out, initially in the BBC's North East and Cumbria branch office and then on BBC2, it touched a real nerve. Until then all the Wainwright aficionados had was a few pen-and-ink self-portraits and then, later, the Derry Brabbs' photographs that illustrated the coffee-table Wainwrights. But now they could suddenly see their mysterious hero walking in the hills and talking to them about his work. It was the next best thing to bumping into him at Sticks Pass or on Catbells. Thousands of other people came across Wainwright for the first time. Sales of his books boomed and a whole new audience was introduced to the Lakeland mountains and encouraged to explore them. The same thing happened again when BBC 4 celebrated the centenary of Wainwright's birth with the documentary – *The Man Who Loved The Lakes* – and showed a selection of favourite Wainwright walks. And Granada TV joined the party, marking the centenary year by featuring, in *Wainwright Country*, some of the best lower level routes from the Pictorial Guides.

It's been fascinating to watch the way different production teams approach the Wainwright subject. You'd imagine that as the years slip away a certain objectivity would creep in. An objectivity that it was more difficult for us to apply when out walking with the great man himself. But not a bit of it. The producers and directors on later series are in a way more in awe of him than we were. He's achieved iconic status. There's a certain reverence in the way he's described; an almost missionary zeal in introducing him to a new generation of fell walkers.

Quite what Wainwright himself would have made of all this you'll have to walk up to Haystacks to find out, dear reader. But

I suspect he would have been quite chuffed. He may have been self-effacing but he wasn't daft about it. He used to say to me that he never intended to publish his Pictorial Guides. They were just an *aide memoire* in preparation for the day when he would be too decrepit to go up the hill. Well, that may have been the case with the first volume. Maybe he was nervous about how it would be received. But enough people told him how good it was for him to be left in no doubt. And he became immensely proud of the project, even if he was too shy to be caught saying so. It would have pleased him no end that the books are still finding an audience; still encouraging people to the hill. And he'd have enjoyed the television programmes, too, particularly as he didn't have to appear in them any longer – and just so long as they didn't clash with *Coronation Street* or a televised Blackburn Rovers match.

He would have liked the idea that *Wainwright Country* was made by Granada, producers of his favourite soap opera. Maybe we should have had a cat on a chimney pot in the opening titles. He would have particularly enjoyed the programmes Julia Bradbury presented for BBC4. He always had an eye for a pretty girl. And he would have relished the high definition aerials they included. He loved aerial photography; the different perspective of a beloved landscape that it gives. Maybe, too, because they're the next best thing to angel wings over Great Gable. And you can have them without going to the trouble of dying.

Wainwright's TV Walks

1 Helvellyn
from Glenridding via Striding Edge

The common complaint is that on a sunny summer afternoon the approach to Helvellyn is like the checkout at Sainsbury's. On a sunny Bank Holiday weekend it's like the turnstiles at Old Trafford. From my experience I've got to say that, if that's the case, both our favourite family supermarket and Manchester United Football Club must be doing very badly indeed.

Yes, you're unlikely to get Striding Edge to yourself. Yes, there may be a bit of a queue at the bad step or the Hole in the Wall, generally caused by a momentary loss of nerve. I was responsible for creating a tiny queue the day I filmed there with Bob Allen for the *Great Walks* series. Henry, Bob's Schnauzer dog, managed the manoeuvre with marginally more grace than I did, but Bob was carrying Henry and, for some reason, refused the same service to me.

You probably won't get the summit of Helvellyn to yourself either. If solitude is what you need, there are lots of other mountains in this book that will provide it. But unless you're a recluse, have taken a vow of silence or have strange personal habits unsuitable or illegal in the outside world, don't turn your back on Helvellyn. It's a giant of a mountain. A gentle giant from the west, an ogre from the east in bad weather. It's probably the most climbed of all the Lakeland summits but that doesn't make it a bad person, even in Wainwright's book. Even he was prepared to put up with company to experience its delights. He wrote twenty-six detailed pages about it which meant that, even in those far-off days when he was compiling the Pictorial Guides, he must have had to nod the occasional hello to a fellow walker.

BBC4's Julia Bradbury, like Bob Allen and me, took his advice, avoided the carpet-slippers western approaches and headed for Striding Edge. Of course, it lived up to its reputation for airy exposure. But more than that, it offered one of the great mountain moments. The deep views into Red Tarn and beyond that the soaring staircase of Swirral Edge with Catstycam beyond are worth any number of bad steps and cursing queues. In fact they're the real reason that people bunch up on the Edge. It's just too good to leave. When I was there, a couple of people enjoyed it so much that they turned round, went back and did it all over again. Two-way traffic on a narrow edge of rock slows things down a bit.

But eventually you tear yourself away and head for the summit which, in truth, isn't pretty. But you don't have to study the shaley surface and the silly cairns and the wide footpaths. Instead raise your eyes to any horizon and have your fill of a panorama that takes in, by my reckoning, 105 summits. Take time to learn them all. It's a great party piece. And if you do happen to bump into someone really objectionable on Helvellyn, just start reeling them off, starting in the north and working clockwise. By the time you get somewhere near SSE, the offending character will be glazing over and by SW he'll be slouching away and cursing himself for not having taken a vow of silence when he had the chance.

Practical bits
Map: OL5.

Ascent. Start at Patterdale (NY395161). The *Wainwright Walks* route went up from there in the way described on Helvellyn 15 in *The Eastern Fells*. The route ascends 2700 feet over 5 miles.

Descent: Television programmes, of course, tend to finish on the summit – a bit like Wainwright himself – but the descent from Helvellyn by Swirral Edge to Glenridding deserves special mention. Follow Helvellyn 16 in reverse

Helvellyn

3118'

from the south-west ridge of St Sunday Crag

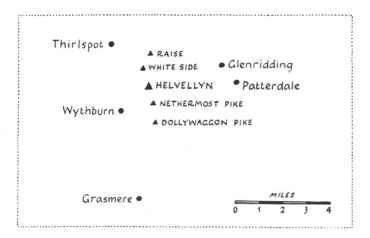

Legend and poetry, a lovely name and a lofty altitude
combine to encompass Helvellyn in an aura of romance; and
thousands of pilgrims, aided by its easy accessibility, are
attracted to its summit every year. There is no doubt that
Helvellyn is climbed more often than any other mountain
in Lakeland, and, more than any other, it is the objective
and ambition of the tourist who does not normally climb;
moreover, the easy paths leading up the western flanks
make it particularly suitable for sunrise expeditions, and,
in a snowy winter, its sweeping slopes afford great sport
to the ski parties who congregate on these white expanses.
There are few days in any year when no visitor calls at
the wall-shelter on the summit to eat his sandwiches. It
is a great pity that Helvellyn is usually ascended by its
western routes, for this side is unattractive and lacking
in interest. From the east, however, the approach is quite
exciting, with the reward of an extensive panorama as a
sudden and dramatic climax when the top is gained; only
to the traveller from this direction does Helvellyn display
its true character and reveal its secrets. There is some
quality about Helvellyn which endears it in the memory
of most people who have stood on its breezy top; although
it can be a grim place indeed on a wild night, it is, as a
rule, a very friendly giant. If it did not inspire affection
would its devotees return to it so often ?

NATURAL FEATURES

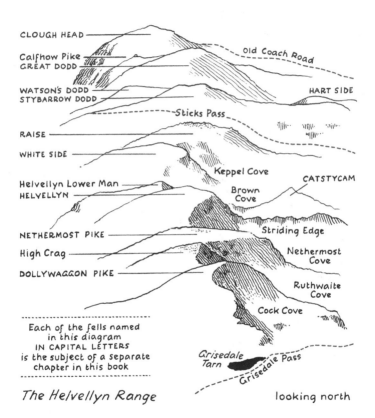

CLOUGH HEAD

Calfhow Pike
GREAT DODD

Old Coach Road

WATSON'S DODD
STYBARROW DODD

HART SIDE

Sticks Pass

RAISE

WHITE SIDE

Keppel Cove

CATSTYCAM

Helvellyn Lower Man
HELVELLYN

Brown
Cove

NETHERMOST PIKE

Striding Edge

High Crag

Nethermost
Cove

DOLLYWAGGON PIKE

Ruthwaite
Cove

Cock Cove

Each of the fells named
in this diagram
IN CAPITAL LETTERS
is the subject of a separate
chapter in this book

Grisedale
Tarn

Grisedale Pass

The Helvellyn Range

looking north

The altitude of these fells and the main connecting ridges
is consistently above 2500 feet from Dollywaggon Pike (2815')
to Great Dodd (2812') except for the depression of Sticks Pass,
which is slightly below. This is the greatest area of high fells
in Lakeland, and the traverse of the complete range from south
to north (the better way) is a challenge to all active walkers.
(As a preliminary canter, strong men will include the Fairfield group,
starting at Kirkstone Pass and reaching Grisedale Tarn over the tops
of Red Screes, Little Hart Crag, Dove Crag, Hart Crag and Fairfield)

NATURAL FEATURES

The Helvellyn range is extremely massive, forming a tremendous natural barrier from north to south between the deep troughs of the Thirlmere and Ullswater valleys. The many fells in this vast upland area are each given a separate chapter in this book, and the following notes relate only to Helvellyn itself, with its main summit at 3118′ (the third highest in Lakeland) and a subsidiary at 3033′.

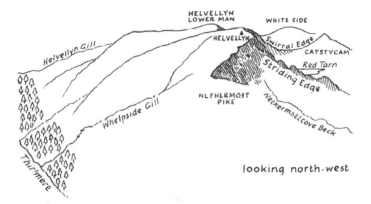

looking north-west

Helvellyn is a high point on a high ridge and therefore is substantially buttressed by neighbouring heights, the connecting depressions, north and south, being relatively slight. Westwards, however, after a gentle incline from the summit the slope quickens and finally plunges steeply down to Thirlmere, the total fall in height being nearly half a mile in a lateral distance of little more than one mile. This great mountain wall below the upper slopes is of simple design, consisting of two broad buttresses each bounded by swift-flowing streams and scarred by broken crags and occasional scree gullies. The base of the slope is densely planted with conifers.

continued

NATURAL FEATURES

continued

The smooth slopes curving up from the west break abruptly along the ridge, where, in complete contrast, a shattered cliff of crag and scree falls away precipitously eastwards : here are the most dramatic scenes Helvellyn has to offer. From the edge of the declivity on the summit Red Tarn is seen directly below, enclosed between the bony arms of Swirral Edge on the left and Striding Edge on the right. Swirral Edge terminates in the grassy cone of Catstycam, a graceful peak, but Striding Edge is all bare rock, a succession of jagged fangs ending in a black tower. The Edges are bounded by deep rough hollows, silent and very lonely. Beyond the Edges is the bulky mass of Birkhouse Moor, Helvellyn's long east shoulder, a high wedge separating Grisedale and Glenridding and descending to the lovely shores of Ullswater.

Striding Edge

Early writers regarded Striding Edge as a place of terror; contemporary writers, following a modern fashion, are inclined to dismiss it as of little account. In fact, Striding Edge is the finest ridge there is in Lakeland, for walkers — its traverse is always an exhilarating adventure in fair weather or foul, and it can be made easy or difficult according to choice. The danger of accident is present only when a high wind is blowing or when the rocks are iced : in a mist on a calm day, the Edge is a really fascinating place.

Swirral Edge

Helvellyn from Red Tarn

MAP

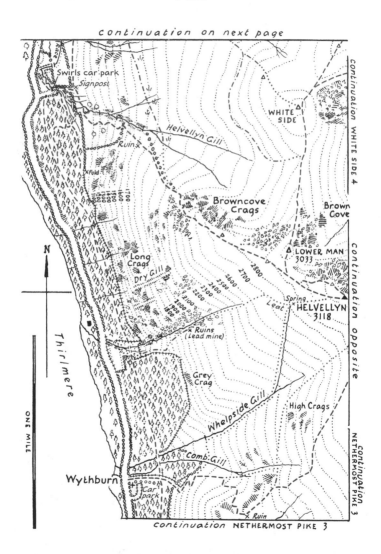

continuation on next page

Swirls car park
Signpost

continuation WHITE SIDE 4

Helvellyn Gill

WHITE SIDE

Brown Cove

Ruin

Fold

1700

Browncove Crags

LOWER MAN 3033

continuation opposite

N

Long Crags

Dry Gill

2800

2700

2600

2500

2400

2300

2200

2100

2000

1900

1800

Spring

Lead

HELVELLYN 3118

Ruins (Lead mine)

Thirlmere

ONE MILE

Grey Crag

High Crags

Whelpside Gill

continuation NETHERMOST PIKE 3

Comb Gill

Wythburn

Car park

Ruin

continuation NETHERMOST PIKE 3

MAP

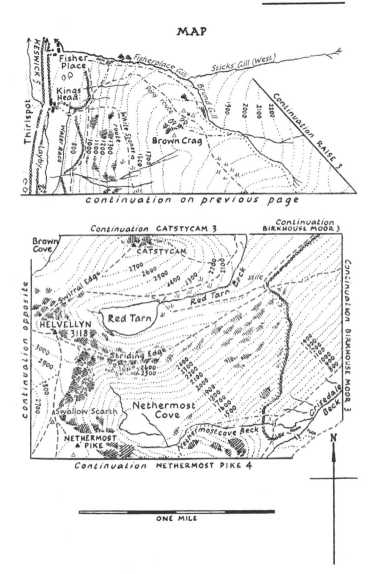

continuation on previous page

ONE MILE

THE WESTERN APPROACHES

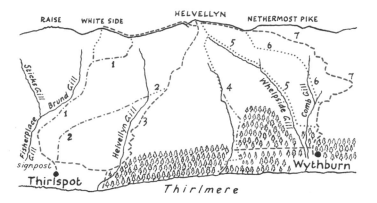

1 : **The old pony-route :** The original, longest and easiest route.
The path is now becoming intermittent owing to disuse. This
route is preferable to the Helvellyn Gill route because it avoids
the crowds. It is hard to imagine ponies coming this way now.

2 : **The 'White Stones' route :** Once the usual and popular way
up from Thirlspot, this route is now going out of use. To find it
turn right at the signpost for fifty paces and head up the hill.

3 : *via Helvellyn Gill :* A very popular route, starting at the Swirls
car park. The start is clearly signposted. Much of the steepness
has been relieved by the construction of a zigzag path, and
recent improvements eliminate the need to negotiate scree.

4 : *via the old lead mine :* The shortest way to the top from the
road, taking advantage of a breach in the plantation. Very steep
and rough for 2,200 feet. Solitary walkers with weak ankles should
avoid this route: it is *not* recognised and is not attractive. It is
linked to the car park at Wythburn by a forest road.

5 : *via Whelpside Gill :* A good route on a hot day, with water
close almost to the summit. Rough scrambling in the gill. No path.

6 : *via Comb Gill :* A route of escape from the crowds on the
popular Birk Side path. Steep up by the gill, but generally easy
walking most of the way, on grass.

7 : **The 'Wythburn' route, *via Birk Side* :** One of the most popular
ways up Helvellyn, and the usual route from Wythburn. Good
path throughout. Steep for the first mile, then much easier.

These routes are illustrated on pages 11 and 12 following

THE WESTERN APPROACHES

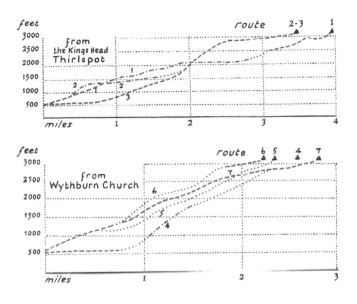

Helvellyn Gill

In mist:

Route 1 is impossible to find in descent.

Route 2 is difficult to find in ascent and impossible to find in descent.

Route 3 is easy to find and easy to follow.

Route 4 is safe but seems even rougher in mist.

Route 5 is safe if the gill is kept alongside.

Route 6 is better avoided.

Route 7 is best of all, the path being distinct throughout its length.

Whelpside Gill

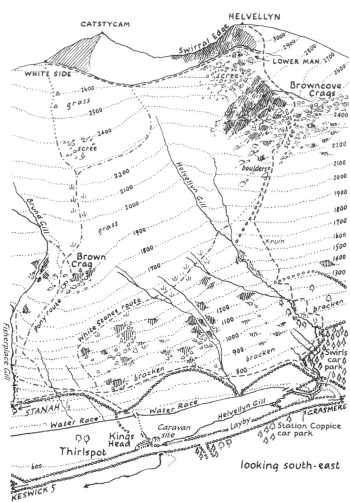

ASCENT FROM THIRLSPOT
2600 feet of ascent : 3½ - 4 miles

looking south-east

See Helvellyn 9 for details of the routes illustrated

ASCENT FROM WYTHBURN
2550 feet of ascent : 2¼-2¾ miles

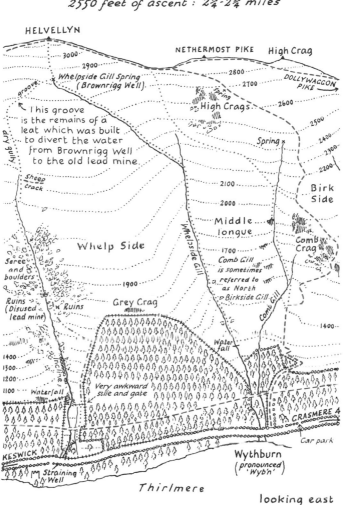

HELVELLYN

3000

2900

NETHERMOST PIKE   High Crag

2800

Whelpside Gill Spring
(Brownrigg Well)

groove

2700

DOLLYWAGGON PIKE

High Crags

2600

I his groove
is the remains of a
leat which was built
to divert the water
from Brownrigg Well
to the old lead mine

Spring

2500

2400

2300

2200

Sheep
crack

2100

2000

Birk
Side

Middle
longue

Comb
Crag

Whelp Side

Whelpside Gill

1700

Comb Gill
is sometimes
referred to
as North
Birkside Gill

Comb Gill

Scree
and
boulders

1900

Grey Crag

Ruins (Disused
lead mine)

Ruins

1400

Water
fall

1400
1300
1200
1100

Incline

Waterfall

Very awkward
stile and gate

CRASMERE 4

Car park

KESWICK

Straining
Well

Wythburn
(pronounced
'Wyb'n)

Thirlmere

looking east

See Helvellyn 9 for details of the routes illustrated

THE EASTERN APPROACHES

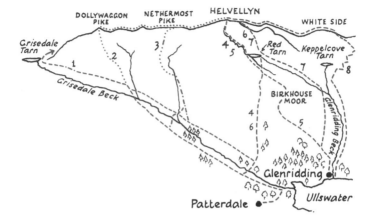

1 :   *via* Grisedale Tarn :   A long easy walk on a good path, with only one steep section. An interesting and pleasant route, which can be improved by following the edge of the escarpment between Dollywaggon Pike and the summit, instead of the path.

2 :   *via* Ruthwaite Cove and Dollywaggon Pike : A very fine route for the more adventurous walker, cutting off a big corner of Route 1 – but the variation is steep and pathless.

3 :   *via* Nethermost Cove and Nethermost Pike : A twin to Route 2, with a steep enjoyable scramble. Not for novices.

4 and 5: *via* Striding Edge : The best ways of all, well known, popular, and often densely populated in summer. The big attraction is an airy rock ridge, very fine indeed. Good paths throughout.

6 :   *via* Red Tarn and Swirral Edge, from Patterdale :   An easier variation finish to Route 4, marshy by Red Tarn, ending in a good scramble up a steep rock staircase.

7 :   *via* Red Tarn and Swirral Edge, from Glenridding : An easy walk finishing in a good scramble up a steep rock staircase.

8 :   The old pony-route *via* Keppel Cove : The original route from Glenridding. A long but easy and interesting walk.

Routes 4, 6, 7 and 8 are illustrated on pages 15 and 16 following. For Routes 1, 2 and 3, the diagrams on Dollywaggon Pike 5 and 7 and Nethermost Pike 6, respectively, will be helpful. Further details of Route 5 are to be found on Birkhouse Moor 6.

THE EASTERN APPROACHES

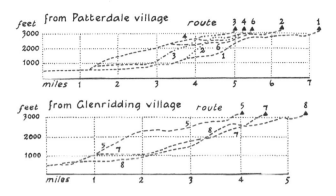

feet — from Patterdale village — route 3 4 6 2 1
3000
2000
1000
miles 1 2 3 4 5 6 7

feet — from Glenridding village — route 5 7 8
3000
2000
1000
miles 1 2 3 4 5

In mist:

Route 1 is easy to follow every inch of the way.

Routes 2 and 3 should be avoided absolutely.

Routes 4 and 5 are safe for anyone already familiar with them.

Route 6 is safe, but there will be uncertainty near Red Tarn.

Routes 7 and 8 are distinct all the way.

The summit, from Striding Edge

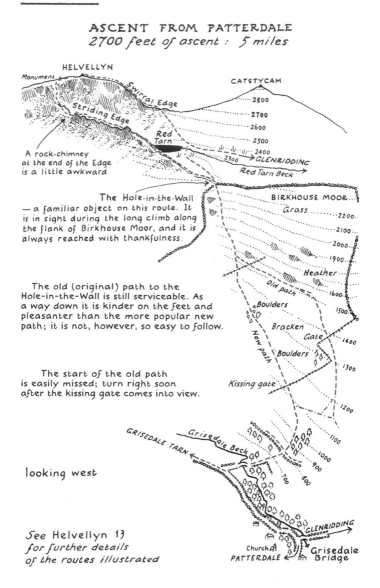

ASCENT FROM PATTERDALE
2700 feet of ascent : 5 miles

HELVELLYN
Monument
CATSTYCAM
Swirral Edge
2800
Striding Edge
2700
2600
Red
2500
Tarn
2400
GLENRIDDING
A rock-chimney
2300
at the end of the Edge
Red Tarn Beck
is a little awkward.

The Hole-in-the-Wall
BIRKHOUSE MOOR
— a familiar object on this route. It
Grass
is in sight during the long climb along
2200
the flank of Birkhouse Moor, and it is
2100
always reached with thankfulness.
2000
1900
Heather
The old (original) path to the
1600
Hole-in-the-Wall is still serviceable. As
Old path
a way down it is kinder on the feet and
Boulders
1500
pleasanter than the more popular new
path; it is not, however, so easy to follow.
Bracken
Gate
New path
1400
Boulders
1300
The start of the old path
is easily missed; turn right soon
Kissing gate
after the kissing gate comes into view.
1200

GRISEDALE TARN
Grisedale Beck
1100

1000
looking west
900
700
800

See Helvellyn 13
GLENRIDDING
for further details
of the routes illustrated
Church
PATTERDALE
Grisedale
Bridge

ASCENT FROM GLENRIDDING
2750 feet of ascent : 4½ or 5½ miles

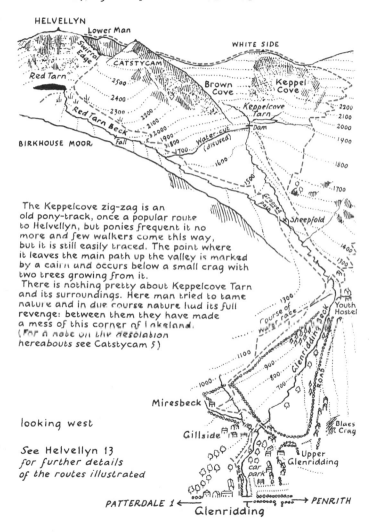

HELVELLYN
Lower Man
WHITE SIDE
Squirrel Edge
CATSTYCAM
Red Tarn
2500
Brown Cove
Keppel Cove
2400
Keppelcove Tarn
2300
2200
2100
2000
Red Tarn Beck
2200
2100
2000
1900
BIRKHOUSE MOOR
Fall
Dam
1800
Water-cut (disused)
1700
1600
1500
1800
Crossed path
1700
Sheepfold
1400
1300

The Keppelcove zig-zag is an
old pony-track, once a popular route
to Helvellyn, but ponies frequent it no
more and few walkers come this way,
but it is still easily traced. The point where
it leaves the main path up the valley is marked
by a cairn and occurs below a small crag with
two trees growing from it.
There is nothing pretty about Keppelcove Tarn
and its surroundings. Here man tried to tame
nature and in due course nature had its full
revenge: between them they have made
a mess of this corner of Lakeland.
(For a note on the desolation
hereabouts see Catstycam 5)

Course of water race
Youth Hostel
1300

looking west

1100

1000
900
800
700

Glenridding Beck
ROAD

Miresbeck

See Helvellyn 13
for further details
of the routes illustrated

Gillside
Blaes Crag
Upper Glenridding
car park

PATTERDALE 1 ←—— Glenridding ——→ PENRITH

ASCENT FROM GRASMERE
3050 feet of ascent : 6½ miles from Grasmere Church

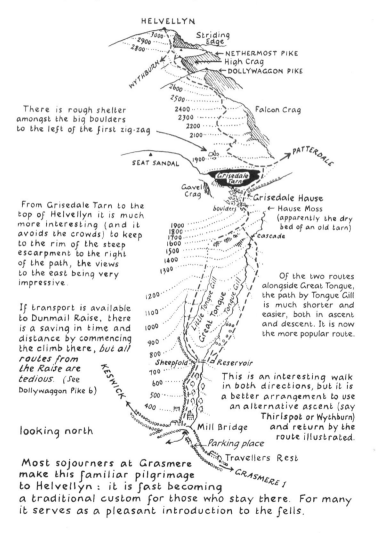

HELVELLYN

Striding Edge

3000
2900
2800

WYTHBURN

← NETHERMOST PIKE
← High Crag
← DOLLYWAGGON PIKE

2600
2500
2400
2300
2200
2100

Falcon Crag

PATTERDALE

There is rough shelter
amongst the big boulders
to the left of the first zig-zag

SEAT SANDAL

1900

Grisedale Tarn

Gavel Crag

Grisedale Hause

boulders

← Hause Moss
(apparently the dry
bed of an old tarn)

From Grisedale Tarn to the
top of Helvellyn it is much
more interesting (and it
avoids the crowds) to keep
to the rim of the steep
escarpment to the right
of the path, the views
to the east being very
impressive.

1900
1800
1700
1600
1500
1400
1300

cascade

1200

Little Tongue Gill
Great Tongue
Tongue Gill

1100

If transport is available
to Dunmail Raise, there
is a saving in time and
distance by commencing
the climb there, *but all
routes from
the Raise are
tedious.* (See
Dollywaggon Pike 6)

1000
900
800

Sheepfold

Reservoir

Of the two routes
alongside Great Tongue,
the path by Tongue Gill
is much shorter and
easier, both in ascent
and descent. It is now
the more popular route.

KESWICK

700
600
500
400

This is an interesting walk
in both directions, but it is
a better arrangement to use
an alternative ascent (say
Thirlspot or Wythburn)
and return by the
route illustrated.

looking north

Mill Bridge

Parking place
Travellers Rest

GRASMERE 1

Most sojourners at Grasmere
make this familiar pilgrimage
to Helvellyn : it is fast becoming
a traditional custom for those who stay there. For many
it serves as a pleasant introduction to the fells.

Helvellyn Lower Man

looking northwest

Helvellyn Lower Man, half a mile northwest of the principal top, occupies a key position on the main ridge, which here changes its direction subtly and unobtrusively. Walkers intending to follow

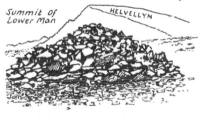

Summit of Lower Man

HELVELLYN

the ridge north may easily go astray hereabouts. The wide path from Helvellyn skirts the Lower Man and continues clearly along a broad spur which appears to be the main ridge, but is not (*this is the direct way to the car park at Swirls*).

Browncove Crags — oddly named because Brown Cove is on the other side of the ridge.

THE SUMMIT

It might be expected that the summit of so popular a mountain would be crowned with a cairn the size of a house, instead of which the only adornment is a small and insignificant heap of stones that commands no respect at all, untidily thrown together on the mound forming the highest point. It is a disappointment to have no cairn to recline against, and as there is no natural seat anywhere on the top visitors inevitably drift into the nearby wall-shelter and there rest ankle-deep in the debris of countless packed lunches. The summit is covered in shale and is lacking in natural features, a deficiency which man has attempted to remedy by erecting thereon, as well as the shelter, a triangulation column and two monuments. And until many walkers learn better manners there is a crying need for an incinerator also, to dispose of the decaying heaps of litter they leave behind to greet those who follow.

The paths across the summit are wide and so well-trodden as to appear almost metalled: they are unnecessarily and amply cairned.

The dull surroundings are relieved by the exciting view down the escarpment to Red Tarn and Striding Edge below.

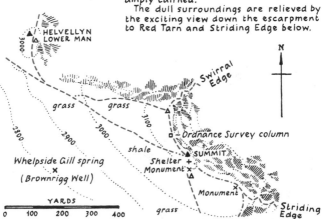

DESCENTS

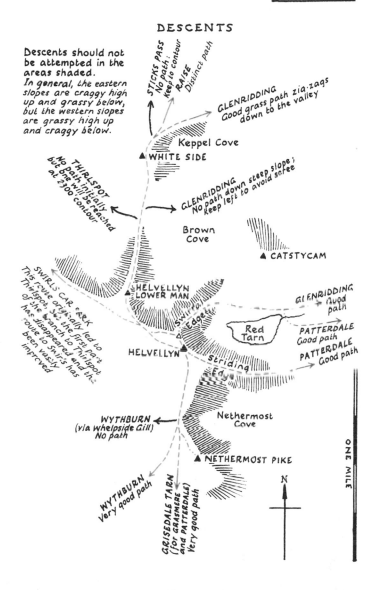

Descents should not be attempted in the areas shaded.
In general, the eastern slopes are craggy high up and grassy below, but the western slopes are grassy high up and craggy below.

STICKS PASS
No path;
keep to contour

RAISE
Distinct path

GLENRIDDING
Good grass path zig-zags down to the valley

Keppel Cove

▲ WHITE SIDE

THIRLSPOT
No path
but one will be reached at 2300 contour

GLENRIDDING
No path down steep slope;
keep left to avoid scree

Brown Cove

▲ CATSTYCAM

SWIRLS CAR PARK
This route originally led to Thirlspot, via the first part of the branch to Thirlspot has disappeared and the route to Swirls has been vastly improved

▲ HELVELLYN
LOWER MAN

Swirl

Edge

GLENRIDDING
Good path

Red Tarn

PATTERDALE
Good path

▲ HELVELLYN

Striding Edge

PATTERDALE
Good path

WYTHBURN
(via Whelpside Gill)
No path

Nethermost Cove

ONE MILE

▲ NETHERMOST PIKE

N

WYTHBURN
Very good path

GRISEDALE TARN
(for Grasmere and Patterdale)
Very good path

RIDGE ROUTES

To HELVELLYN LOWER MAN, 3033': ½ mile : NW
Depression at 2975': 60 feet of ascent
A simple stroll, safe in mist.

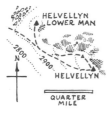

Take the Thirlspot path, forking right below the cone of Lower Man. Or, better, follow the edge of the escarpment all the way.

NOTE : *Helvellyn Lower Man stands at the point where the main ridge makes an abrupt and unexpected right-angled turn. Its summit must be traversed for White Side, Sticks Pass or Glenridding.*

To CATSTYCAM, 2917': 1 mile : NW (200 yards), then NE
Depression at 2600': 320 feet of ascent
A splendid walk with a fine rock scramble.
Safe in mist; dangerous in ice and snow.

200 yards north-west of the top of Helvellyn is a cairn (the Ordnance Survey column is midway), and just beyond, over the rim, is the start of the steep rock stairway going down to Swirral Edge: the descent is less formidable than it looks. Midway along the Edge the main path turns off to the right: here continue ahead up the grass slope to the summit.

The Monuments of Helvellyn ⟶

The Gough Memorial

Erected 1890 on the edge of the summit above the path to Striding Edge.

This small stone tablet, 40 yards S of the shelter, commemorates the landing of an aeroplane in 1926. (Playful pedestrians may have hidden it with stones)

The Dixon Memorial 1858

Situated on a platform of rock on Striding Edge overlooking Nethermost Cove (often not noticed)

RIDGE ROUTES

To BIRKHOUSE MOOR, 2356': 2 miles : ESE then NE
Minor depressions only : 100 feet of ascent

An unpleasant descent on loose scree, followed by an exhilarating scramble along a narrow rock ridge and an easy walk. Dangerous in snow and ice; care necessary in gusty wind; safe in mist.

Turn down the scree for Striding Edge 30 yards beyond the monument. The Edge begins with a 20' chimney, well furnished with holds: this is the only difficulty. From the rock tower at the far end the path slants across the slope but it is pleasanter to follow the crest.

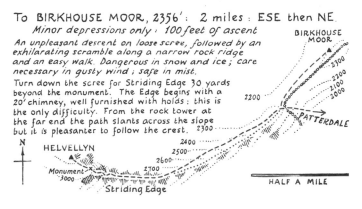

HALF A MILE

To NETHERMOST PIKE, 2920'
¾ mile : S then SE
Depression at 2840': 80 feet of ascent
A very easy walk. Safe in mist.

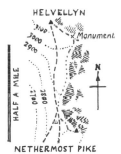

A broad path leads south to the depression known as Swallow Scarth. Here the path divides, one branch descending to Wythburn, and the other continuing over the flat top of Nethermost Pike. To visit the summit-cairn bear left at the fork, and left again in about fifty yards, along a faint path.

In clear weather a more interesting route follows the edge of the escarpment, the views being very impressive.

Whelpside Gill Spring
(Brownrigg Well)

Few visitors to Helvellyn know of this spring (the source of Whelpside Gill), which offers unfailing supplies of icy water. To find it, walk 500 yards south of west from the top in the direction of Pillar.

THE VIEW

The figures following the names of fells
indicate distances in miles

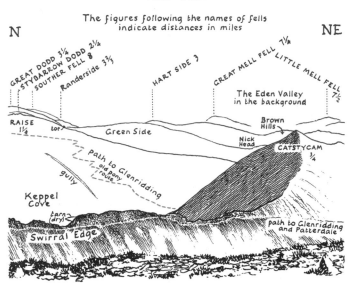

N   NE

GREAT DODD 3¼
STYBARROW DODD 2¼
SOUTHER FELL 8
Randerside 3⅔

HART SIDE 3

GREAT MELL FELL 7⅛
LITTLE MELL FELL 7½

The Eden Valley
in the background

RAISE 1¼   tor

Green Side

Brown
Hills

Nick
Head

CATSTYCAM 3/4

Path to Glenridding
old pony route

gully

Keppel
Cove

tarn (dry)

Swirral Edge

path to Glenridding
and Patterdale

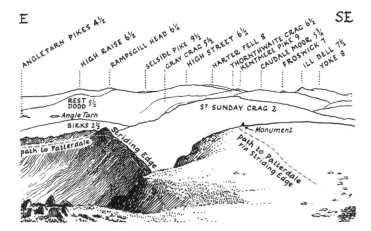

E   SE

ANGLETARN PIKES 4½

HIGH RAISE 6½

RAMPSGILL HEAD 6¼

SELSIDE PIKE 9½
GRAY CRAG 5½
HIGH STREET 6½

HARTER FELL 8
THORNTHWAITE CRAG 6½
KENTMERE PIKE 9
CAUDALE MOOR 5¾
FROSWICK 7
ILL BELL 7½
YOKE 8

REST
DODD 5½

Angle Tarn

St SUNDAY CRAG 2

BIRKS 2⅓

Striding Edge

Monument

path to Patterdale

Path to Patterdale
via Striding Edge

THE VIEW

NE   E

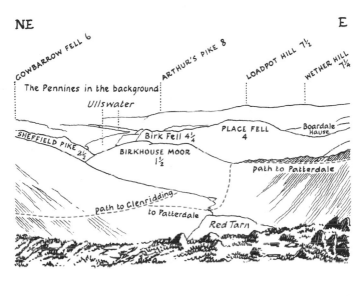

SE   S

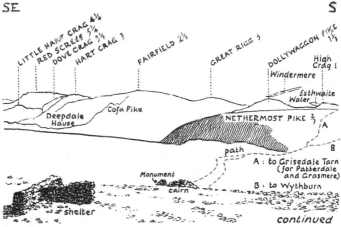

A : to Grisedale Tarn
(for Patterdale
and Grasmere)

B : to Wythburn

continued

THE VIEW

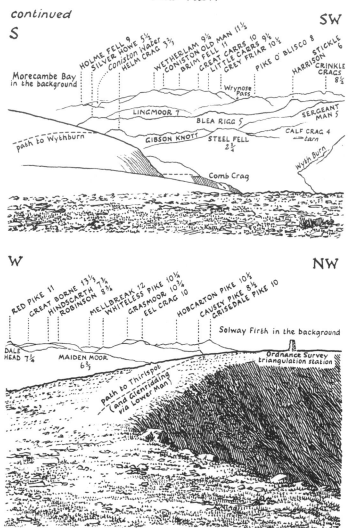

continued

S — **SW**

HOLME FELL 9
SILVER HOWE 5½
Coniston Water
HELM CRAG 3⅓
WETHERLAM 9¼
CONISTON OLD MAN 11½
BRIM FELL 11
GREAT CARRS 10
LITTLE CARRS 9½
GREY FRIAR 10½
PIKE O' BLISCO 8
HARRISON
STICKLE 6
CRINKLE CRAGS 8½

Morecambe Bay
in the background

Wrynose
Pass

LINGMOOR 7

BLEA RIGG 5

SERGEANT
MAN 5

path to Wythburn

GIBSON KNOTT

STEEL FELL 2¾

CALF CRAG 4
← tarn

Wyth Burn

Comb Crag

W — **NW**

RED PIKE 11
GREAT BORNE 13⅓
HINDSCARTH 7¾
ROBINSON 8¾
MELLBREAK 12
WHITELESS PIKE 10½
GRASMOOR 10¾
EEL CRAG 10
HOBCARTON PIKE 10½
CAUSEY PIKE 8½
GRISEDALE PIKE 10

Solway Firth in the background

DALE
HEAD 7¼

MAIDEN MOOR 6⅓

Ordnance Survey
triangulation station

path to Thirlspot
(and Glenridding
via Lower Man)

THE VIEW

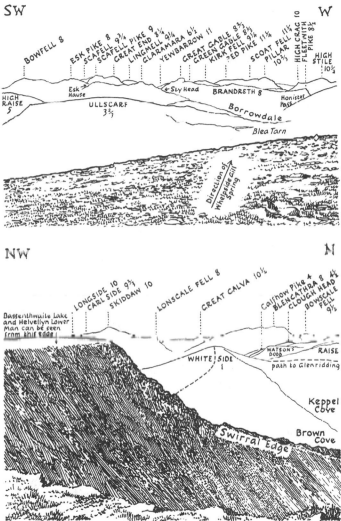

2   Stybarrow Dodd
from Sticks Pass

Wainwright was fascinated by maps. He read them the way other people read novels. Footpaths and tracks provided the plot, with its twists and turns and the occasional surprise ending. The summits were his cast list, each with its own character and secrets to discover as the story unfolded. There were villains, rotten with peat hags or grassy, featureless tops. But there were heroes too, in a Jack-the-Lad mould, strutting their stuff in rocky outcrops and pinnacled summits.

The problem with Wainwright was that by the time he became a celebrity, he was an old man. His reputation for grumpiness had taken hold. And stuck. But when we filmed together, against all the odds flashes of the younger, more vibrant Wainwright shone through the protective shell. He couldn't help it, however hard he tried.

He was determined not to enjoy filming because filming wasn't what proper people did – not a real job, like being Borough Treasurer. It was too easy-going. It allowed space for silliness. He tried his best to rise above it but his instincts very occasionally outstripped his professional reserve.

Apart from Betty, I must be one of the few people who ever heard Wainwright giggle. It was a small, stifled giggle, but a giggle nevertheless. We were filming at Black Sail Youth Hostel and, as often happens, something went wrong with a shot. We re-did it. It went wrong again, probably because A.W. was more interested in the Herdwick sheep looking for a crust of cheese sandwich than he was in the process of making a television programme. We tried again to get the shot of Britain's greatest fell walker emerging from a hut. Action! He walked out through the door, looked straight into the camera, and said, 'I didn't look at the sheep.' The director gave a groan. It was a small, stifled groan, but a groan nevertheless. And Wainwright giggled. Then he fumbled his way back into the hut and made a perfect exit. Unfortunately the camera wasn't running so nobody ever saw A.W. become a television professional. And he never attempted to be the consummate presenter ever again.

Not that it mattered. Blundering as he was, he had a real screen presence, the kind that comes from being master of your art and also from being inaccessible for years. He could have read bits from Enid Blyton and his fans would have oohed and aahed. It was Wainwright. To this day I'm still approached by people who shake my hand and ask me to sign a scrap of paper because, once, I walked with Wainwright. They can't remember my name but that doesn't matter – the Wainwright aura lingers. I was very lucky to have spent time with him, despite my early misgivings. Very lucky to have heard, first hand, his epic tale of the Lakeland mountains – both the stars and the walk-on parts.

Stybarrow Dodd, where we're going next, rather hides its star qualities. If we're going to apply Wainwright's anthropomorphism, it's a shy, retiring mountain hiding away behind the rather dreary approach over Sticks Pass.

'So why bother going there?' I asked at the time.

'Because it's one of those character actors you can't remember the name of that always gives a great performance,' said he. Or words to that effect. 'And when you get to the top of Stybarrow Dodd, just savour the view. Just because it's not a household name doesn't mean it isn't one of the best viewing platforms in Lakeland.'

Overture and beginners then.

Practical bits
Map: OL5.

Ascent: You can get to Sticks Pass from Patterdale or from the Thirlmere side. I'd suggest you start at Stannah above Thirlmere (NY320190). Follow the Stybarrow Dodd 5 ascent from *The Eastern Fells* (2½ miles and 2300 feet).

Descent: A few options, but for *Wainwright Country* we took the ridge route to Watson's Dodd from Stybarrow Dodd 8 and then the descent by way of Castle Rock of Triermain, the reverse of Watson's Dodd 3 (see the Appendix on page 338).

Stybarrow Dodd 2770'

from Brown Crag

Dockray

▲ GREAT DODD

Stanah
Thirlspot

STYBARROW
▲ DODD

Glencoyne

▲ RAISE

Glenridding

▲ HELVELLYN

MILES

0   1   2   3   4

NATURAL FEATURES

Stybarrow Dodd is the first of the group of fells north of the Sticks Pass and it sets the pattern for them all: sweeping grassy slopes, easy walking for the traveller who likes to count his miles but rather wearisome for those who prefer to see rock in the landscape. Rock is so rare that the slightest roughnesses get undeserved identification on most maps, either by distinctive name or extravagant hachures: thus Deepdale Crag is hardly more than a short stony slope. Stybarrow Dodd sends out a long eastern spur that rises to a minor height, Green Side (which, incidentally, gave its name to the lead mine in nearby Glenridding) before falling steeply to Glencoyne; on Green Side there are both crags and dangerous quarries, now disused.

Stybarrow Dodd's one proud distinction is that on its slopes it carries the well-known path over Sticks Pass throughout most of its length. Far more people ascend the slopes of Stybarrow Dodd than reach its summit!

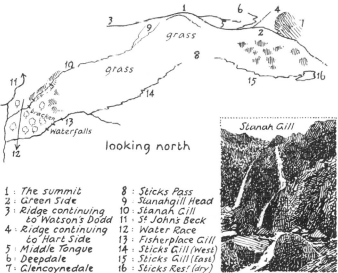

looking north

Stanah Gill

1 : The summit
2 : Green Side
3 : Ridge continuing to Watson's Dodd
4 : Ridge continuing to Hart Side
5 : Middle Tongue
6 : Deepdale
7 : Glencoynedale
8 : Sticks Pass
9 : Stanahgill Head
10 : Stanah Gill
11 : St John's Beck
12 : Water Race
13 : Fisherplace Gill
14 : Sticks Gill (West)
15 : Sticks Gill (East)
16 : Sticks Res! (dry)

MAP

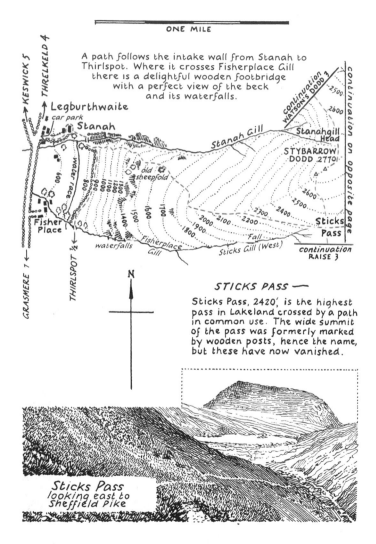

ONE MILE

A path follows the intake wall from Stanah to Thirlspot. Where it crosses Fisherplace Gill there is a delightful wooden footbridge with a perfect view of the beck and its waterfalls.

KESWICK 5
THRELKELD 4

Legburthwaite
car park
Stanah
Stanah Gill
continuation WATSON'S DODD 7
continuation on opposite page
Stanahgill Head
STYBARROW DODD 2770'
old sheepfold
Fisher Place
GRASMERE 7
THIRLSPOT ½
waterfalls
Fisherplace Gill
Sticks Gill (West)
Fall
Sticks Pass
continuation RAISE 3

N

STICKS PASS —

Sticks Pass, 2420', is the highest pass in Lakeland crossed by a path in common use. The wide summit of the pass was formerly marked by wooden posts, hence the name, but these have now vanished.

Sticks Pass
looking east to
Sheffield Pike

MAP

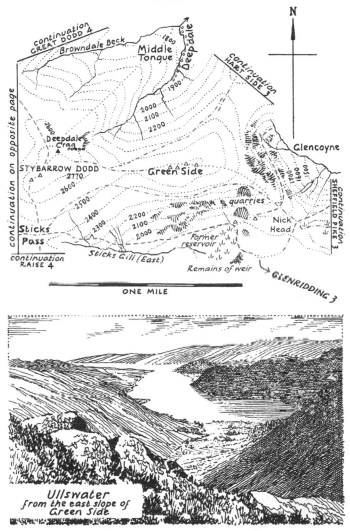

continuation GREAT DODD 4

Browndale Beck

Middle Tongue

1800

Deepdale

continuation HART SIDE 3

N

continuation on opposite page

2000
2100
2200

1900

Deepdale Crag

2600

Glencoyne

1600
1500

1700

STYBARROW DODD
2770

Green Side

continuation SHEFFIELD PIKE 3

2600

2500

quarries

2400

2300

2200

Nick Head

2100

Sticks
Pass

2000

continuation RAISE 4

Sticks Gill (East)

former reservoir

Remains of weir

GLENRIDDING 3

ONE MILE

Ullswater
from the east slope of
Green Side

ASCENT FROM STANAH
2300 feet of ascent : 2½ miles

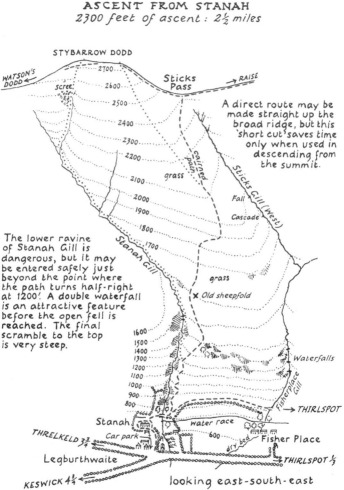

STYBARROW DODD

WATSON'S DODD ←

scree

Sticks Pass

→ RAISE

A direct route may be made straight up the broad ridge, but this 'short cut' saves time only when used in descending from the summit.

2700
2600
2500
2400
2300
2200
2100
2000
1900
1800
1700

cairned path

grass

Sticks Gill (west)

Fall
Cascade

The lower ravine of Stanah Gill is dangerous, but it may be entered safely just beyond the point where the path turns half-right at 1200'. A double waterfall is an attractive feature before the open fell is reached. The final scramble to the top is very steep.

Stanah Gill

grass

× Old sheepfold

1600
1500
1400
1300
1200
1100
1000
900
800

Waterfalls

Fisherplace Gill

→ THIRLSPOT

Stanah

Car park

water race

600

dry bed

Fisher Place

THRELKELD 3¾

→ THIRLSPOT ½

Legburthwaite

KESWICK 4¾ ←

looking east-south-east

Conveniently, the path to Sticks Pass climbs the slopes of Stybarrow Dodd, the summit being easily gained from the top of the pass. Stanah Gill is a rough alternative, affording some relief from the dull grassiness of the path.

ASCENT FROM DOCKRAY
1900 feet of ascent: 5½ miles

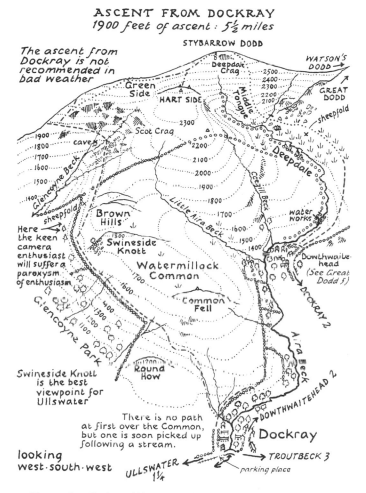

STYBARROW DODD

The ascent from Dockray is not recommended in bad weather

WATSON'S DODD →

Deepdale Crag

Green Side

HART SIDE

GREAT DODD

Middle Tongue

sheepfold

2500
2400
2300
2200
2100

Scot Crag

2300
2200
2100
2000
1900
1800
1700
1600
1500

Deepdale

Cecil Beck

Glencoyne Beck

1900
1800
1700
1600
1500
1400

caves

sheepfold

Little Aira Beck

water works

Brown Hills

1800

Swineside Knott

Watermillock Common

Here the keen camera enthusiast will suffer a paroxysm of enthusiasm

1700

1600

Common Fell

Dowthwaite head (See Great Dodd f)

DOCKRAY 2

Glencoyne Park

1400
1300
1100

1200

Round How

Aira Beck

Swineside Knott is the best viewpoint for Ullswater

looking west·south·west

There is no path at first over the Common, but one is soon picked up following a stream.

BOWTHWAITEHEAD 2

Dockray

ULLSWATER 1¼ ←

→ TROUTBECK 3

parking place

There is all the difference in the world between the two routes depicted. The direct way up, by Deepdale, is dreary and depressing; that by the Brown Hills is (after a dull start) a splendid high·level route, with excellent views of Ullswater below.

THE SUMMIT

When this book was first published there was no spot height on Stybarrow Dodd and the author suggested that walkers should pass their time on the summit estimating its altitude by this method:

The usually accepted top is the upright slate slab at the south-western end, (2756'), but there is higher ground 300 yards north-east, indicated by a very loose (at the time of writing!) estate-boundary iron post That it *is* higher is easily proved : from here, the slate slab at 2756' is seen to cover a part of Esk Pike, 9½ miles away, at about 2400; therefore the view is *downward*. Q.E.D.

The altitude of the highest point can be roughly decided mathematically. It will be noted that the summit of Raise (2889', 7 furlongs) is directly below the summit of Helvellyn (3080' say, 18 furlongs). The walker didn't climb up here to do sums, and is not likely to challenge the statement that the altitude may, from the data, be calculated at 2770' approximately.

Today no such complex calculations are necessary. The 2½" Ordnance Survey map gives the altitude of the highest point as 843 metres (2766'), which is remarkably close to the author's estimate.

On the highest point there is now a large cairn which incorporates the slate slab. The iron post has gone.

DESCENTS : All ways off are obvious in clear weather. Think twice before dropping down into Deepdale. *In bad conditions aim south for Sticks Pass.*

RIDGE ROUTE

To RAISE, 2897' : 1 mile : SW then S
Depression at 2420' (Sticks Pass)
470 feet of ascent
An easy walk, mostly on grass. Safe in mist.

From the south-west top, descend south to cross Sticks Pass at its highest point. The long facing slope of Raise becomes stony towards the summit

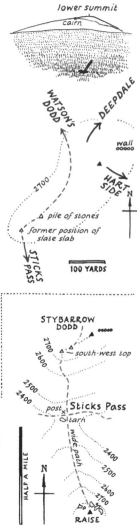

RIDGE ROUTES

To WATSON'S DODD, 2589' : ⅔ mile : NW
Depression slight : Ascent negligible
A very easy stroll.
Safe in mist.

A short distance beyond the tarn the path divides into three, the left fork slightly ascending across the flat plateau to the summit-cairn. Beware of marshy ground.

To HART SIDE, 2481' : 1½ miles : E then NE
Depressions at 2525' and 2250': 300 feet of ascent.
An easy walk on grass. Not recommended in mist.

Descend east, leaving the wall well to the left, to the obvious ridge rising gently to Green Side. Skirt the cairns there and aim directly for Hart Side ahead. Alternatively, bear left in the depression onto the path that skirts Green Side to the north.

To SHEFFIELD PIKE, 2215' : 2 miles : E then SE and E
Depressions at 2525' and 1925' : 400 feet of ascent
An easy walk. Not recommended in mist.

Descend east, leaving the wall well to the left, to the obvious ridge rising gently to Green Side. Beyond the cairns there, follow the grassy slope down to Nick Head, whence a broad marshy ridge rises to the summit. *This walk is dangerous in mist.*

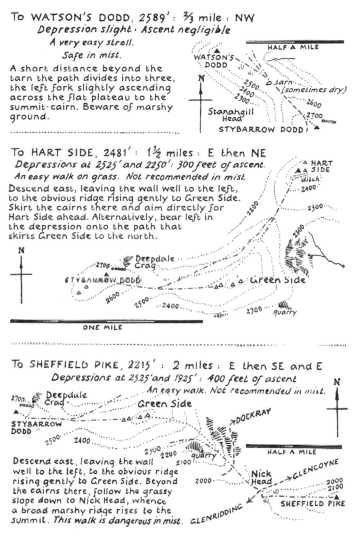

THE VIEW

An extensive and excellent panorama
is seen above a dull and dreary foreground

Principal Fells

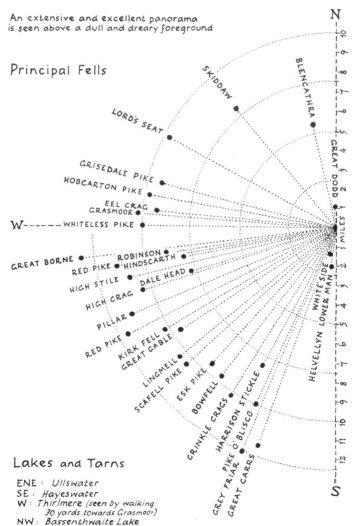

Lakes and Tarns

ENE : *Ullswater*
SE : *Hayeswater*
W : *Thirlmere (seen by walking
30 yards towards Grasmoor)*
NW : *Bassenthwaite Lake*

THE VIEW

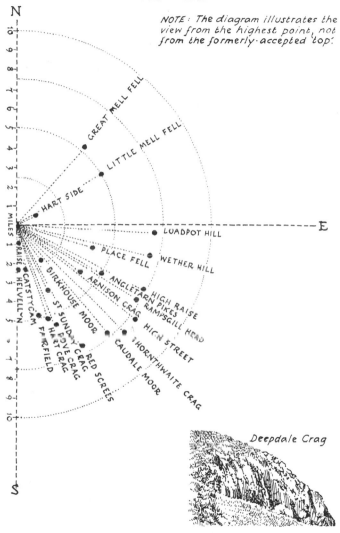

NOTE: The diagram illustrates the view from the highest point, not from the formerly-accepted top.

Deepdale Crag

3 High Street
from Mardale Head via Rough Crag

'We're going racing.'

That's how the researcher introduced High Street to me.

'There was once a horse-racing track up there.'

Leaving aside the fact that it was a bloody silly place to put a race track (if you've ever seen the crowds leaving the enclosures at Cheltenham during Gold Cup week you'll realise that 2718 feet of descent is the very last thing they need at the end of the day) we did seem to be missing out quite a lot of High Street's more interesting history.

While most of high Lakeland was a mysterious place so far as the historical record is concerned, a brooding, dangerous region of legend and superstition (a place to be avoided if you had any sense), High Street was on the map. It was put there by the Romans who built one of their straight roads across the top of it, apparently ignoring the fact that there was a mountain in the way. So when you've made the effort and got to the top, just remember that all you had to carry up there was your sandwiches. Once, squads of Roman auxiliaries had to labour their way up carrying the tools to build a motorway in the sky.

BBC4 chose to film the ascent from Mardale where Wainwright and I spent a lot of time. He never forgave Manchester for drowning the Mardale Valley, a place he imagined with meandering lanes and hedges bursting with wild flowers. What he saw as the rape of Mardale, the damming of remote Haweswater and the consequent destruction of the hamlet of Mardale Green, rankled with him. He mourned the ancient church which was pulled down and its stone used in the building of the dam. He regretted the destruction of the old Dun Bull Hotel which had been such a convenient place to get refreshment after a day in the hills.

He grudgingly accepted that when the graveyard at Mardale Green was emptied and the bodies taken for re-burial to Shap history had come full circle. Until the eighteenth century there was no burial right in Mardale. Coffins were strapped to the back of horses and taken across the track still known as the corpse road.

We stood one day at the end of the reservoir at Mardale Head and after a particularly long silence he spoke softly and said he had to admit there was one benefit that flowed from clearing the people out of the valley. In the old, bucolic days golden eagles were regarded as vermin that took the newborn lambs. There was a price on their head. Some time after the people went, the eagles returned to Riggindale, the great bowl carved into the craggy side of High Street.

As you climb out over Eagle Crag and Rough Crag you may see the eagles soaring over the lonely valley landscape. That day I was with Wainwright, he imagined that he could see them through the eyes of Riggindale's first recorded visitor. In 1208 the conspirator Hugh Holme was on the run from King John. Here he found refuge. Here he stayed and became known as the King of Mardale. A.W. said that sounded really rather appealing. But then shattered the illusion by asking Betty if they'd get home in time for *Coronation Street*.

Practical bits
Map: OL5.
Ascent: BBC4 took Wainwright's spectacular route up the nose of crags that soar above Riggindale – it's shown on High Street 6 in *The Far Eastern Fells* (2050 feet of ascent over 3 miles). Start at Mardale Head car park (NY469106)
Descent: You can come down by way of Blea Water using the reverse of the left-hand route on High Street 6. Alternatively, and more excitingly, you can push on along High Street and over Mardale Ill Bell using the ridge route shown on High Street 13, and descend by way of the Nan Bield Pass and Small Water – the reverse of one of the routes shown on Mardale Ill Bell 5 (see the Appendix on page 339).

High Street

2718'

from the north ridge of Branstree

NATURAL FEATURES

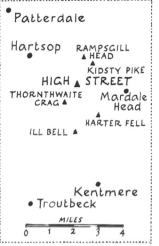

Patterdale

Hartsop   RAMPSGILL
▲ HEAD

▲ KIDSTY PIKE

HIGH ▲ STREET

THORNTHWAITE   Mardale
CRAG ▲   Head
                ▲
            HARTER FELL

ILL BELL ▲

Kentmere
• Troutbeck

MILES
0   1   2   3   4

Most of the high places in Lakeland have no mention in history books, and, until comparatively recent times, when enlightened men were inspired to climb upon them for pleasure and exercise, it was fashionable to regard them as objects of awe and terror, and their summits were rarely visited.   Not so High Street, which has been known and trodden, down through the ages, by a miscellany of travellers on an odd variety of missions: by marching soldiers, marauding brigands, carousing shepherds, officials of the Governments, and now by modern hikers. Its summit has been in turn a highway and a sports arena and a racecourse, as well as, as it is today, a grazing ground for sheep.

The long whale-backed crest of High Street attains a greater altitude than any other fell east of Kirkstone. Walking is easy on the grassy top: a factor that must have influenced the Roman surveyors to throw their road along it.   But High Street is much more than an elevated and featureless field, for its eastern flank, which falls precipitously from the flat top to enclose the splendid tarn of Blea Water in craggy arms, is a striking study in grandeur and wildness; on this side a straight narrow ridge running down to Mardale is particularly fine. The western face drops roughly to Hayeswater. To north and south, high ground continues to subsidiary fells along the main ridge.

The River Kent has its birth in marshes on the south slope but most of the water draining from the fell flows northwards to Haweswater and Hayeswater.

Rough Crag
from
Long Stile

NATURAL FEATURES

The main High Street range
illustrating the complexity of the valley systems

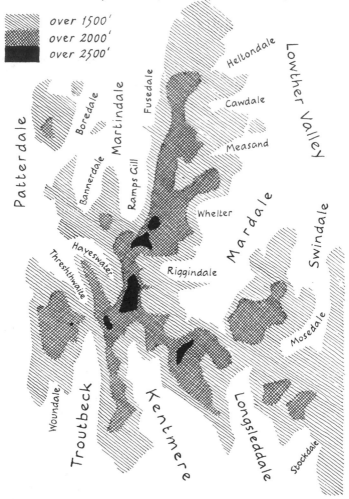

over 1500'
over 2000'
over 2500'

Patterdale

Boredale

Martindale

Fusedale

Heltondale

Lowther Valley

Cawdale

Measand

Bannerdale

Ramps Gill

Whelter

Mardale

Swindale

Hayeswater

Threshthwaite

Riggindale

Mosedale

Woundale

Troutbeck

Kentmere

Longsleddale

Stockdale

MAP

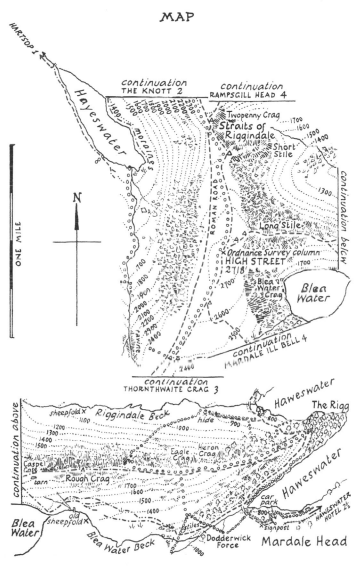

ASCENTS FROM PATTERDALE AND HARTSOP
2450 feet of ascent : 5½ miles from Patterdale
2300 feet of ascent : 3¾ miles from Hartsop

Proceed from the Straits of Riggindale to the summit
not by the wall *nor* by the Roman Road (which are
dull trudges) but by following the edge of the eastern
face (which has excellent views) until the Ordnance
Survey column comes into sight.

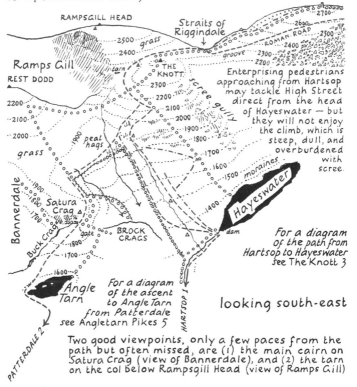

looking south-east

Enterprising pedestrians
approaching from Hartsop
may tackle High Street
direct from the head
of Hayeswater — but
they will not enjoy
the climb, which is
steep, dull, and
overburdened
with
scree.

For a diagram
of the path from
Hartsop to Hayeswater
see The Knott 3

For a diagram
of the ascent
to Angle Tarn
from Patterdale
see Angletarn Pikes 5

Two good viewpoints, only a few paces from the
path but often missed, are (1) the main cairn on
Satura Crag (view of Bannerdale), and (2) the tarn
on the col below Rampsgill Head (view of Ramps Gill)

This is the least exciting approach to High Street; it
is, nevertheless, a very enjoyable walk, with a series
of varied and beautiful views; and the tracking of
the indistinct path, which has many unexpected
turns and twists, is interesting throughout.

ASCENT FROM MARDALE

2050 feet of ascent   *3 miles from the road end*

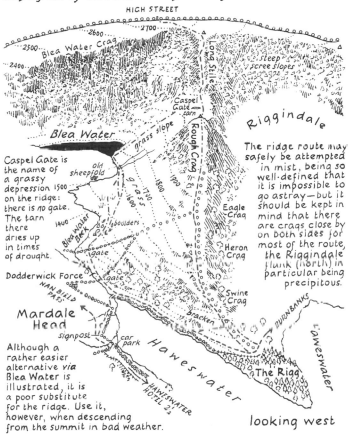

HIGH STREET

2600
2700
2500
Blea Water Crag
2400
Long Stile
steep scree slopes
Caspel Gate - tarn
Blea Water
grass slope
Rough Crag
Riggindale
Caspel Gate is the name of a grassy depression on the ridge: there is *no* gate. The tarn there dries up in times of drought.
old sheepfold
1500
1800
1900
1700
1600
grass
1400
Eagle Crag
The ridge route may safely be attempted in mist, being so well-defined that it is impossible to go astray—but it should be kept in mind that there are crags close by on both sides for most of the route, the Riggindale flank (north) in particular being precipitous.
Bleawater Beck
boulders
gate
Heron Crag
Dodderwick Force
gate
NAN BIELD PASS.
Swine Crag
Mardale Head
bracken
BURNBANKS
Lawswater
signpost
car park
Haweswater
The Rigg
Lawswater
Although a rather easier alternative *via* Blea Water is illustrated, it is a poor substitute for the ridge. Use it, however, when descending from the summit in bad weather.
HAWESWATER HOTEL 2½

looking west

The ridge of Rough Crag and the rocky stairway of Long Stile together form the connoisseur's route up High Street, the only route that discloses the finer characteristics of the fell. The ascent is a classic, leading directly along the crest of a long, straight ridge that permits of no variation from the valley to the summit. The views are excellent throughout.

ASCENT FROM TROUTBECK
2350 feet of ascent : 6 miles

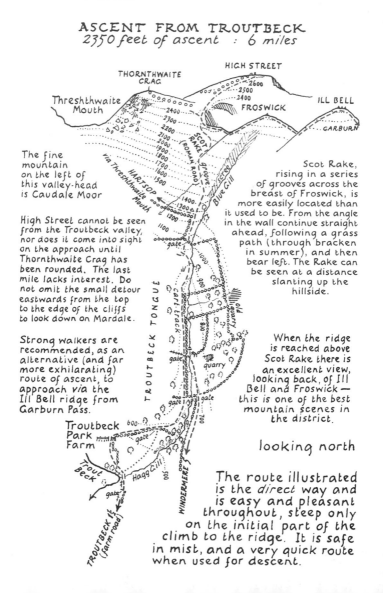

The fine mountain on the left of this valley-head is Caudale Moor

High Street cannot be seen from the Troutbeck valley, nor does it come into sight on the approach until Thornthwaite Crag has been rounded. The last mile lacks interest. Do not omit the small detour eastwards from the top to the edge of the cliffs to look down on Mardale.

Strong walkers are recommended, as an alternative (and far more exhilarating) route of ascent, to approach via the Ill Bell ridge from Garburn Pass.

Scot Rake, rising in a series of grooves across the breast of Froswick, is more easily located than it used to be. From the angle in the wall continue straight ahead, following a grass path (through bracken in summer), and then bear left. The Rake can be seen at a distance slanting up the hillside.

When the ridge is reached above Scot Rake there is an excellent view, looking back, of Ill Bell and Froswick — this is one of the best mountain scenes in the district.

looking north

The route illustrated is the *direct* way and is easy and pleasant throughout, steep only on the initial part of the climb to the ridge. It is safe in mist, and a very quick route when used for descent.

ASCENT FROM KENTMERE
2300 feet of ascent
5½ miles via Hall Cove : 6 miles via Nan Bield Pass

HIGH STREET

THORNTHWAITE CRAG

MARDALE ILL BELL

FROSWICK

source of River Kent

Bleathwaite Crag

Hall Cove

Gavel Crag

sheepfold

Nan Bield Pass

Lingmell End

waterfalls

scree

grass

sheepfold

FROSWICK

Lingmell Gill

ILL BELL

sheepfold

River Kent

bracken

Consult
Mardale Ill Bell 6
& Thornthwaite Crag 6
for additional
notes on the routes
illustrated

This is the usual route
to Nan Bield from
Kentmere (for
details of the start
see Harter Fell 6)

Kentmere Reservoir

Smallthwaite Knott

bracken

KENTMERE via Overend 3

looking
north·north·west

fold

Kentmere Quarries

quarries

KENTMERE via Hartrigg 2½

High Street is commonly
ascended from Kentmere by
way of the Ill Bell ridge (the best
route) or via Mardale Ill Bell, but it
may be climbed direct from Hall Cove
(or by a variation over Gavel Crag):
an interesting expedition.

Haweswater, from above Long Stile

Hayeswater, from the Roman Road

THE SUMMIT

The summit is barren of scenic interest, and only visitors of lively imagination will fully appreciate their surroundings. Any person so favoured may recline on the turf and witness, in his mind's eye, a varied pageant of history, for he has been preceded here, down the ages, by the ancient Britons who built their villages and forts in the valleys around; by the Roman cohorts marching between their garrisons at Ambleside and Brougham; by the Scots invaders who were repulsed on the Troutbeck slopes; by the shepherds, dalesmen and farmers who, centuries ago, made the summit their playground and feasting-place on the occasion of their annual meets; by racing horses (the summit is still named Racecourse Hill on the large-scale Ordnance Survey maps).....and let us not forget Dixon of immortal legend, whose great fall over the cliff while fox-hunting is an epic in enthusiasm.

Nowadays all is quiet here and only the rising larks disturb the stillness. A pleasant place, but — to those unfortunate folk with no imagination — so dull!

DESCENTS should be made only by the regular routes. It must be emphasised that there is only one direct way to Mardale — by Long Stile, the top of which is indicated by a cairn. Direct descents into Kentmere may lead to trouble, the best plan being to aim for Nan Bield Pass, in clear weather.

In mist, consult the maps. For Mardale, stick to the crest of Long Stile, but at Caspel Gate turn down right to Blea Water. Kentmere is best reached by descending into Hall Cove at a point 100 yards south-east of the end of the High Street wall. Avoid the Hayeswater face.

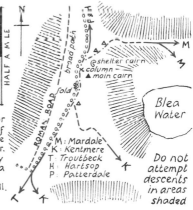

HALF A MILE

ROMAN ROAD
broad path
fold
column
shelter cairn
main cairn
Blea Water

M: Mardale
K: Kentmere
T: Troutbeck
H: Hartsop
P: Patterdale

Do not attempt descents in areas shaded

THE VIEW

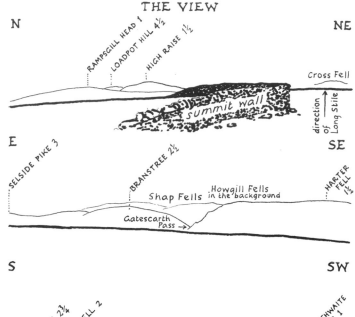

N — NE

RAMPSGILL HEAD 1 — LOADPOT HILL 4½ — HIGH RAISE 1½

Cross Fell

summit wall

direction of Long Stile

E — SE

SELSIDE PIKE 3

BRANSTREE 2½

Shap Fells — Howgill Fells in the background

HARTER FELL 1½

Gatescarth Pass →

S — SW

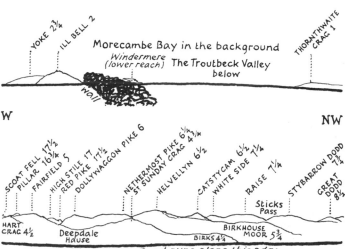

YOKE 2¾ — ILL BELL 2

Morecambe Bay in the background

Windermere (lower reach) — The Troutbeck Valley below

THORNTHWAITE CRAG 1

wall

W — NW

SCOAT FELL 17½ — PILLAR 16½ — FAIRFIELD 5 — HIGH STILE 17 — RED PIKE 17½ — DOLLYWAGGON PIKE 6 — NETHERMOST PIKE 6½ — ST SUNDAY CRAG 4¾ — HELVELLYN 6½ — CATSTYCAM 6½ — WHITE SIDE 7¼ — RAISE 7¼ — STYBARROW DODD 7¾ — GREAT DODD 8½

HART CRAG 4½ — Deepdale Hause — BIRKS 4¼ — BIRKHOUSE MOOR 5¾ — Sticks Pass

The Roman Road runs along this edge

THE VIEW

NE   E

The figures following the names of fells
indicate distances in miles

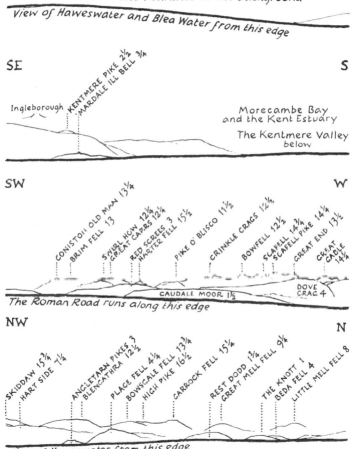

The Pennines in the background

View of Haweswater and Blea Water from this edge

SE   S

Ingleborough   KENTMERE PIKE 2½ ³/₄ MARDALE ILL BELL ½

Morecambe Bay
and the Kent Estuary

The Kentmere Valley
below

SW   W

CONISTON OLD MAN 13¼ BRIM FELL 13 SWIRL HOW 12½ GREAT CARRS 12¼ RED SCREES 3 HARTER FELL 1½ PIKE O' BLISCO 11½ CRINKLE CRAGS 12½ BOWFELL 12½ SCAFELL 14¼ SCAFELL PIKE 14¼ GREAT END 13½ GREAT GABLE 14¼

CAUDALE MOOR 1½   DOVE CRAG 4

The Roman Road runs along this edge

NW   N

SKIDDAW 15¾ HART SIDE 7¼ ANGLETARN PIKES 3 BLENCATHRA 12½ PLACE FELL 4¼ BOWSCALE FELL 13¾ HIGH PIKE 16½ CARROCK FELL 15¼ REST DODD 1¾ GREAT MELL FELL 9¾ THE KNOTT 1 BEDA FELL 4 LITTLE MELL FELL 8

View of Hayeswater from this edge

RIDGE ROUTES

To RAMPSGILL HEAD, 2598': 1¼ miles : N then NE
Depression at 2340': 250 feet of ascent
An easy and interesting walk

Follow the edge of the escarpment north to the narrow Straits of Riggindale. Beyond, watch for the divergence to the right from the main path, and bear left when the top of the fell is reached.

To MARDALE ILL BELL, 2496': ⅘ mile : SE then ESE
Depression at 2350': 150 feet of ascent
An easy walk with fine views

Follow the edge of the escarpment south-east — the cross on the map marks an excellent view of Blea Water. Incline left when the marshy depression is crossed. In mist, it is better to use the path.

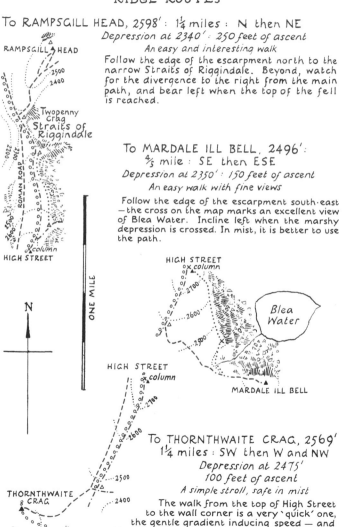

To THORNTHWAITE CRAG, 2569' 1¼ miles : SW then W and NW
Depression at 2475'
100 feet of ascent
A simple stroll, safe in mist

The walk from the top of High Street to the wall corner is a very 'quick' one, the gentle gradient inducing speed — and there is little of interest to detain the walker.

High Street from Mardale Ill Bell

Blea Water Crag

4 Thornthwaite Crag
from Hartsop

You find me sheltering by Thornthwaite Beacon, the 14 ft high stone-built pillar above Thornthwaite Crag and one of the most distinctive cairns in the Lake District. I was filming *Wainwright's Memorial Walk* and feeling a serious bond with the young Wainwright. When he came to this spot during the Whitsun holiday in 1931 he was on the first leg of his planned walking tour during which he would see every lake, valley and mountain in the district. He and his mates from work weren't getting off to a good start. It was raining that day in 1931 and it was raining the day I was there as well. In fact I went one better and had thunder.

On that trip, following in Wainwright's inexperienced footsteps, we'd walked across from Orrest Head, up the Garburn Pass and over Ill Bell and Froswick. If I hear the sound of Wainwright devotees bridling at the conjunction of 'Wainwright' and 'inexperienced', he was just that: a mountain novice. It's hard to credit now. But the Whitsun walk was his first tentative step into the big mountains. If the rain had continued for all six days, if he'd turned an ankle, if he'd got unbearable blisters, if his mates had said 'You must be off your trolley, Alf, we're out of here' (or whatever young men said to each other in a similar vein in 1931) we might never have had the Pictorial Guides. Wainwright might have become famous for bird-watching or making models out of bottle tops rather than as the master of the mountains. Fortunately, he shook off the rain and pressed on and so will we.

Because we were looking for rather easier ways into the mountains for the Granada series *Wainwright Country* we chose a different approach to Thornthwaite Crag, starting from the village of Hartsop by Brothers Water. And we're heading for a spot that has really great views. To the west, Pillar 16 miles away, Crinkle Crags 11 or 12 miles distant and, closer to in the east, Kentmere Pike, Shipman Knotts and High Street.

Even before you get to the summit you're going to have to spend time at the saddle of Threshthwaite Mouth, where you'll find Ullswater sparkling in its northern panorama and Windermere to the south. And then, once you've toasted the distant summits with a glass of champagne on Thornthwaite Crag (doesn't everyone?), you really have to stroll along the narrow ridge to Gray Crag above Hayeswater to look out over Patterdale to the sweep of Ullswater beyond. It will be a canny day's walking. All we've got to hope for now is that it's third time lucky and the rain stays away.

Practical bits
Map: OL5.
Ascent: The *Wainwright Country* route (3¼ miles and 2000 feet) starts at Hartsop village (NY408132) and follows Threshthwaite Glen up into Threshthwaite Cove. Turn for the summit at Threshthwaite Mouth as on Thornthwaite Crag 4 in *The Far Eastern Fells*.
Descent. Also shown on Thornthwaite Crag 4 is the route over Gray Crag to Wath Bridge and back to Hartsop. Distance and feet of descent are the same as the ascent. If you have a friendly driver, you could walk back to the summit from Gray Crag and then go down into Kentmere as on Thornthwaite Crag 6 in reverse. It's just 2 miles and 1650 feet down to the reservoir but then another 3 miles down the reservoir road to Kentmere. Leaving a car in Kentmere is a problem because there's a real shortage of parking space.

Thornthwaite Crag   2569'

Hartsop

HIGH STREET

CAUDALE MOOR ▲

▲ THORNTHWAITE CRAG

▲ ILL BELL

Kentmere

Troutbeck

MILES
0   1   2   3   4

from Caudale Moor

NATURAL FEATURES

Occupying a commanding position overlooking four valleys, Thornthwaite Crag is one of the better-known fells east of Kirkstone, owing not a little of its fame to its tall pillar of stones, a landmark for miles around. Its name derives from the long shattered cliff facing west above the upper Troutbeck valley; there are also crags fringing the head of Hayeswater Gill and above the early meanderings of the River Kent. Apart from these roughnesses the fell is grassy, the ground to the east of the summit forming a wide plateau before rising gently to the parent height of High Street, of which Thornthwaite Crag is a subsidiary; it has, however, a ridge in its own right, this being a narrow steep-sided shoulder that ends in Gray Crag, northwards. Streams flow in three directions: north to Ullswater, south to Windermere and south-east along the Kentmere valley.

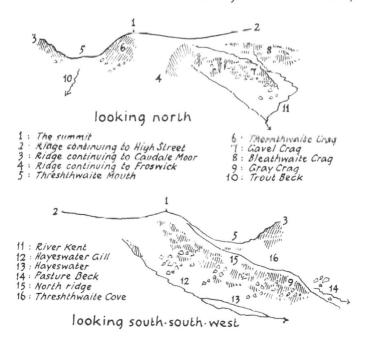

looking north

1 : The summit
2 : Ridge continuing to High Street
3 : Ridge continuing to Caudale Moor
4 : Ridge continuing to Froswick
5 : Threshthwaite Mouth
6 : Thornthwaite Crag
7 : Gavel Crag
8 : Bleathwaite Crag
9 : Gray Crag
10 : Trout Beck

11 : River Kent
12 : Hayeswater Gill
13 : Hayeswater
14 : Pasture Beck
15 : North ridge
16 : Threshthwaite Cove

looking south-south-west

MAP

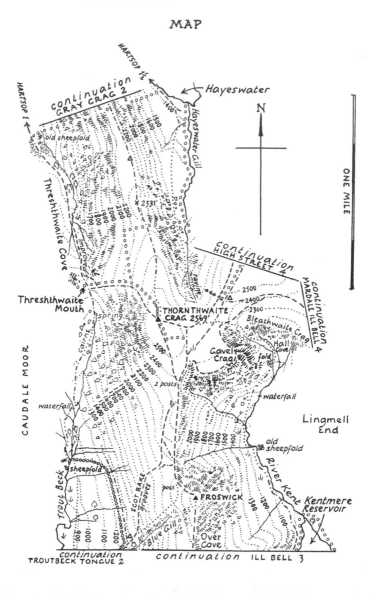

ONE MILE

N

continuation GRAY CRAG 2

HARTSOP 1½

HARTSOP 1

Hayeswater

Hayeswater Gill

old sheepfold

Threshthwaite Cove

improved

× 2331'

Threshthwaite Mouth

Threshthwaite Mouth

spring

cairns

CAUDALE MOOR

waterfall

Trout Beck

sheepfold

SCOT RAKE

groove

post

continuation TROUTBECK TONGUE 2

Blue Gill

continuation ILL BELL 3

Over Cove

▲ FROSWICK

continuation HIGH STREET 4

continuation MARDALE ILL BELL 4

2500
2400
2300

THORNTHWAITE CRAG 2569'

Bleathwaite Crag

Hall Cove

Gavel Crag

fold

2 posts

waterfall

Lingmell End

old sheepfold

River Kent

Kentmere Reservoir

ASCENT FROM HARTSOP
2000 feet of ascent : 3¼ miles

THORNTHWAITE CRAG

CAUDALE MOOR

HIGH STREET

Threshthwaite Mouth

grass

HIGH STREET

ravine

2500
2400
2300
2200
2100
2000
1900
1800
1700
1600
1500

GRAY CRAG

Hayeswater Gill

Threshthwaite Cove

grass

Pasture Beck

Raven Crag

HARTSOP DODD

Hayeswater

moraine

grass

1800
1500
1600

dam

1500
1400
1300
1200

grass

Threshthwaite Glen

sheepfold

There is shelter among the boulders below Raven Crag

Pronounce 'Threshthwaite' Thresh'et

stile
filter house

old mine

Wath

Wall mine

ruin

gate

gate

gate

700

gate

600

Hayeswater is a reservoir for Penrith

In mist, use the Threshthwaite route only

looking south-south-east

car park

Hartsop

This is a very interesting and enjoyable expedition. Of the three routes illustrated, that via Hayeswater starts well but has a tame and tiring conclusion. If the return is to be made to Hartsop, Threshthwaite is the best approach, the descent being made along the north ridge over Gray Crag, which itself has an airy situation and good views.

ASCENT FROM TROUTBECK
2200 feet of ascent
5 miles via Scot Rake; 5½ via Threshthwaite Mouth

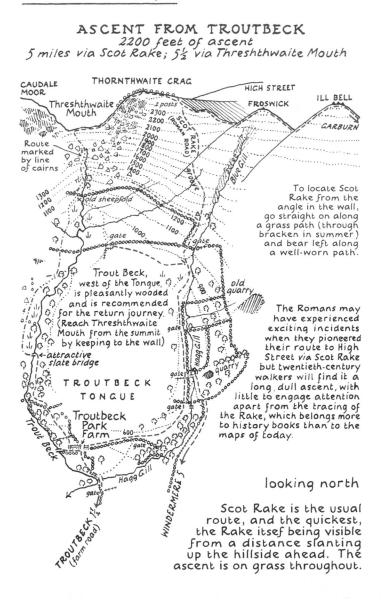

CAUDALE MOOR

THORNTHWAITE CRAG

HIGH STREET

ILL BELL

Threshthwaite Mouth

FROSWICK

GARBURN

2 posts

2300
2200
2100
2000
1900
1800
1700
1600
1500

SCOT RAKE (ROMAN ROAD)

Route marked by line of cairns

1300
1200
1100

old sheepfold

1200

gate

1000

1100

gate

To locate Scot Rake from the angle in the wall, go straight on along a grass path (through bracken in summer) and bear left along a well-worn path.

old quarry

Trout Beck, west of the Tongue, is pleasantly wooded and is recommended for the return journey. (Reach Threshthwaite Mouth from the summit by keeping to the wall)

gate

The Romans may have experienced exciting incidents when they pioneered their route to High Street via Scot Rake but twentieth-century walkers will find it a long, dull ascent, with little to engage attention apart from the tracing of the Rake, which belongs more to history books than to the maps of today.

attractive slate bridge

TROUTBECK TONGUE

gate

quarry

Hagg Gill

gate

Troutbeck Park Farm

600

gate

gate

Trout Beck

Hagg Gill

gate

WINDERMERE 5

looking north

Scot Rake is the usual route, and the quickest, the Rake itself being visible from a distance slanting up the hillside ahead. The ascent is on grass throughout.

TROUTBECK 1¼ (farm road)

ASCENT FROM KENTMERE RESERVOIR
1650 feet of ascent : 2 miles

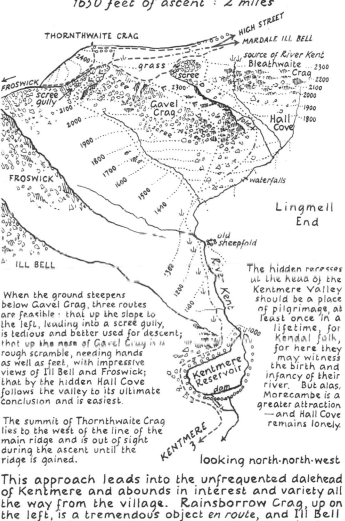

THORNTHWAITE CRAG

HIGH STREET

MARDALE ILL BELL

FROSWICK

grass

scree

source of River Kent
Bleathwaite
Crag

Gavel
Crag

Hall
Cove

scree
gully

scree

FROSWICK

waterfalls

Lingmell
End

ILL BELL

old
sheepfold

River Kent

When the ground steepens
below Gavel Crag, three routes
are feasible : that up the slope to
the left, leading into a scree gully,
is tedious and better used for descent;
that up the nose of Gavel Crag is a
rough scramble, needing hands
as well as feet, with impressive
views of Ill Bell and Froswick;
that by the hidden Hall Cove
follows the valley to its ultimate
conclusion and is easiest.

The summit of Thornthwaite Crag
lies to the west of the line of the
main ridge and is out of sight
during the ascent until the
ridge is gained.

The hidden recesses
at the head of the
Kentmere Valley
should be a place
of pilgrimage, at
least once in a
lifetime, for
Kendal folk,
for here they
may witness
the birth and
infancy of their
river. But alas,
Morecambe is a
greater attraction
— and Hall Cove
remains lonely.

Kentmere
Reservoir

dam

KENTMERE 3

looking north-north-west

This approach leads into the unfrequented dalehead
of Kentmere and abounds in interest and variety all
the way from the village. Rainsborrow Crag, up on
the left, is a tremendous object *en route*, and Ill Bell
and Froswick reveal themselves most effectively.

THE SUMMIT

Thornthwaite Beacon

It is sometimes difficult to recall the details of familiar summits but surely all who have climbed Thornthwaite Crag will identify it in memory by its remarkable 14-feet column, one of the most distinctive cairns in Lakeland. It stands in the angle of a wall that traverses the summit. A few outcrops of flaky rock in the vicinity relieve the general grassiness of the top of the fell.

DESCENTS: In clear weather all the routes of ascent may be reversed, but that to Kentmere *via* Gavel Crag is not suggested nor should routes be 'invented' as there is rough ground about. *In bad conditions*, descend to Troutbeck or Hartsop *via* Threshthwaite Mouth — to which the wall leads when followed north-west. For Kentmere, go to the end of the wall eastwards; here turn right along a faint path for 200 yards to a scree gully on the left, which descend.

looking north to
Ullswater

Threshthwaite Mouth

looking south to
Windermere

THE VIEW

Principal Fells

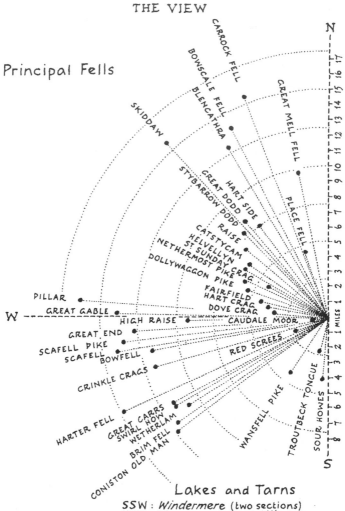

Lakes and Tarns

SSW: *Windermere* (two sections)
NNW: The upper reach of *Ullswater* may be seen by descending the west slope for 50 yards, or by following the wall north. N: *Hayeswater* is brought into view by a short walk (130 yards) in the direction of High Street.

THE VIEW

The tall column, the wall, and adjacent high ground
northwards between them interrupt the panorama —
and various 'stations' must be visited to see all there
is to see. The view is good, but not amongst the best;
the northern prospect, in particular, is best surveyed
from the slope going down to Threshthwaite Mouth.

The best feature in the scene is Windermere, to which
the Troutbeck valley leads the eye with excellent effect.

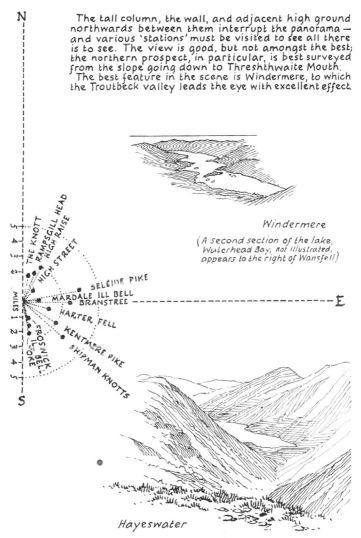

Windermere

*(A second section of the lake,
Waterhead Bay, not illustrated,
appears to the right of Wansfell)*

N

THE KNOTT
RAMPSGILL HEAD
HIGH RAISE
HIGH STREET
SELSIDE PIKE
MARDALE ILL BELL
BRANSTREE
HARTER FELL
KENTMERE PIKE
FROSWICK
ILL BELL
YOKE
SHIPMAN KNOTTS

MILES 5 4 3 2 1 1 2 3 4 5

E

S

Hayeswater

RIDGE ROUTES

To CAUDALE MOOR, 2502' : 1 mile : NW, W and WSW
Depression at 1950' : 560 feet of ascent
A rough scramble, made safe in mist by walls

There is more to this walk than appears at first sight, for the gap of Threshthwaite Mouth is deep and it links slopes that are steep and rough. Keep by the wall until the broken crag of Caudale is left behind. The Caudale flank above the gap can be dangerous when the rocks are iced or under snow.

To GRAY CRAG, 2286' : 1¼ miles : slightly W of N
Two minor depressions : 150 feet of ascent
An easy, interesting walk, better avoided in mist.

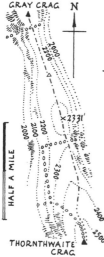

Straightforward walking along the descending and narrowing north ridge leads first to the nameless conical height of point 2331', then to the flat top of Gray Crag.   Two broken walls are crossed en route.   Both flanks are heavily scarped and dangerous in mist.

To FROSWICK, 2359'
1 mile
SSE then S and SE
Depression at 2100'
300 feet of ascent
A very easy walk

Follow the path by the broken wall to the south-south-east. When the wall bends left, continue straight on along the path to a junction marked by two posts. A long grassy descent leads to the final rise to the top of Froswick.

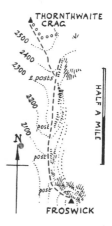

RIDGE ROUTES

To HIGH STREET, 2718': 1¼ miles : SE, then E and NE
Depression at 2475' : 250 feet of ascent
A very simple walk; safe in mist

Take the prominent path east from Thornthwaite Crag and follow it as far as the wall corner. Then follow the broken wall to the top of High Street. All is grass.

To MARDALE ILL BELL, 2496'
1½ miles : SE, then E, ENE and ESE
Depressions at 2475' and 2350' : 200 feet of ascent
Easy walking, but a confusing area in mist

Leave the corner of the High Street wall by a plain track trending eastwards and when this curves right go straight on over long grass in the same direction, descending slightly to the depression ahead. In mist, take care not to descend to the right into Hall Cove.

*Thornthwaite Crag
from the south ridge of
Caudale Moor*

5 Eagle Crag
from Stonethwaite

When I showed Wainwright's picture of Eagle Crag to Fred Talbot, who was presenting the Granada series *Wainwright Country*, he said with commendable honesty, 'You really expect me to go up that?' You should know that the previous television series Fred made was about canals, and given that feet of ascent for canal builders involved impressive civil engineering and cost serious brass, they obviously tried to avoid them wherever they could. That's not an option in the central fells of Lakeland.

There's no avoiding Eagle Crag on foot.

It's a bold upstart, as Wainwright himself might have said if there had been enough space left on one of his impeccably balanced pages. There wasn't and he didn't, so I've made up for the omission.

When we were filming together, he and I talked often about his system of classification of mountains – how high they had to be and how they needed to look to qualify for the accolade. The consensus was that, ideally, they should be big – certainly over 2000 feet.

'So Eagle Crag isn't one because it's only 1650 feet?'

Consensus evaporated. Long pause.

'Well, no.' Long pause. 'Because there are other factors to take into account such as whether or not they have a rocky aspect and a fine summit.'

'So Eagle Crag is a mountain?'

The pause extended until it was time for him to go home that day.

In *The Central Fells* Wainwright hedged his bets, called it a beautiful fell, often admired, seldom ascended; called it a splendidly situated giant cornerstone. In Wainwright's book it was a continuous rampart of repelling crags. In mine it's a mountain. I first saw it on an expedition to Castle Crag in Borrowdale. It beckons to lovers of mountains, tempting them down the Stonethwaite valley. It's impressive even at a distance but the views of it from just below, by Stonethwaite Beck, are as majestic as any mountain needs to be.

It looks impossible without resorting to ropes and the swathes of high-tech hardware that make modern climbers look like mediaeval peddlers selling gew-gaws when they arrive in the valley. Its vertical faces harbour sinister shadows. From the bottom you can't spot a way past them. But Wainwright found a way past the repelling crags and charted one of the most enervating and satisfying mountain ascents in Lakeland. Even though it's only a little mountain.

As A.W. hadn't made up his mind last time I talked to him about it, when you're on Eagle Crag listen out for a deep harrumph and a grudging 'Yes' carried on the mountain wind. You might just hear it, because Wainwright wasn't a man to leave loose ends.

Practical bits

Map: OL 4

Ascent: Start at Stonethwaite Bridge (NY264138) and follow Route A on Eagle Crag 3 and 4 in Wainwright's *The Central Fells* (2 miles and 1300 feet). The walk out via Greenup Gill to High Raise is worth doing if you've time and weather on your side

Descent: If the weather turns, use the reverse of Route B as the descent and if the weather's bad before you set off, don't. The final ascent over Heron Crag is dodgy in poor visibility and, anyhow, a view of nothing more than a wall of grey emulsion paint wouldn't do this mountain justice.

Eagle Crag

1650'
approx.

The latest 2½" O.S. map shows
a 520-metre contour, suggesting
an altitude in excess of 1700'.

- **Rosthwaite**
- **Stonethwaite**
  - ▲ ▲ ULLSCARF
  - **EAGLE CRAG**
  - ▲ HIGH RAISE

MILES
0   1   2   3

from Stonethwaite Beck

MAP

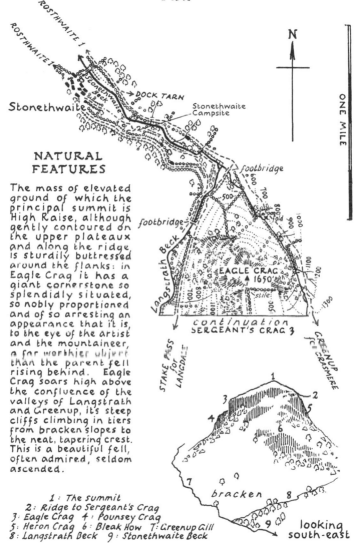

ROSTHWAITE ↑

ROSTHWAITE ↑

N

ONE MILE

Stonethwaite

DOCK TARN

Stonethwaite Campsite

DOCK TARN

footbridge

footbridge

fold

Langstrath Beck

EAGLE CRAG ▲ 1650'

stile

continuation
SERGEANT'S CRAG 3

STAKE PASS for LANGDALE

GREENUP for GRASMERE

NATURAL FEATURES

The mass of elevated ground of which the principal summit is High Raise, although gently contoured on the upper plateaux and along the ridge, is sturdily buttressed around the flanks: in Eagle Crag it has a giant cornerstone so splendidly situated, so nobly proportioned and of so arresting an appearance that it is, to the eye of the artist and the mountaineer, a far worthier object than the parent fell rising behind. Eagle Crag soars high above the confluence of the valleys of Langstrath and Greenup, its steep cliffs climbing in tiers from bracken slopes to the neat, tapering crest. This is a beautiful fell, often admired, seldom ascended.

bracken

looking south-east

1: The summit
2: Ridge to Sergeant's Crag
3: Eagle Crag 4: Pounsey Crag
5: Heron Crag 6: Bleak How 7: Greenup Gill
8: Langstrath Beck 9: Stonethwaite Beck

ASCENT FROM STONETHWAITE
1300 feet of ascent : 2 miles

GREENUP

moraines

Greenup Gill

grass

EAGLE CRAG

B

B bracken

sheepfold

Eagle Pouncey Crag Crag

Heron Crag

A

From the summit, with ample time in hand, the walk may be continued around the head of Greenup Gill and across rising grass slopes to High Raise (poor path initially, then none. Aim right of Long Crag)

Leave the Greenup path at a sheepfold on an island. Bear left at first and then right horizontally along the upper bracken limit to the wall

A 1200

A

900

800 bracken

700

old sheepfold

A bracken

600

bracken

A bracken

500

STAKE PASS

Langstrath Beck

Langstrath

When surveyed from the valley, Eagle Crag seems well-nigh unassailable, a continuous rampart of crags defending the crest above other steep rocks rising in tiers from the lower slopes. The crags are undoubtedly repelling (the main cliff is quite vertical) and a direct *straight* ascent is out of the question, but there is just one line of weakness on this front by which the top may be gained by ordinary walking: tracing this line amid its impressive surroundings is enjoyable and interesting. This route is marked A on the diagram, and its complicated upper portion is repeated in more detail on the opposite page. Route B is easy, and without thrills; it gains the summit by the 'back door', and is very suitable as a way down. In bad weather Route B is the *only* way, either up or down, *but in bad weather the climb should not be attempted at all.*

600 500 Footbridge

Galleny Force 400

DOCK TARN

stile

400

Stonethwaite Beck

Stonethwaite

The beginning of Route A, beyond the footbridge, is difficult to negotiate in late summer because of the bracken. (There are gates, or gateways, in both walls just above the stream.)

ROSTHWAITE

ROSTHWAITE

looking south-south-east

continued

ASCENT FROM STONETHWAITE

continued

The upper section of Route A

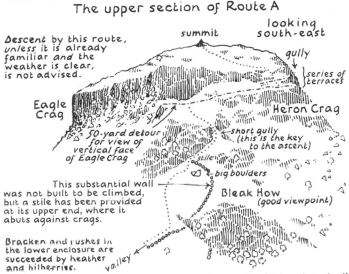

looking south-east

summit

gully

series of terraces

Descent by this route, unless it is already familiar and the weather is clear, is not advised.

Eagle Crag

Heron Crag

50-yard detour for view of vertical face of Eagle Crag

short gully (this is the key to the ascent)

stile

big boulders

This substantial wall was not built to be climbed, but a stile has been provided at its upper end, where it abuts against crags.

Bleak How (good viewpoint)

Bracken and rushes in the lower enclosure are succeeded by heather and bilberries.

valley

Here, and in other craggy places, sheep should be disturbed as little as possible, even at inconvenience to the walker; otherwise they may become casualties. The walls are not put there for ornament: they serve a vital purpose, and if stones are displaced they should be put back, and firmly.

Eagle Crag is the most distinctive object in the Stonethwaite landscape and its ascent reveals all the beauty of the valley in a pleasant half-day's (or summer evening's) expedition.

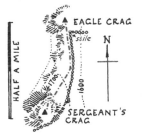

▲ EAGLE CRAG

stile

N

1700

1600

▲ SERGEANT'S CRAG

HALF A MILE

RIDGE ROUTE

TO SERGEANT'S CRAG, 1873'
½ mile : S. then SSW
Minor depressions
250 feet of ascent
Easy, but not safe in mist

A rough little path leads down to the head of a gully at the wall-corner. Do not cross the wall, but accompany it south, finally inclining away from it.

THE SUMMIT

HINDSCARTH   GRASMOOR   EEL CRAG   GRISEDALE PIKE   CAUSEY PIKE   LORD'S SEAT   BARF   CATBELLS   Bassenthwaite Lake

A small cairn sits proudly on the apex of a tilted slab of rock and indicates the summit. Nothing can be seen of the crags that fall away to the valley because of an upper plateau of grass and heather, broken by many outcrops. Eastwards from the cairn there is an acre of flat marshy ground before the slopes descend from sight.

DESCENTS: There must be no thought of a quick romp straight down to the valley immediately below: *it cannot be done.* Unless the route on the Stonethwaite face (Route A) is already known, it should not be sought from above: the crags form an almost continuous barrier here. Palpitations and alarms may be avoided by following the wall down towards Greenup (away from the direction of Stonethwaite) after first crossing it at the corner, and, when rough ground appears ahead, making a wide detour to the right to join the Greenup path down easy bracken slopes. *In bad weather, or if there is deep snow, this is the only route that will ensure the due arrival of the walker at Stonethwaite in one unbroken piece.*

THE VIEW

Principal Fells

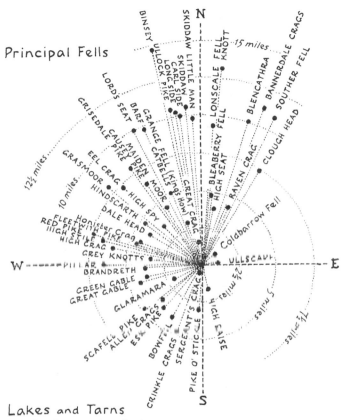

Lakes and Tarns
NNW : Bassenthwaite Lake

The view of the Stonethwaite valley, which might be expected
to be excellent, is not quite that, the summit being set rather
too far back from the edge of the crags to enable all of it to
be seen; a short and easy descent of the upper slope leads to
better points of vantage. But generally the valley is too short
to be really effective in a view, although the whole picture is
very pleasing to west and north. Eastwards the scene is drab.

6 Helm Crag

from Grasmere

For most people, it's a mountain framed in the car or bus window. A Howitzer, an old woman playing a mighty Wurlitzer and a lion and lamb are what you're looking out for. Find them and you've found Helm Crag above Grasmere. It's probably the most recognisable summit in the whole of Lakeland, rising, as it does, beside the main road from Keswick to Ambleside. It's known to tens of thousands of people for whom the high point of their holiday visit has been a vertiginous bar stool or a high kerb in Keswick.

But Helm Crag goes beyond being merely a vicarious thrill. It's also the end point of *Wainwright's Memorial Walk*, which tracked A.W.'s early attempt at a comprehensive walking tour of the Lake District. I thought, when we were making the film version, that Helm Crag was bound to be an anticlimax after all the really big summits. What could this 1299 feet pimple offer that they couldn't?

Having marched down to it along the gentle ridge from Calf Crag and Rough Crag and Gibson Knott, I discovered that the answer was quite a lot, really. This is the perfect spot from which to see the real glories of the Vale of Grasmere.

Wainwright liked Helm Crag very much and often went there when poor weather kept him off the high fells. In rather the same way that Ruskin counted the scene from Friar's Crag on Derwent Water as one of the greatest landscape spectacles in the world, Wainwright put Helm Crag in the first division of great views. In fact it was on a par with the outlook from Orrest Head, his first revelation of Lakeland – that moment when the young lad from mill town walked off the edge of the real world and found himself in a sort of heaven.

As Julia Bradbury showed when she walked up from Grasmere village for the *Wainwright Walks* film made here, heaven and the modern world aren't so very far apart.

From Helm Crag can be seen the blend of Lakeland textures that make this place one of the great landscapes of Europe. Wild and rocky uplands framing lower slopes won back from the mountain by generations of hard farming labour. And below those, held by them as if in the palm of a hand, fertile and gently-watered valley bottoms, with their clusters of farms and hamlets. Up here, away from traffic and crowds that are the inevitable, essential beating economic heart of these communities, it's not a great deal different from the way it was in Wordsworth's day.

The essence of the Lake District is here for all to find and, hopefully, understand. If you want wilderness, you've come to the wrong place. If what touches a nerve with you, as it did with Wainwright, is that here man and landscape have achieved an impossible harmony, then Helm Crag is the place to be.

Practical bits

Map: OL7.

Ascent: Unless you're going to do the long hike in that we did on *Wainwright's Memorial Walk*, there is really only one route, the one taken for *Wainwright Walks*. It's detailed on Helm Crag 4 in *The Central Fells* (1100 feet of ascent over 1½ miles). Start in Grasmere main car park (NY336076).

Descent: The only sensible descent is to retrace your steps but the repetition is made bearable by the glorious views ahead of you most of the way.

Helm Crag

1329'

affectionately known as
'The Lion and The Lamb'

HELM ▲
CRAG

Grasmere •

MILES
0   1   2

This is the smallest (and most accurate!) map in the book

from Grasmere

NATURAL FEATURES

Helm Crag may well be the best-known of all Lakeland fells, and possibly even the best-known hill in the country. Generations of waggonette and motor-coach tourists have been tutored to recognise its appearance in the Grasmere landscape: it is the one feature of their Lakeland tour they hail at sight, and in unison, but the cry on their lips is not "Helm Crag!" but "The Lion and the Lamb!" — in a variety of dialects. The resemblance of the summit rocks to a lion is so striking that recognition, from several viewpoints, is instant; yet, oddly, the outline most like Leo is not the official 'Lion' at all: in fact there are two lions, each with a lamb, and each guards one end of the summit ridge as though set there by architectural design. The summit is altogether a rather weird and fantastic place, well worth not merely a visit but a detailed and leisurely exploration. Indeed the whole fell, although of small extent, is unusually interesting; its very appearance is challenging; its sides are steep, rough and craggy; its top bristles; it *looks* irascible, like a shaggy terrier in a company of sleek foxhounds, for all around are loftier and smoother fells, circling the pleasant vale of Grasmere out of which Helm Crag rises so abruptly.

The fell is not isolated, nor independent of others, for it is the termination of a long ridge enclosing Far Easedale in a graceful curve on north and east and rising, finally, to the rocky peak of Calf Crag. It drains quickly, is dry underfoot, and has no streams worthy of mention.

The virtues of Helm Crag have not been lauded enough. It gives an exhilarating little climb, a brief essay in real mountaineering, and, in a region where all is beautiful, it makes a notable contribution to the natural charms and attractions of Grasmere.

outline of
STEEL FELL

DUNMAIL
RAISE

THE
GREENBURN
VALLEY

*summit
scene*

MAP

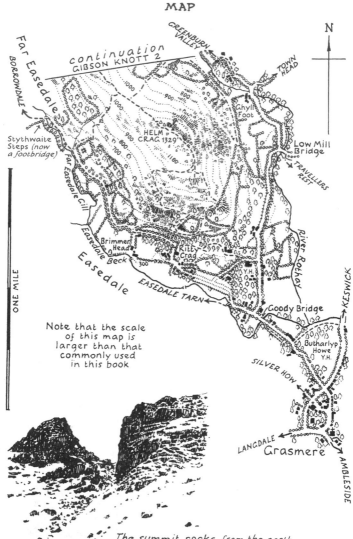

N

continuation
GIBSON KNOTT 2

GREENBURN VALLEY

Far Easedale

BORROWDALE

TOWN HEAD

Ghyll Foot

Stythwaite Steps *(now a footbridge)*

HELM CRAG 1329

Low Mill Bridge

TRAVELLERS REST

Far Easedale Gill

Easedale Beck

Brimmer Head

Kilt Crag

Y.H.

River Rothay

KESWICK

Easedale

EASEDALE TARN

Goody Bridge

Butharlyp Howe Y.H.

ONE MILE

Note that the scale of this map is larger than that commonly used in this book

SILVER HOW

LANGDALE

Grasmere

AMBLESIDE

The summit rocks from the north

ASCENT FROM GRASMERE
1100 feet of ascent : 1½ miles

HELM CRAG

bracken

new path

White Crag

bracken

Raven Crag

scree

Jackdaw Crag

old path

FAR EASEDALE & BORROWDALE (footpath)

Easedale

EASEDALE TARN

Lancrigg Crag

Kitty Crag

LOW MILL BRIDGE and GYLL FOOT

Goody Bridge

Easedale Beck

Butharlyp Howe Y.H.

studio

LANGDALE

KESWICK

car park

Red Lion Hotel

Grasmere

Church

This is one of the few hills where ascent and descent by the same route is recommended, the new path depicted here being much the best way both up and down. An alternative route (shown on the map but not on this diagram) has nothing in its favour.

If, however, Helm Crag is to be a part only of the day's programme (e.g. the circuit of Far Easedale or the Greenburn valley) it is better reserved for descent, for then the Vale of Grasmere will be directly in view ahead; and this fair scene is at its best when the shadows of evening are lengthening, with the Langdales silhouetted in rugged outline against the sunset. Tarry long over this exquisite picture of serenity and peace, and memorise it for the long winter of exile!

looking north-west

This is a splendid little climb ; if it has a fault it is that it is too short. But for the evening of the day of arrival in Grasmere on a walking holiday it is just the thing : an epitome of Lakeland concentrated in the space of two hours — and an excellent foretaste of happy days to come.

THE SUMMIT

Rocks at the north-west
end of the summit ridge,
known by various names:
(a) **The Lion Couchant**,
or, more popularly, **The
Lion and The Lamb**,
(as seen from the road
below Dunmail Raise)
(b) **The Howitzer**
(as seen from
Dunmail Raise)

The highest
point of the
rocks is the
true summit
of the fell

In scenic values, the summits of many high mountains are a disappointment after the long toil of ascent, yet here, on the top of little Helm Crag, a midget of a mountain, is a remarkable array of rocks, upstanding and fallen, of singular interest and fascinating appearance, that yield a quality of reward out of all proportion to the short and simple climb. The uppermost inches of Scafell and Helvellyn and Skiddaw can show nothing like Helm Crag's crown of shattered and petrified stone : indeed, its highest point, a pinnacle of rock airily thrust out above a dark abyss, is not to be attained by walking and is brought underfoot only by precarious manœuvres of the body. This is one of the very few summits in Lakeland reached only by climbing rocks, and it is certainly (but not for that reason alone) one of the very best.

continued

THE SUMMIT

continued

The summit ridge is 250 yards in length and is adorned at each end by fangs of rock overtopping the fairly level path. Between these towers there have been others in ages past but all that remains of them now is a chaos of collapsed boulders, choking a strange depression that extends the full length of the summit on the north-east side. The depression is bounded by a secondary ridge, and this in turn descends craggily to an even more strange depression, in appearance resembling a huge ditch cleft straight as a furrow across the breast of the fell for 300 yards; or, more romantically, a deep moat defending the turreted wall of the castle above. This surprising feature, which will not be seen unless searched for, will doubtless be readily explained by geologists (or antiquaries?); to the unlearned beholder it seems likely to be the result of some ancient natural convulsion that caused the side of the fell to slip downwards a few yards before coming to rest. This ditch is also bounded on its far side by a parallel ridge or parapet (narrow, and an interesting walk) beyond which the fellside plunges down almost precipitously to the valley, falling in juniper-clad crags.

Care is necessary when exploring the boulder-strewn depressions on the summit, especially if the rocks are greasy. There are many good natural shelters here, and some dangerous clefts and fissures and holes, so well protected from the weather that summer flowers are to be found in bloom in their recesses as late as mid-winter.

The south west side of the summit ridge consists mainly of bracken slopes and are of little interest in their upper reaches.

DESCENTS : Always use the ridge-path for descent to Grasmere. Watch for the path to the right from the ridge, especially in mist, and ignore the misleading green path going straight on : this ends above crags.

THE SUMMIT

Rocks at the north-west end of the summit-ridge known as The Old Woman Playing the Organ *from their appearance when seen from Tongue Gill and the vicinity of Easedale Tarn*

Rocks at the south-east end of the summit-ridge. *These form the* OFFICIAL Lion and The Lamb *(as seen from the Swan Hotel, Grasmere). The lion's head is the O.S. 'station' (altitude 1306') but is not quite the highest point of the fell*

THE VIEW

This is the view from the cairn on the summit ridge — whether it coincides with the view from the highest point the author will never know for his several attempts to mount to the rocky pate of the Lion Couchant have all been defeated by a lack of resolution; but probably it is the same. In any case, most visitors will be content to study the prospect from the comparative security of the cairn on the ridge.

continued

continued

The Vale of Grasmere is best displayed from the head of the other (official) Lion, which even the author found a simple ascent, (although deeply conscious of precipices all around).

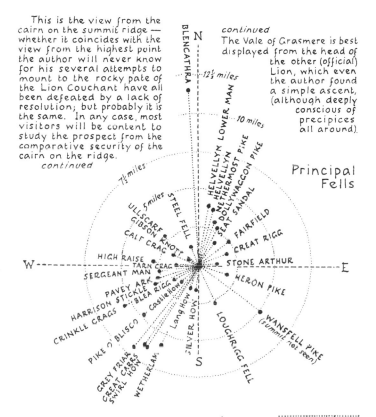

Principal Fells

N

BLENCATHRA · 12½ miles

HELVELLYN LOWER MAN · 10 miles

HELVELLYN
HELVELLYN
NETHERMOST PIKE
DOLLYWAGGON PIKE
SEAT SANDAL

FAIRFIELD

GREAT RIGG

STEEL FELL · 7½ miles

ULLSCARF · 5 miles
GIBSON KNOTT
CALF CRAG

HIGH RAISE
TARN CRAG
SERGEANT MAN

STONE ARTHUR

E

W

PAVEY ARK
HARRISON STICKLE
BLEA RIGG
CRINKLE CRAGS
CASTLE HOW

HERON PIKE

PIKE O' BLISCO

LANG HOW

SILVER HOW

LOUGHRIGG FELL

WANSFELL PIKE (summit not seen)

GREY FRIAR
GREAT CARRS
SWIRL HOW
WETHERLAM

S

The prominent height south-south-east (to the right of Loughrigg Fell) is Gummers How, 13 miles distant at the foot of Windermere.

Lakes and Tarns

SE: *Windermere (upper reach)*
SSE: *Grasmere*
SSE: *Esthwaite Water*
WSW: *Easedale Tarn*

This corner was reserved for an announcement that the author had succeeded in surmounting the highest point. Up to the time of going to press, however, such an announcement cannot be made.

Tarn Crag
across Far Easedale
from the slopes of Helm Crag

The north-east face
from Low Mill Bridge

RIDGE ROUTE

To GIBSON KNOTT, 1379'
  1 mile : NW, then W
  Depression at 1050'
  400 feet of ascent
   An interesting ridge climb

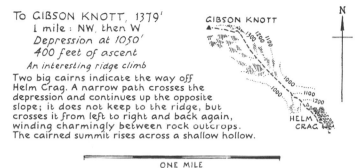

Two big cairns indicate the way off
Helm Crag. A narrow path crosses the
depression and continues up the opposite
slope; it does not keep to the ridge, but
crosses it from left to right and back again,
winding charmingly between rock outcrops.
The cairned summit rises across a shallow hollow.

ONE MILE

Helm Crag, from the path to Gibson Knott

7 Bowfell via Crinkle Crags
from Langdale

We're heading for a world of shattered crags and tumbled rocks, of gullies too deep to catch the sun and slabs hurled petulantly about as if by the hand of an angry giant. It's one of the most dramatic mountain landscapes in Britain. It is pure Lakeland, the sort of mountain scenery for which fell walkers were invented.

When Wainwright finished his exploration of 'this bit of heaven fallen upon the earth', he said he left with that hollow feeling you get when taking leave of friends, knowing that it may be for the last time. Both Bowfell and Crinkle Crags appear in his list of the six finest fells. I couldn't disagree. When we went there during the filming of *Wainwright's Memorial Walk* it was perfection, apart from a very noisy group of picnickers on Crinkle Crags who were given a short, sharp lecture by our sound recordist to the effect that there are many places in the Lake District where you can play silly games, shout to your heart's content and throw stones at one another. But this wasn't one of them. There are times when I think Wainwright had more influence on our film crew than we've so far admitted.

We didn't get him to the summit of Bowfell when we were filming the 1980s BBC series. That really would have been pushing our luck. So Wainwright and I looked out of Langdale towards that jagged mountain horizon. Looked up the well-tramped path called the Band. I said I thought it was a fairly boring flog. Wainwright humphed. He said he thought it was designed that way by the maker of mountains to keep you waiting; to sharpen your sense of expectation. It was an overture to a symphony of mountain landscapes and anyone who thought it was boring obviously had no soul. Good job I appreciate bluntness.

I changed the subject. He ticked off the summits. Bowfell itself, brooding under cloud. He said a strange thing, that

Bowfell was a mountain that roared. On a couple of occasions there he'd apparently noticed the way the mountain wind seemed to wail with a deep resonance among the rocks on the summit. I told Julia Bradbury when she was about to climb Bowfell for her series on BBC4. She was going to listen out for it.

It took some time to get off Bowfell by the time he'd run through the memories of his first time on Great Slab and the blood-racing views from there of Bowfell Buttress and Cambridge Crag. All recounted in almost as much pen sharp detail as the drawings he left us.

But then we were among gentler memories. Him resting by Three Tarns, sitting on a rock and splashing his boots in the water before climbing out over Shelter Crags and Gunson Knott and, eventually, Crinkle Crags. He remembered the details of the walk he'd done twenty-five years before with such precision that we were almost travelling in real time. I joked that, at this rate, there was a chance of not getting off the mountain before dark. And he said another strange thing, that the mountains had always looked after him. But then, as if he'd given away a secret too many, it was his turn to change the subject.

Practical bits
Map: OL6.
Ascent: For *Wainwright Walks*, BBC4 planned their route up the Band from the junction of Mickleden and Oxendale, as shown in *The Southern Fells* on Bowfell 5. Start at the car park at the Old Dungeon Ghyll Hotel (NY286061). 2700 feet of ascent over 3 miles or 3¼ miles if you go by Three Tarns. If you choose to go to the summit of Bowfell first, take the A route shown in more detail on Bowfell 6. Then make your way back to Three Tarns and follow the ridge plan in Crinkle Crags 13.
Descent: A fine descent which takes you back to your car is via Red Tarn, the reverse of Wainwright's route on Crinkle Crags 5.

Bowfell

2960'

'Bow Fell' (two words)
on Ordnance Survey maps

from Lingmoor Fell

NATURAL FEATURES

A favourite of all fellwalkers, Bowfell is a mountain that commands attention whenever it appears in a view.   And more than attention, respect and admiration, too; for it has the rare characteristic of displaying a graceful outline and a sturdy shapeliness on all sides. The fell occupies a splendid position at the hub of three well-known valleys, Great Langdale, Langstrath and Eskdale, rising as a massive pyramid at the head of each, and it is along these valleys that its waters drain, soon assuming the size of rivers. The higher the slopes rise the rougher they become, finally rearing up steeply as a broken rim of rock around the peaked summit and stony top.   These crags are of diverse and unusual form, natural curiosities that add an exceptional interest and help to identify Bowfell in the memory. Under the terraced northern precipices, in a dark hollow, is Angle Tarn.

As much as any other mountain, the noble Bowfell may be regarded as affording an entirely typical Lakeland climb, with easy walking over grass giving place to rough scrambling on scree, and a summit deserving of detailed exploration and rewarding visitors with very beautiful views.

Rank Bowfell among the best half-dozen! ✳

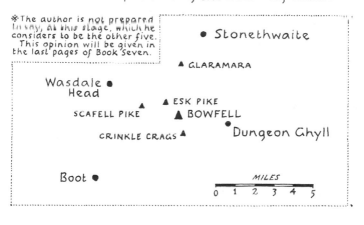

✳ The author is not prepared to say, at this stage, which he considers to be the other five. This opinion will be given in the last pages of Book Seven.

• Stonethwaite

▲ GLARAMARA

Wasdale • Head

▲ ESK PIKE

SCAFELL PIKE ▲   ▲ BOWFELL

CRINKLE CRAGS ▲   • Dungeon Ghyll

Boot •

MILES
0 1 2 3 4 5

MAP

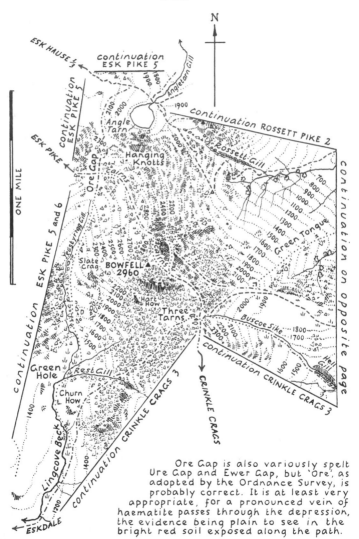

Ore Gap is also variously spelt Ure Gap and Ewer Gap, but 'Ore', as adopted by the Ordnance Survey, is probably correct. It is at least very appropriate, for a pronounced vein of haematite passes through the depression, the evidence being plain to see in the bright red soil exposed along the path.

MAP

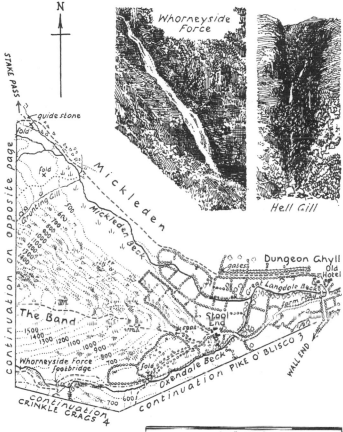

Whorneyside Force

Hell Gill

ONE MILE

The county boundary between Cumberland and Westmorland passed over the top of Bowfell, coming up from Wrynose Pass via Crinkle Crags and Three Tarns. From the summit it followed the height of land to Hanging Knotts, where the main ridge was left in favour of the lesser watershed of Rossett Pass, whence it continued the circuit of Mickleden.   Thus, Great Langdale and all the waters thereof were wholly within Westmorland.

ASCENT FROM DUNGEON GHYLL
2700 feet of ascent : 3 miles (3¼ via Three Tarns)

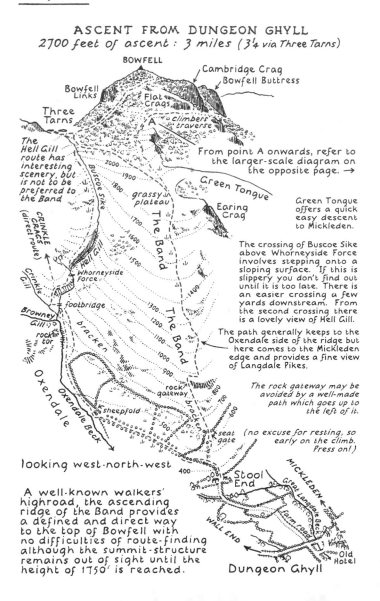

BOWFELL

Cambridge Crag
Bowfell Buttress

Bowfell
Links

Flat
Crags

Three
Tarns

climbers
traverse

A

The Hell Gill route has interesting scenery, but is not to be preferred to the Band

From point A onwards, refer to the larger-scale diagram on the opposite page. →

Green Tongue

Earing Crag

grassy plateau

Green Tongue offers a quick easy descent to Mickleden.

2000
1900
1800
1700
1600
1500
1400
1300
1200
1100
1000
900
800
700
600
500
400

Buscoe Sike

The Band

The crossing of Buscoe Sike above Whorneyside Force involves stepping onto a sloping surface. If this is slippery you don't find out until it is too late. There is an easier crossing a few yards downstream. From the second crossing there is a lovely view of Hell Gill.

CRINKLE CRAGS (direct route)

Hell Gill

Crinkle Gill

Whorneyside Force

footbridge

The path generally keeps to the Oxendale side of the ridge but here comes to the Mickleden edge and provides a fine view of Langdale Pikes.

Browney Gill

rock tor

bracken

Oxendale

Oxendale Beck

The Band

rock gateway

The rock gateway may be avoided by a well-made path which goes up to the left of it.

sheepfold

bracken

seat

gate

(no excuse for resting, so early on the climb. Press on!)

looking west-north-west

Stool End

MICKLEDEN

Great Langdale Beck

A well-known walkers' highroad, the ascending ridge of the Band provides a defined and direct way to the top of Bowfell with no difficulties of route-finding although the summit-structure remains out of sight until the height of 1750' is reached.

farm road

WALL END

Old Hotel

Dungeon Ghyll

ASCENT FROM DUNGEON GHYLL

The upper section,
looking west

BB : Bowfell Buttress
CC : Cambridge Crag
FC : Flat Crags

BOWFELL

THREE TARNS

direct route

bilberry

Great Slab

FC

small col

A

climbers' traverse

CC

ORE GAP

EG

BB

waterspout

THE BAND

└─ corresponds with point A on diagram on opposite page.

The stony path coming up the ridge from the Band leads to, and is continued as, the climbers' traverse. Ten yards below the point where the horizontal traverse commences the direct route wiggles away up to the left and may be passed unnoticed.

The climbers' traverse is a very enjoyable, high-level route leading to excellent rock-scenery. The path is quite distinct and perfectly easy, with a little very mild scrambling, hardly worth mentioning. The traverse is a series of little ups and downs, but generally keeps to a horizontal course. Except at the small col the ground falls away steeply on the valley side of the path.
The best way off the traverse to the summit lies up the fringe of a 'river' of boulders along the south side of Cambridge Crag, or, more tediously, the wide scree gully between Cambridge Crag and Bowfell Buttress may be ascended. (Cambridge Crag is identifiable, beyond all doubt, by the waterspout gushing from the base of the cliff — and nothing better ever came out of a barrel or a bottle).

The climbers' traverse

The striations of Flat Crags are of particular interest, even to non-geologists. Note how the angle of tilt is repeated in the slope of the Great Slab.

ASCENT FROM WASDALE

Although Bowfell is well hidden from Wasdale Head it is not too distant to be climbed from there in comfortable time, but the walk has the disadvantage (for those who object to re-tracing footsteps) that very little variation of route is possible on the return journey to Wasdale Head. Esk Pike stands in the way and must be climbed first (and traversed later).
For a diagram of the ascent of Esk Pike from Wasdale Head see Esk Pike 8

ASCENT FROM MICKLEDEN
2500 feet of ascent : 1¼ miles from the sheepfold

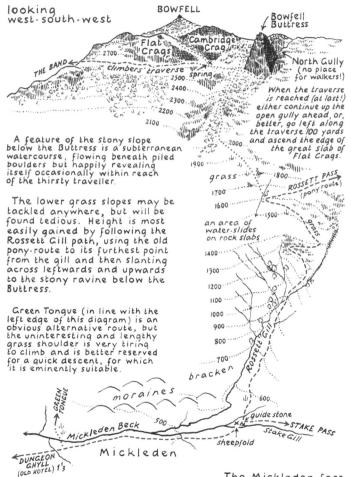

looking
west-south-west

BOWFELL

Bowfell
↓ Buttress

Flat
Crags

Cambridge
Crag

THE BAND ←

2700

climbers traverse

2500
2400
2300
2200
2100

spring

North Gully
(no place
for walkers!)

When the traverse
is reached (at last!)
either continue up the
open gully ahead, or,
better, go left along
the traverse 100 yards
and ascend the edge of
the great slab of
Flat Crags

2000

A feature of the stony slope below the Buttress is a subterranean watercourse, flowing beneath piled boulders but happily revealing itself occasionally within reach of the thirsty traveller.

1900

grass

1800

ROSSETT PASS
(pony route)

The lower grass slopes may be tackled anywhere, but will be found tedious. Height is most easily gained by following the Rossett Gill path, using the old pony-route to its furthest point from the gill and then slanting across leftwards and upwards to the stony ravine below the Buttress.

1700
1600
1500

an area of
water-slides
on rock slabs

grass

1400
1300
1200
1100
1000
900
800

Green Tongue (in line with the left edge of this diagram) is an obvious alternative route, but the uninteresting and lengthy grass shoulder is very tiring to climb and is better reserved for a quick descent, for which it is eminently suitable.

Rossett Gill

bracken

700

moraines

600

GREEN
TONGUE

500

guide stone

STAKE PASS

Mickleden Beck

sheepfold

Stake Gill

← DUNGEON
GHYLL
(OLD HOTEL) 1⅓

Mickleden

The Mickleden face, 2500 feet of continuous ascent, is a route for scramblers rather than walkers. The rock-scenery becomes imposing as height is gained, Bowfell Buttress in particular being an impressive object when seen at close quarters.

ASCENT FROM ESKDALE
2900 feet of ascent : 7½ miles from Boot

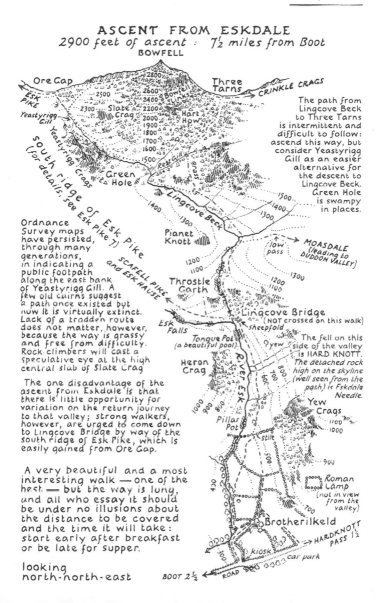

BOWFELL

Ore Gap — Three Tarns — CRINKLE CRAGS

ESK PIKE

Yeastyrigg Gill

south ridge of Esk Pike (for details, see Esk Pike 7)

Yeastyrigg Crags

Slate Crag

Bowfell LINKS

Hart How

Green Hole

Lingcove Beck

The path from Lingcove Beck to Three Tarns is intermittent and difficult to follow: ascend this way, but consider Yeastyrigg Gill as an easier alternative for the descent to Lingcove Beck. Green Hole is swampy in places.

Ordnance Survey maps have persisted, through many generations, in indicating a public footpath along the east bank of Yeastyrigg Gill. A few old cairns suggest a path once existed but now it is virtually extinct. Lack of a trodden route does not matter, however, because the way is grassy and free from difficulty. Rock-climbers will cast a speculative eye at the high central slab of Slate Crag.

The one disadvantage of the ascent from Eskdale is that there is little opportunity for variation on the return journey to that valley; strong walkers, however, are urged to come down to Lingcove Bridge by way of the south ridge of Esk Pike, which is easily gained from Ore Gap.

A very beautiful and a most interesting walk — one of the best — but the way is long, and all who essay it should be under no illusions about the distance to be covered and the time it will take: start early after breakfast or be late for supper.

Pianet Knott

SCAFELL PIKE and ESK HAUSE

Throstle Garth

Esk Falls

Tongue Pot (a beautiful pool)

Heron Crag

Pillar Pot

MOASDALE (leading to DUDDON VALLEY)

low pass

Lingcove Bridge (NOT crossed on this walk)

sheepfold

yew

The fell on this side of the valley is HARD KNOTT. The detached rock high on the skyline (well seen from the path) is Eskdale Needle.

Yew Crags

Roman Camp (not in view from the valley)

stile

Brotherilkeld

HARDKNOTT PASS 1½

kiosk

car park

BOOT 2½   ROAD

looking north-north-east

ASCENT FROM STONETHWAITE
2650 feet of ascent : 6½ miles

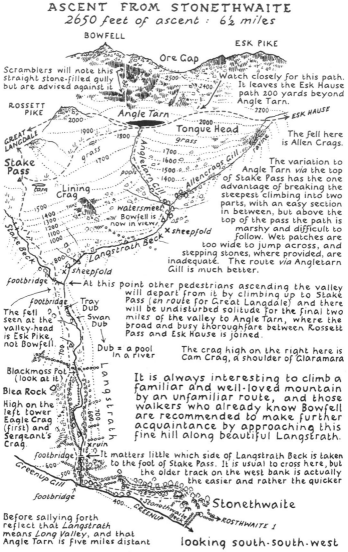

BOWFELL

ESK PIKE

Ore Gap

Scramblers will note this straight stone-filled gully but are advised against it

Watch closely for this path. It leaves the Esk Hause path 200 yards beyond Angle Tarn.

ROSSETT PIKE

Angle Tarn

ESK HAUSE

GREAT LANGDALE

Tongue Head

The fell here is Allen Crags.

grass

grass

Stake Pass

Lining Crag

Allencrags Gill

The variation to Angle Tarn *via* the top of Stake Pass has the one advantage of breaking the steepest climbing into two parts, with an easy section in between, but above the top of the pass the path is marshy and difficult to follow. Wet patches are too wide to jump across, and stepping stones, where provided, are inadequate. The route *via* Angletarn Gill is much better.

pools

watersmeet

Bowfell is now in view.

✗ sheepfold

Langstrath Beck

✗ sheepfold

footbridge

← At this point other pedestrians ascending the valley will depart from it by climbing up to Stake Pass (en route for Great Langdale) and there will be undisturbed solitude for the final two miles of the valley to Angle Tarn, where the broad and busy thoroughfare between Rossett Pass and Esk Hause is joined.

footbridge

Tray Dub

Swan Dub

The fell seen at the valley-head is Esk Pike, not Bowfell.

Dub = a pool in a river

The crag high on the right here is Cam Crag, a shoulder of Glaramara.

Langstrath

Blackmoss Pot (look at it)

Blea Rock

High on the left tower Eagle Crag (first) and Sergeant's Crag.

It is always interesting to climb a familiar and well-loved mountain by an unfamiliar route, and those walkers who already know Bowfell are recommended to make further acquaintance by approaching this fine hill along beautiful Langstrath.

footbridge

✗ ruin

It matters little which side of Langstrath Beck is taken to the foot of Stake Pass. It is usual to cross here, but the older track on the west bank is actually the easier and rather the quicker

Greenup Gill

footbridge

Stonethwaite Beck

Stonethwaite

CREENUP

ROSTHWAITE 1

Before sallying forth reflect that *Langstrath* means *Long Valley*, and that Angle Tarn is five miles distant

looking south-south-west

Cambridge Crag and Bowfell Buttress
from the top of the Great Slab

THE SUMMIT

Bowfell's top is a shattered pyramid, a great heap of stones and boulders and naked rock, a giant cairn in itself.

The rugged summit provides poor picking for the Bowfell sheep, who draw the line at mosses and lichens and look elsewhere for their mountain greenery, and reserves its best rewards for the walkers who climb the natural rocky stairway to its upper limit for here, spread before them for their delectation, is a glorious panorama, which, moreover, may be surveyed and appreciated from positions of repose on the comfortable flat seats of stone (comfortable in the sense that everybody arriving here says how nice it is to sit down) with which the summit is liberally equipped. The leisurely contemplation of the scene will not be assailed by doubts as to whether the highest point has in fact been gained for rough slopes tumble away steeply on all sides.

The top pyramid stands on a sloping plinth which, to the east, extends beyond the base of the pyramid and forms a shelf or terrace where stones are less in evidence. It is from this shelf that Bowfell's main crags fall away, and from which, with care, they may be viewed; care is necessary because the boulders to be negotiated in carrying out this inspection are in a state of balance, in places, and liable to heel over and trap a leg.

It is possible, and does happen, that walkers ascend Bowfell and traverse its top quite unaware of the imposing line of crags overlooking Mickleden : from the summit and the shelf-track there is little to indicate the presence of steep cliffs.   But to miss seeing the crags is to miss seeing half the glory of Bowfell.

THE SUMMIT

continued

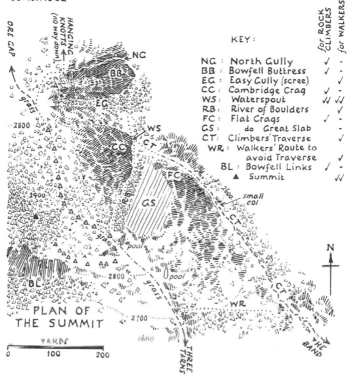

KEY:

		for ROCK CLIMBERS	for WALKERS
NG :	North Gully	✓	-
BB :	Bowfell Buttress	✓	-
EG :	Easy Gully (scree)	-	✓
CC :	Cambridge Crag	✓	-
WS :	Waterspout	√√	√√
RB :	River of Boulders	-	✓
FC :	Flat Crags	✓	-
GS :	do Great Slab	-	-
CT :	Climbers' Traverse	-	✓
WR :	Walkers' Route to avoid Traverse	-	✓
BL :	Bowfell Links	✓	-
▲	Summit	-	√√

PLAN OF THE SUMMIT

DESCENTS : The sloping grass shelf, east of the actual summit, carries the only cairned route across the top. It links the path to Ore Gap with that to Three Tarns, and each cairn is visible from the last. There is a further line of cairns to the south of the summit, but this cannot be seen from the summit or from the path from Three Tarns. For Langdale the steep lower section of the Three Tarns path may be avoided by using a terrace on the left at a gap in the wall of rocks (WR on the plan above); but this is difficult to locate. Direct descents to Eskdale over the steepening boulder slopes are not feasible.

‖ *In mist,* the only safe objectives are Ore Gap (for Wasdale, ‖ Borrowdale or Eskdale) and Three Tarns (for Langdale *via* the ‖ Band, or Eskdale) avoiding Bowfell Links on the way thereto.

The Great Slab of Flat Crags

RIDGE ROUTES

To CRINKLE CRAGS, 2816' : 1½ miles
SE, E, SE and then generally S
*Main depression (Three Tarns) at 2320'
600 feet of ascent*
A rough ridge-walk of high quality

A bee-line for Three Tarns runs foul of Bowfell Links, and the summit notes should be consulted for getting down to the gap. From there onwards the gradual climb to Crinkle Crags, with its many turns and twists and ups and downs is entirely delightful, *but not in mist.* (See Crinkle Crags 13.)

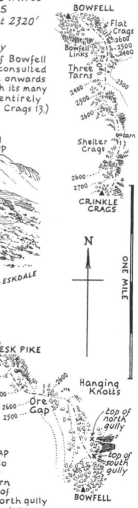

Crinkle Crags, as seen on the descent to Three Tarns from the summit of Bowfell. The path is indicated. The first three Crinkles are hidden behind Shelter Crags.

To ESK PIKE, 2903' : 1 mile
NW, W and NW
*Depression (Ore Gap) at 2575'
340 feet of ascent*
A straightforward, rather rough, walk

The path going up Esk Pike from Ore Gap is visible from afar, but the way thereto across Bowfell's stony top is less clearly marked but well indicated by cairns. Turn aside to look down the wide gully south of Bowfell Buttress ; the more impressive north gully may also be reached by a short and easy detour.

*Three views
from the Band*

Right:
Browney Gill and Cold Pike

Bottom Right:
Pike o' Blisco

Below:
Pike o' Stickle

THE VIEW

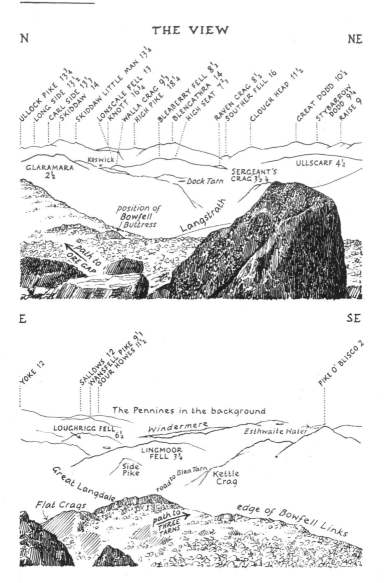

N

NE

ULLOCK PIKE 13¾
LONG SIDE 13¼
CARL SIDE 13½
SKIDDAW 14
SKIDDAW LITTLE MAN 13¼
LONSCALE FELL 13
KNOTT 16¾
WALLA CRAG 9½
HIGH PIKE 18¼
BLEABERRY FELL 8½
BLENCATHRA 14
HIGH SEAT 7¾
RAVEN CRAG 8½
SOUTHER FELL 16
CLOUGH HEAD 11½
GREAT DODD 10½
STYBARROW DODD 9¾
RAISE 9

GLARAMARA 2½

Keswick

Dock Tarn

SERGEANT'S CRAG 3½

ULLSCARF 4½

position of
Bowfell
Buttress

Langstrath

path to
ORE GAP

E

SE

YOKE 12

SALLOWS 12
WANSFELL PIKE 9¾
SOUR HOWES 11½

PIKE O' BLISCO 2

The Pennines in the background

LOUGHRIGG FELL
6½

Windermere

Esthwaite Water

LINGMOOR
FELL 3¾

Side
Pike

Great Langdale

road to Blea Tarn

Kettle
Crag

Flat Crags

path to
THREE
TARNS

edge of Bowfell Links

THE VIEW

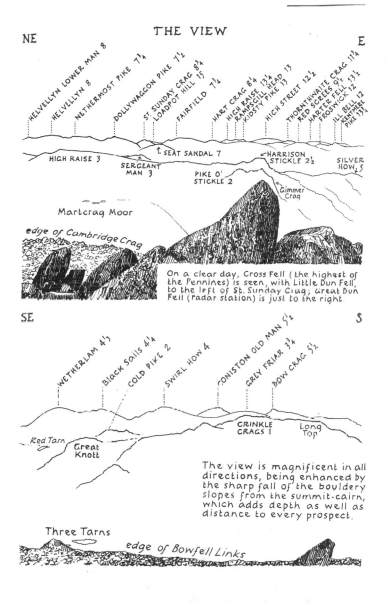

NE

HELVELLYN LOWER MAN 8
HELVELLYN 8
NETHERMOST PIKE 7¾
DOLLYWAGGON PIKE 7½
ST. SUNDAY CRAG 8¾
LOADPOT HILL 15
FAIRFIELD 7¾
HART CRAG 8¼
HIGH RAISE 13¼
RAMPSGILL HEAD 13
KIDSTY PIKE 13
HIGH STREET 12½
THORNTHWAITE CRAG 11¼
RED SCREES 9½
HARTER FELL 13½
FROSWICK 12
ILL BELL 12
KENTMERE PIKE 13¼

E

HIGH RAISE 3

SERGEANT MAN 3

SEAT SANDAL 7

PIKE O' STICKLE 2

HARRISON STICKLE 2½

SILVER HOW 5

Gimmer Crag

Martcrag Moor

edge of Cambridge Crag

On a clear day, Cross Fell (the highest of the Pennines) is seen, with Little Dun Fell, to the left of St. Sunday Crag; Great Dun Fell (radar station) is just to the right.

SE

WETHERLAM 4⅓
BLACK SAILS 4¼
COLD PIKE 2
SWIRL HOW 4
CONISTON OLD MAN 5½
GREY FRIAR 3¾
DOW CRAG 5½

S

Red Tarn

Great Knott

CRINKLE CRAGS 1

Long Top

The view is magnificent in all directions, being enhanced by the sharp fall of the bouldery slopes from the summit-cairn, which adds depth as well as distance to every prospect.

Three Tarns

edge of Bowfell Links

THE VIEW

S   SW

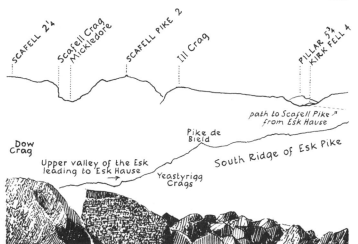

Caw 7½

Stickle Pike 8¾

HARTER FELL 4½

Black Combe 14¾
GREEN CRAG 5¾

Duddon
Estuary

Devoke
Water

Duddon
Valley

HARD KNOTT
2½

Eskdale

Moasdale

River Esk   Heron Crag

Rest Gill

← Lingcove
Beck

W   NW

SCAFELL 2¼

Scafell Crag
Mickledore

SCAFELL PIKE 2

Ill Crag

PILLAR 5¾
KIRK FELL 4

path to Scafell Pike ↗
from Esk Hause

Dow
Crag

Pike de
Bield

South Ridge of Esk Pike

Upper valley of the Esk
leading to Esk Hause →   Yeastyrigg
Crags

THE VIEW

SW · W

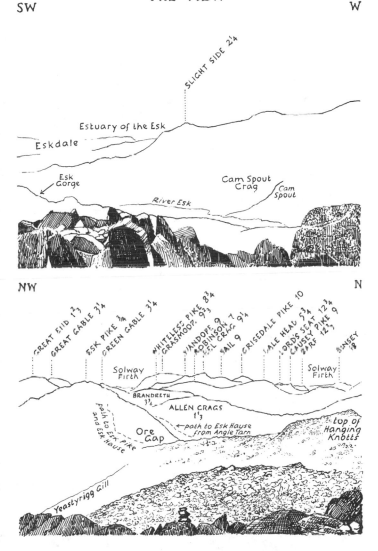

SLIGHT SIDE 2¼

Estuary of the Esk

Eskdale

Esk Gorge

Cam Spout Crag

Cam Spout

River Esk

NW · N

GREAT END 1¾ · GREAT GABLE 3¼ · ESK PIKE ⅜ · GREEN GABLE 3¼ · WHITELESS PIKE 8¾ · GRASMOOR 9½ · WANDOPE 9 · ROBINSON 7 · EEL CRAGS 9¼ · SAIL 9 · GRISEDALE PIKE 10 · LORD'S SEAT 5¾ · CAUSEY PIKE 12¾ · BARF 12¾ · SKIDDAW 9 · BINSEY 8

Solway Firth

Solway Firth

BRANDRETH 3¾

ALLEN CRAGS 1⅓

← path to Esk Hause from Angle Tarn

path to Esk Pike and Esk Hause

Ore Gap

Top of Hanging Knotts

Yeastyrigg Gill

Crinkle Crags

2816'

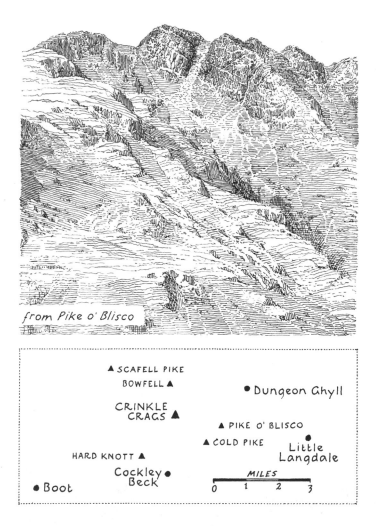

from Pike o' Blisco

▲ SCAFELL PIKE

BOWFELL ▲

● Dungeon Ghyll

CRINKLE
CRAGS ▲

▲ PIKE O' BLISCO

▲ COLD PIKE

Little
Langdale ●

HARD KNOTT ▲

Cockley ●
Beck

● Boot

MILES

0   1   2   3

NATURAL FEATURES

Some mountains are obviously named by reference to their physical characteristics. Crinkle Crags is one of these, and it was probably first so called by the dalesfolk of the valleys to the east and around the head of Windermere, whence its lofty serrated ridge, a succession of knobs and depressions, is aptly described by the name. These undulations, seeming trivial from a distance, are revealed at close range as steep buttresses and gullies above wild declivities, a scene of desolation and rugged grandeur equalled by few others in the district. Nor is the Eskdale flank any gentler, for here too are gaunt shattered crags rising from incredibly rough slopes. The high pass of Three Tarns links the ridge with Bowfell to the north while southwards Wrynose Bottom is the boundary.

Crinkle Crags is much too good to be missed. For the mountaineer who prefers his mountains rough, who likes to see steep craggy slopes towering before him into the sky, who enjoys an up-and-down ridge walk full of interesting nooks and corners, who has an appreciative eye for magnificent views, this is a climb deserving of high priority. But it is not a place to visit in bad weather for the top is confusing, with ins and outs as well as ups and downs and a sketchy path that cannot be relied on. Crinkle Crags merits respect, and should be treated with respect; then it will yield the climber a mountain walk long to be remembered with pleasure.

Is it 'Crinkle Crags IS ...' or 'Crinkle Crags ARE ...'?
Is it 'Three Tarns IS ....' or 'Three Tarns ARE ...'?

IS sounds right but looks wrong!

The outline of Crinkle Crags from Great Langdale

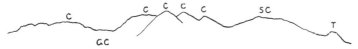

C : The five Crinkles   GC : Great Cove
T : Rock tower near Three Tarns   SC : Shelter Crags

The highest Crinkle (2816') is second from the left on the diagram. When seen from the valley it does not appear to be the highest, as it is set back a little from the line of the others.

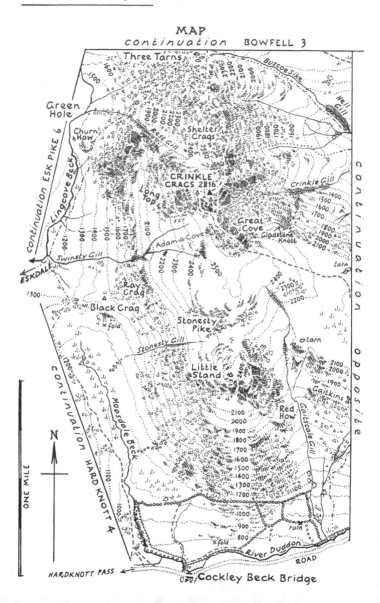

MAP
continuation BOWFELL 3

Three Tarns

Buscoe Sike

Hell

Green Hole

Churn How

Shelter Crags

Red Gill

continuation ESK PIKE 6

Lingcove Beck

CRINKLE CRAGS 2816

Crinkle Gill

Long Top

Great Cove

Gladstone Knott

Adam-a-Cove

Swinsty Gill

ESKDALE

tarn

continuation opposite

Ray Crag

Black Crag

x fold

Stonesty Pike

Stonesty Gill

tarn

Little Stand

Gaitkins

Coatscale Gill

Red How

Moasdale Beck

continuation HARD KNOTT 4

N

ONE MILE

ruin

x fold

River Duddon

ROAD

HARDKNOTT PASS

Cockley Beck Bridge

MAP

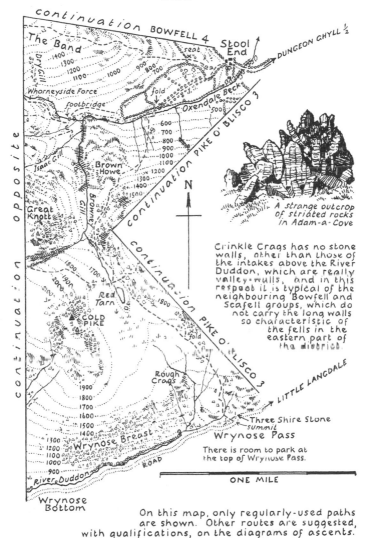

continuation BOWFELL 4

The Band

Dry Gill

1400
1300
1200
1100
1000
900
800
700

seat

Stool End

DUNGEON GHYLL ½

fold

Whorneyside Force

footbridge

Oxendale Beck

500

Isaac Gill

Brown Howe

600
700
800
900
1000
1100
1200
1300
1400
1500

continuation PIKE O' BLISCO 3

Great Knott

Browney

N

continuation PIKE O' BLISCO 3

A strange outcrop of striated rocks in Adam-a-Cove

Crinkle Crags has no stone walls, other than those of the intakes above the River Duddon, which are really valley-walls, and in this respect it is typical of the neighbouring Bowfell and Scafell groups, which do not carry the long walls so characteristic of the fells in the eastern part of the district.

1500
1700
2000
1900

Red Tarn

COLD PIKE

1800

fold

LITTLE LANGDALE

Rough Crags

1900
1800
1700
1600
1500
1400
1300
1200
1100
1000
900

Wrynose Breast

Three Shire Stone summit

Wrynose Pass

There is room to park at the top of Wrynose Pass.

River Duddon

ROAD

Wrynose Bottom

ONE MILE

On this map, only regularly-used paths are shown. Other routes are suggested, with qualifications, on the diagrams of ascents.

ASCENT FROM DUNGEON GHYLL (via RED TARN)
2600 feet of ascent : 4 miles

As far as Red Tarn, the route is that used for the ascent of Pike o' Blisco (the craggy slopes of which tower up on the left throughout) and for the high-level walk to Wrynose Pass.

CRINKLE CRAGS

COLD PIKE

prominent path

Consult the Ridge Plan here (page 11)

Some walkers 'cut the corner' by using a terrace route on the south side of Great Knott, reached from the west bank of Browney Gill. It is rough (and dangerous in mist, for the sheer wall of the ravine is just below) and not to be preferred to the longer path via Red Tarn.

Red Tarn

WRYNOSE

Great Knott

fall

Here the path passes close to the confluence of two ravines, with another confluence farther downstream. There is much red soil in this area.

grass

Browney Gill

Isaac Gill

Crinkle Gill

CRINKLE CRAGS (direct route)

The usual route passes through the farmyard of Stool End and crosses Oxendale Beck at the sheepfold by way of a footbridge (rebuilt in 2005). Beyond the sheepfold the route climbs a well-made path (not distinct at the start). Other routes, in use before the bridge at the sheepfold was built, follow the north bank of Oxendale Beck and the west bank of Browney Gill, or keep to the south bank all the way from Stool End Bridge to the sheepfold.

Brown Howe

footbridge

tor

Oxendale Beck

Rising high on the right here is The Band, a spur of Bowfell

The wide, bouldery course of Oxendale Beck testfies to its power in flood. The valley is outstanding for its impressive ravines.

sheepfold

BOWFELL

looking west-south-west

Stool End

gate

bridge

gate

DUNGEON GHYLL

The climb to Brown Howe from the beck, once rough, is one of many in the district that have been improved in recent years by being paved with stones. The scenery throughout is excellent. Descend via Three Tarns in order to make the complete traverse of the summit ridge. This is a popular walk.

ASCENT FROM DUNGEON GHYLL (via THREE TARNS)
2650 feet of ascent : 4 miles

CRINKLE CRAGS
Gunson Knott
Shelter Crags
Consult the Ridge Plan when Three Tarns is (or are) reached (page 13)
Three Tarns
BOWFELL

2600
2500

The path on the ridge alternates between the Langdale and the Eskdale sides of the watershed.

Turn left just short of the three tarns (one of which is now very small).

CRINKLE CRAGS (direct route)

2000
1900
1800
1700
grassy plateau
1800
1700
view down into Mickleden
1600
1500
1400
1300

Ruscoe Sike

Crinkle Gill
Hell Gill

A variation route to Three Tarns by way of Hell Gill is shown. For walkers who have already trodden the Band several times it makes a pleasant change and gives striking views of the huge Hell Gill ravine; but generally this route lacks the airiness and the views of the Band and is not to be preferred. Its one advantage is a supply of running water all the way to Three Tarns.

waterfall (Whorneyside Force)

footbridge

Browney Gill

RED TARN

bracken

The Band

juniper

Oxendale Beck

sheepfold

seat inscribed 'Rest and remember the work of S.H. Hamer, Secretary of the National Trust 1911-1934'

gate

bracken

The Three Tarns route should be combined with that via Red Tarn to make a full traverse of the ridge and a splendid mountain excursion; the easier way round is to ascend by Red Tarn and descend by the Band.

Stool End

looking west

The Band is among the best known of Lakeland walks. It is a shoulder of, and the usual way to, Bowfell, but is equally convenient for the ascent of Crinkle Crags.

WALL END

Farm road

Great Langdale Beck

MICKLEDEN

Old Hotel
Dungeon Ghyll

ASCENT FROM DUNGEON GHYLL
(DIRECT CLIMB FROM OXENDALE)
2550 feet of ascent : 3½ miles

looking
west

CRINKLE CRAGS

Gunson
Knott

Shelter
Crags

2600
2500
2400
2300
2200
2100

curious
channel
of scree

High
Bleaberry
Knott

1900
bilberry   bilberry   1800
1700

Low
Bleaberry
Knott

1600

1500

grass

1400

THREE TARNS

1300

Hell Gill

1200

Dry Gill

1100

fall

1000

RED TARN

Isaac Gill

Crinkle Gill

bracken

900

1000

footbridge

800

Browney Gill

tor

700

The ridge may
be reached by
determined walkers
at any one of five
different points by
a direct climb from
Oxendale, each of them
avoiding solid rock but
encountering oceans of scree
and boulders.   The simplest
(least steep and fewest stones)
and most obvious way is that
shown, gaining
the ridge at
2600' just north
of Gunson Knott; in
the final scree gully
keep to the right side.
  A more direct route,
admittedly, would be to
follow Crinkle Gill on its
north bank, keeping high
above the ravine, the rock
scenery being very impressive,
but the weariness of the last
thousand feet of boulders and
scree rule it out of account for
walkers who walk for pleasure.
On this route the ridge is gained
immediately to the north of the
main summit by toiling up a steep
loose gully enclosed between high
rock walls (Mickle Door). This gully,
a river of stones, cannot be seen from
Oxendale; its position is indicated on
the diagram by two arrows.

Features
to note on
the ascent
are the deep
black gash
of Hell Gill
and the fall
just below it.
Oxendale is
particularly
notable in its
ravine scenes

Oxendale

sheepfold

600

BOWFELL

500

Oxendale Beck

Stool
End

DUNGEON GHYLL

The summit-ridge overlooking Oxendale
tops a series of precipitous buttresses of
formidable appearance.   The route shown,
however, is quite simple, becoming rough (but
not difficult) only in the concluding stages.

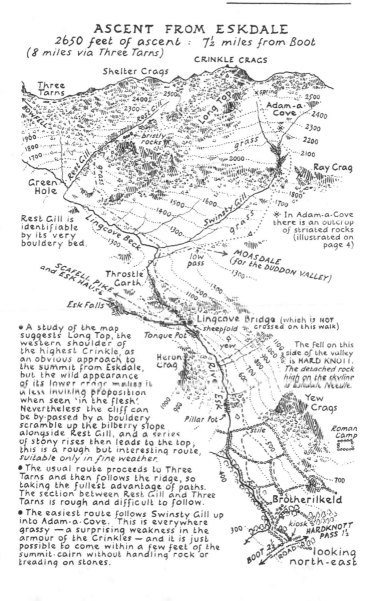

ASCENT FROM ESKDALE
2650 feet of ascent : 7½ miles from Boot
(8 miles via Three Tarns)

CRINKLE CRAGS

Shelter Crags

Three Tarns

Long Top

Adam-a-Cave

2500
2400
2300
bristly rocks
grass
2000

2500
2400
2300
2200
2100

Ray Crag

BOWFELL

1900
1800
1700

Rest Gill

1800

Green Hole

Rest Gill is identifiable by its very bouldery bed.

1500
1600
Swinsty Gill
grass
1700

Lingcove Beck
1400
1300

1300

❋ In Adam-a-Cove there is an outcrop of striated rocks (illustrated on page 4)

low pass

MOASDALE
(for the DUDDON VALLEY)
1300

SCAFELL PIKE and ESK HAUSE

Throstle Garth

1200
1100
1300

Esk Falls

Lingcove Bridge (which is NOT crossed on this walk)
sheepfold

• A study of the map suggests Long Top, the western shoulder of the highest Crinkle, as an obvious approach to the summit from Eskdale, but the wild appearance of its lower crags makes it a less inviting proposition when seen 'in the flesh'. Nevertheless the cliff can be by-passed by a bouldery scramble up the bilberry slope alongside Rest Gill, and a series of stony rises then leads to the top; this is a rough but interesting route, *suitable only in fine weather.*

• The usual route proceeds to Three Tarns and then follows the ridge, so taking the fullest advantage of paths. The section between Rest Gill and Three Tarns is rough and difficult to follow.

• The easiest route follows Swinsty Gill up into Adam-a-Cove. This is everywhere grassy — a surprising weakness in the armour of the Crinkles — and it is just possible to come within a few feet of the summit-cairn without handling rock or treading on stones.

Tongue Pot

Heron Crag

River Esk

1000
900
Pillar Pot
800

The fell on this side of the valley is HARD KNOTT. The detached rock high on the skyline is Eskdale Needle.

Yew Crags

stile
Roman Camp

700

Brotherilkeld

kiosk
HARDKNOTT PASS 1½

300
BOOT 2½
ROAD

looking north-east

ASCENT FROM COCKLEY BECK BRIDGE
2350 feet of ascent : 3 miles

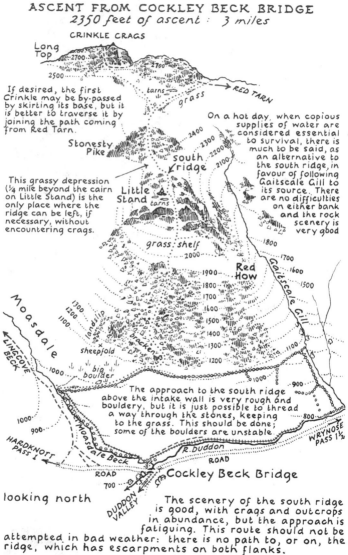

CRINKLE CRAGS

Long Top
2700
2500

CRINKLE CRAGS

tarns
grass → RED TARN

If desired, the first Crinkle may be by-passed by skirting its base, but it is better to traverse it by joining the path coming from Red Tarn.

Stonesty Pike

2400
2300
2200
2100

south ridge

On a hot day, when copious supplies of water are considered essential to survival, there is much to be said, as an alternative to the south ridge, in favour of following Gaitscale Gill to its source. There are no difficulties on either bank and the rock scenery is very good

This grassy depression (¼ mile beyond the cairn on Little Stand) is the only place where the ridge can be left, if necessary, without encountering crags.

Little Stand
tarns

grass shelf
2000

1800
1700
1600
1500

Red How

1900
1800
1700
1600
1500
1400
1300
1200

Gaitscale Gill

Moasdale

LINGCOVE BECK

1300
1200
1100

landslip

sheepfold

big boulder

bracken

1100

1000

900

The approach to the south ridge above the intake wall is very rough and bouldery, but it is just possible to thread a way through the stones, keeping to the grass. This should be done; some of the boulders are unstable.

1000
900

HARDKNOTT PASS 1

Moasdale Beck

R. Duddon

ROAD

800

WRYNOSE PASS 1½

ROAD

700

Cockley Beck Bridge

looking north

DUDDON VALLEY

The scenery of the south ridge is good, with crags and outcrops in abundance, but the approach is fatiguing. This route should not be attempted in bad weather: there is no path to, or on, the ridge, which has escarpments on both flanks.

ASCENT FROM WRYNOSE PASS
1650 feet of ascent : 2¾ miles

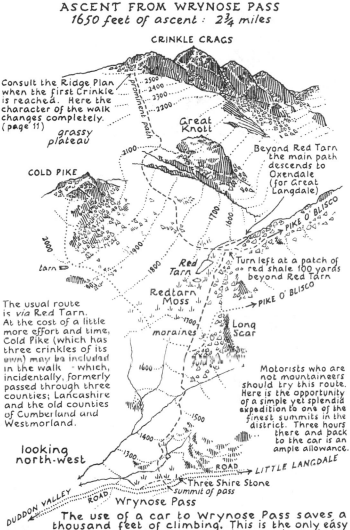

CRINKLE CRAGS

Consult the Ridge Plan when the first Crinkle is reached. Here the character of the walk changes completely. (page 11)

grassy plateau

Great Knott

2500
2400
2300
2200

prominent path

Beyond Red Tarn the main path descends to Oxendale (for Great Langdale)

COLD PIKE

2100

2000

1900

1800

1700

1600

tarn

PIKE O' BLISCO

Red Tarn

Turn left at a patch of red shale 100 yards beyond Red Tarn

Redtarn Moss

PIKE O' BLISCO

1700

moraines

Long Scar

The usual route is *via* Red Tarn. At the cost of a little more effort and time, Cold Pike (which has three crinkles of its own) may be included in the walk — which, incidentally, formerly passed through three counties; Lancashire and the old counties of Cumberland and Westmorland.

1600

1700

Motorists who are not mountaineers should try this route. Here is the opportunity of a simple yet splendid expedition to one of the finest summits in the district. Three hours there and back to the car is an ample allowance.

1500

1400

1300

looking north-west

ROAD → LITTLE LANGDALE

Three Shire Stone summit of pass

DUDDON VALLEY

ROAD

Wrynose Pass

The use of a car to Wrynose Pass saves a thousand feet of climbing. This is the only easy line of approach to Crinkle Crags, the gradients being gentle and the walking pleasant throughout.

RIDGE PLAN
for use when traversing the ridge from SOUTH to NORTH

● Read upwards from the bottom

All heights ending in 0 are approximate and unofficial

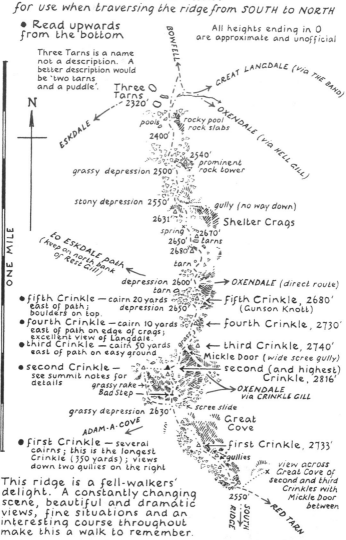

Three Tarns is a name not a description. A better description would be 'two tarns and a puddle'.

Three Tarns 2320'

BOWFELL

GREAT LANGDALE (via THE BAND)

ESKDALE

OXENDALE (via HELL GILL)

pools
rocky pool
rock slabs
2400'
2540' prominent rock tower
grassy depression 2500'
stony depression 2550'
2631'
gully (no way down)
Shelter Crags
spring 2670'
2650' tarns
2680 △
tarn

to ESKDALE path (keep on north bank of Rest Gill)

depression 2600' → OXENDALE (direct route)

● **fifth Crinkle** — cairn 20 yards east of path; boulders on top.
depression 2650'
Fifth Crinkle, 2680' (Gunson Knott)

● **fourth Crinkle** — cairn 10 yards east of path on edge of crags; excellent view of Langdale.
← **fourth Crinkle, 2730'**

● **third Crinkle** — cairn 50 yards east of path on easy ground
← **third Crinkle, 2740'**
Mickle Door (*wide scree gully*)

● **second Crinkle** — see summit notes for details
second (and highest) Crinkle, 2816'

grassy rake
Bad Step →
→ OXENDALE via CRINKLE GILL

grassy depression 2630'
← scree slide

ADAM-A-COVE
Great Cove

● **first Crinkle** — several cairns; this is the longest Crinkle (350 yards); views down two gullies on the right
← **first Crinkle, 2733'**
gullies

view across Great Cove of second and third Crinkles with Mickle Door between

2550'
SOUTH RIDGE
→ RED TARN

This ridge is a fell-walkers' delight. A constantly changing scene, beautiful and dramatic views, fine situations and an interesting course throughout make this a walk to remember.

N
ONE MILE

Looking NORTH along the ridge ....

The second (and highest)
Crinkle, Mickle Door,
and the third Crinkle,
seen across Great Cove

The fourth and fifth
Crinkles (Shelter Crags
and Bowfell behind), seen
from the third Crinkle

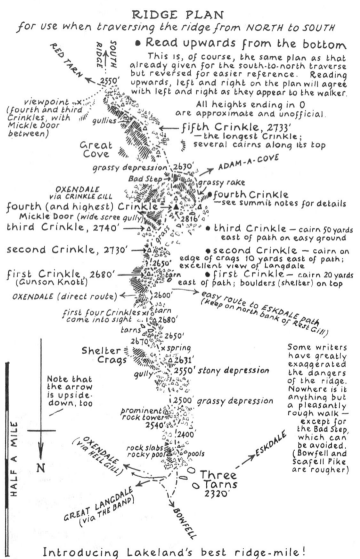

RIDGE PLAN
for use when traversing the ridge from NORTH to SOUTH

● Read upwards from the bottom

This is, of course, the same plan as that already given for the south-to-north traverse but reversed for easier reference. Reading upwards, left and right on the plan will agree with left and right as they appear to the walker.

All heights ending in 0 are approximate and unofficial.

RED TARN

SOUTH RIDGE

2550'

viewpoint x
(fourth and third Crinkles, with Mickle Door between)

gullies

Great Cove

grassy depression 2630'

Bad Step

OXENDALE via CRINKLE GILL

fourth (and highest) Crinkle
Mickle Door (wide scree gully)

third Crinkle, 2740'

second Crinkle, 2730'

first Crinkle, 2680'
(Gunson Knott)

OXENDALE (direct route)

fifth Crinkle, 2733'
—the longest Crinkle; several cairns along its top

ADAM-A-COVE

grassy rake

● fourth Crinkle
—see summit notes for details

2816'

● third Crinkle — cairn 50 yards east of path on easy ground

● second Crinkle — cairn on edge of crags 10 yards east of path; excellent view of Langdale

2650'

tarn

● first Crinkle — cairn 20 yards east of path; boulders (shelter) on top

2600'

easy route to ESKDALE path (keep on north bank of Rest Gill)

first four Crinkles came into sight
2680'

tarns 2650'

2670' x spring

Shelter Crags

△ 2631'

gully 2550' stony depression

2500' grassy depression

prominent rock tower 2540'

Note that the arrow is upside-down, too

2400'

rock slabs rocky pool

pools

HALF A MILE

↓ N

OXENDALE (via HELL GILL)

GREAT LANGDALE (via THE BAND)

Three Tarns 2320'

ESKDALE

BOWFELL

Some writers have greatly exaggerated the dangers of the ridge. Nowhere is it anything but a pleasantly rough walk — except for the Bad Step, which can be avoided. (Bowfell and Scafell Pike are rougher)

Introducing Lakeland's best ridge-mile!

Looking SOUTH along the ridge.........

Four Crinkles come
suddenly into view from
the path as it rounds a
corner of Shelter Crags

The fifth Crinkle
as seen from the main
Crinkle on the descent
to the Bad Step

THE SUMMIT

← BOWFELL

There are five Crinkles (not counting Shelter Crags) and therefore five summits, each with its own summit-cairn. The highest is, however, so obviously the highest that the true top of the fell is not in doubt in clear visibility, and this is the Crinkle (the fourth from the north and second from the south) with which these notes are concerned. It is not the stoniest of the five, nor the greatest in girth, but, unlike the others, it extends a considerable distance as a lateral ridge (Long Top) descending westwards. On the actual summit are two principal cairns separated by 40 yards of easy ground; that to the north, standing on a rock platform, is slightly the more elevated. The eastern face descends in precipices from the easy grass terraces above it; there are crags running down steeply from the south cairn also, but in other directions the top terrain is not difficult although everywhere rough.

1: grassy rake (easy way)
2: direct route (steep scree)
3: the Bad Step (see next page)
4: detour to avoid the Bad Step

The highest Crinkle, from the south   continued

THE SUMMIT

continued

DESCENTS

to GREAT LANGDALE : The orthodox routes are (1) *via* Red Tarn and Brown How, and (2) *via* Three Tarns and the Band, both excellent walks, and in normal circumstances no other ways should be considered. If time is very short, however, or if it is necessary to escape quickly from stormy conditions on the ridge, quick and sheltered routes are provided by (3) the scree gully of Mickle Door or (4) the Gunson Knott gully, which is easier : both are very rough initially but lead to open slopes above Oxendale.

to ESKDALE : Much the easiest way, and much the quickest, is to descend from Adam-a-Cove (no path), keeping *left* of Swinsty Gill where it enters a ravine. Long Top is a temptation to be resisted, for it leads only to trouble.

to COCKLEY BECK BRIDGE : The south ridge is interesting (no path and not safe in mist), but tired limbs had better take advantage of the easy way down from Adam-a-Cove, inclining left below Ray Crag into Moasdale

to WRYNOSE PASS : Reverse the route of ascent. Cold Pike may be traversed with little extra cost in energy.

> In mist, take good care to keep to the ridge-path, which, in many places, is no more than nail-scratches on rocks and boulders but is generally simple to follow. Go nowhere unless there is evidence that many others have passed that way before. (The exception to this golden rule is Adam-a-Cove, which is perfectly safe *if it is remembered to keep to the left bank of the stream*)

The Bad Step

Caution is needed on the descent southwards from the summit. A walker crossing the top from the north will naturally gravitate to the south cairn and start his descent here. A steep path goes down rock ledges to a slope of loose scree, which spills over the lip of a chockstone (two, really) bridging and blocking a little gully. Anyone descending at speed here is asking for a nasty fall. The impasse is usually avoided and the gully regained below the chockstone by an awkward descent of the rock wall to the left, which deserves the name 'The Bad Step', for it is 10 feet high and as near vertical as makes no difference.   This is the sort of place that everybody would get down in a flash if a £20 note was waiting to be picked up on the scree below, but, without such an inducement, there is much wavering on the brink. Chicken-hearted walkers, muttering something about discretion being the better part of valour, will sneak away and circumvent the difficulty by following the author's footsteps around the left flank of the buttress forming the retaining wall of the gully, where grassy ledges enable the foot of the gully to be reached without trouble; here they may sit and watch, with ill-concealed grins, the discomfiture of other tourists who may come along.

The Bad Step from below

The Bad Step is the most difficult obstacle met on any of the regular walkers' paths in Lakeland.

continued

THE SUMMIT

continued

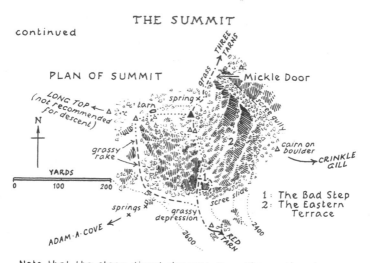

PLAN OF SUMMIT

1: The Bad Step
2: The Eastern Terrace

Note that the steep direct descent from the south cairn may be by-passed altogether (it was formerly customary to do so) by proceeding west from the main cairn for 140 yards to another on grass in a slight depression, whence a grassy rake on the left goes down, skirting completely the rocks of the Crinkle, to join the direct route at its base.

The welcome spring on the summit (usually reliable after recent rain) is remarkable for its proximity to the top cairn (30 yards north-east, in the bend of the path); it is only 20 feet lower than the cairn, and has a very limited gathering-ground. Find it by listening for it — it emerges as a tiny waterfall from beneath a boulder. This is not the highest spring in the district but it is the nearest to a high summit.

The Eastern Terrace

A conspicuous grass terrace slants at an angle of 30° across the eastern cliffs of the main Crinkle, rising from the screes of the Mickle Door gully to the direct ridge-route just above the Bad Step. It is not seen from the ridge but appears in views of the east face clearly, being the middle of three such terraces and most prominent. It is of little use to walkers, except those who (in defiance of advice already given) are approaching the summit from Crinkle Gill: for them it offers

1: the Bad Step
2: the Eastern Terrace
3: Mickle Door
4: scree slide

The Eastern Face

a way of escape from the final screes. The terrace (identified by a little wall at the side of the gully) is wide and without difficulties but is no place for loitering, being subject to bombardments of stones by bloody fools, if any, on the summit above. It is well to remember, too, that the terrace is bounded by a precipice. At the upper end the terrace becomes more broken near the Bad Step and is not quite easy to locate when approached from this direction.

RIDGE ROUTES

To BOWFELL, 2960′ : 1½ miles : Generally N, then WNW
Five depressions; final one (Three Tarns) at 2320′: 850 feet of ascent
Positively one of the finest ridge-walks in Lakeland.

The rough stony ground makes progress slow, but this walk is, in any case, deserving of a leisurely appreciation; it is much too good to be done in a hurry. Every turn of the fairly distinct track is interesting, and in places even exciting, although no difficulty is met except for an occasional awkward stride on rock. *In mist,* the walker will probably have to descend to Three Tarns anyway, but should give Bowfell a miss, especially if the route is unfamiliar.

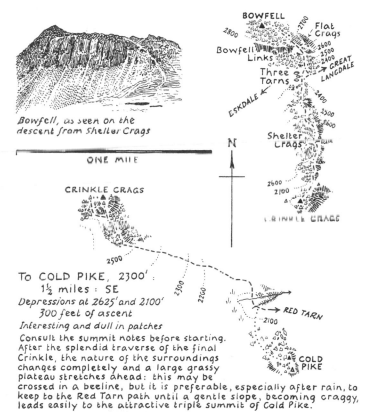

Bowfell, as seen on the descent from Shelter Crags

ONE MILE

N

To COLD PIKE, 2300′: 1½ miles : SE
Depressions at 2625′ and 2100′
300 feet of ascent
Interesting and dull in patches

Consult the summit notes before starting. After the splendid traverse of the final Crinkle, the nature of the surroundings changes completely and a large grassy plateau stretches ahead: this may be crossed in a beeline, but it is preferable, especially after rain, to keep to the Red Tarn path until a gentle slope, becoming craggy, leads easily to the attractive triple summit of Cold Pike.

THE VIEW

The view is not quite as comprehensive as might be expected, the western and north-western fells (with the exception of Eel Crag) being out of sight behind the bulky Scafell group and Bowfell, but is excellent nevertheless. Of special distinction is the supremely beautiful view of the valleys of the Duddon and the Esk winding down to the sea: from no other summit are they so well seen. There is a more dramatic but less attractive picture of Great Langdale, best seen from the edge of the eastern cliffs.

Intruding in the fine array of mountains and lakes and valleys and sea is a comparatively new feature—the cooling towers of the Calder Hall atomic power station, neatly framed in the dip of the skyline between Whin Rigg and Illgill Head, the two heights above Wastwater Screes. The summit of Crinkle Crags is ageless, the cooling towers are symbols of one particular age. Here, on this rugged mountain-top, is an everlasting permanence, something simple, and we can understand; but *there*, on the horizon, is something that is temporary, and complicated beyond our comprehension. Those modern structures, out of place in a landscape that is constant and unchanging, will vanish from the scene with the passing years. The mountains, nature's symbols of power and strength, will remain.

N

ULLOCK PIKE

EEL CRAG

GLARAMARA

BOWFELL
ESK PIKE
GREAT END
Ill Crag
Broad Crag
SCAFELL PIKE
SCAFELL
SLIGHT SIDE

W — — — — — ILLGILL HEAD

WHIN RIGG

MILES 1

GREEN CRAG
HARTER FELL

Stickle Pike
Caw

S

SCAFELL
Mickledore
Scafell Crag
SCAFELL PIKE
Broad Crag
Ill Crag

The Scafell Group

THE VIEW

Principal Fells

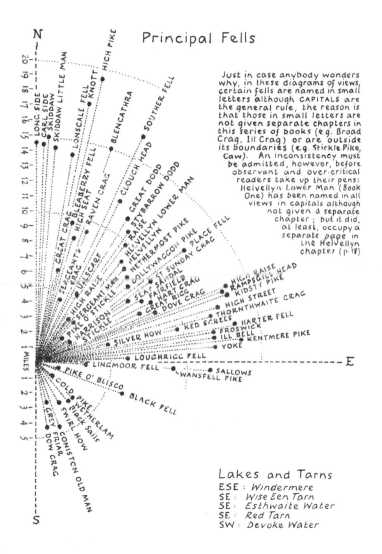

Just in case anybody wonders why, in these diagrams of views, certain fells are named in small letters although CAPITALS are the general rule, the reason is that those in small letters are not given separate chapters in this series of books (e.g. Broad Crag, Ill Crag) or are outside its boundaries (e.g. Stickle Pike, Caw). An inconsistency must be admitted, however, before observant and over-critical readers take up their pens: Helvellyn Lower Man (Book One) has been named in all views in capitals although not given a separate chapter; but it did, at least, occupy a separate page in the Helvellyn chapter (p.18)

Lakes and Tarns
ESE : Windermere
SE : Wise Een Tarn
SE : Esthwaite Water
SE : Red Tarn
SW : Devoke Water

8 Pike o' Blisco
from Wrynose

Here's a route to make you feel smug. You're going to start at the place where most visitors to Lakeland stop: the car park at the Three Shires Stone by the summit of the Wrynose Pass. We certainly felt smug when we filmed it for Granada.

On most summer days it's crammed with people snapping the views over Little Langdale, some with picnic tables set up by the road. While they take their exercise by trimming their sandwiches, you're going to stride past them and march towards Pike o' Blisco, a mountain that Wainwright thought had character, shapeliness and sturdy strength. Just like you.

If you happen to talk to the picnickers, don't, whatever you do, own up to cheating, even though you are, big style. Most people climb Pike o' Blisco from the Old Dungeon Ghyll Hotel in Great Langdale. Starting at Wrynose top saves you about 800 feet of character-building ascent and will dramatically conserves your sturdy strength.

It goes without saying that, even on an official Wainwright route, he wouldn't have approved of the Wrynose picnic table set. He often voiced his suspicion that picnics and the increasing amounts of litter to be found on the fells were synonymous. Anyhow, he just couldn't grasp the fact that anyone could get so close to a mountain and not want to go to the top. Old age and infirmity were no excuse. Even at work on the BBC series, when he was really very frail, he would still insist on trying to get further up the hill than was good for him. Betty often had to be quite firm to keep him in order. He would grumble. He would tell us all to stop fussing. He would give us a rheumy look that said, with more eloquence than frailty really should, 'I know this place better than the lot of you put together; than even people born and bred in the mountains, so ...' But he still did what Betty told him.

She knew how to take the edge off his unwell bloody-mindedness like no other. She knew the passions that still bubbled about within him. Some years before, he had abandoned all hope of getting to his favourite mountains ever again, and suddenly a BBC crew was offering him the chance to get close. One final push was all it would take once we'd organised the four-wheel drive and permission to take it high onto the hill.

At the time I was driving an aged Mercedes G Wagen whose selling point was that if it was good enough for the German and Austrian armies, it was good enough for a humble British off-roader. Leaving aside the fact that the victors really ought to write the motoring reviews, A.W. wasn't happy. Taking cars on mountains was a sin. Moreover, he wasn't at all convinced when I told him the car could lean at an angle of 45 degrees before falling over. (Like his refusal to accept that his mate Percy Duff's motorbike, which took him on some of his early expeditions, had to lean over on corners.) He clung on, white-knuckled, as we headed for the place with great views, constantly checking with Betty that we weren't going to end upside down in a ravine.

Whenever we arrived at the appointed spot he would ease himself out of the car and walk unsteadily away until he'd put distance between himself and the evil machine. Then he'd stand in complete silence for a long time and make his peace with the mountain.

'Sorry, Pike o' Blisco. I shouldn't have let them do this to you.'

'Ah, don't be daft. It's good to have you back.'

'You're looking as good as you ever did.'

'So why did you pick Haystacks?'

A.W. sucks on pipe for a long time.

Practical bits

Map: OL6.

Ascent: Start at Three Shires Stone (NY277027). The route is on Pike o' Blisco 8, *The Southern Fells* (1100 feet and 1¼ miles).

Descent: I'd suggest via Black Crag. Although Wainwright doesn't show the complete route on that page I'm sure by this stage you're capable of picking your way from the summit and joining up with his marked route at Black Crag.

Pike o' Blisco

Sunday name: Pike OF Blisco

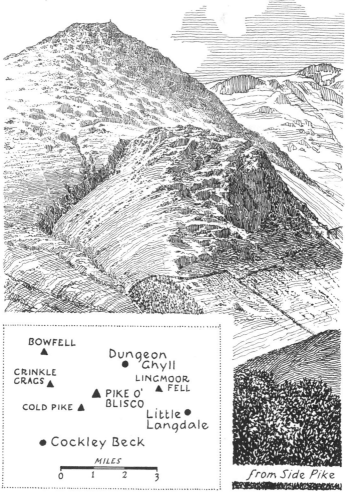

BOWFELL ▲

Dungeon
● Ghyll

CRINKLE
CRAGS ▲

LINGMOOR
▲ FELL

▲ PIKE O'
BLISCO

COLD PIKE ▲

Little ●
Langdale

● Cockley Beck

MILES

0   1   2   3

from Side Pike

NATURAL FEATURES

A mountain has added merit if its highest point can be seen from the valley below, instead of being hidden beyond receding upper slopes as is often the case, for then the objective is clear to the climber, there is no deception about height or steepness, and the full stature from base to summit can readily be comprehended. Such a mountain is Pike o' Blisco, with a well-constructed cairn plainly in view from the floor of Great Langdale and perched high above the steep and rugged flank that forms a massive south wall to the side valley of Oxendale. This peak has great character, for shapeliness and a sturdy strength combine well in its appearance, and that splendid cairn etched against the sky is at once an invitation and a challenge — while the man has no blood in his veins who does not respond eagerly to its fine-sounding swashbuckling name, savouring so much of buccaneers and the Spanish Main. There are higher summits all around, some of far greater altitude; but height alone counts for nothing, and Pike o' Blisco would hold its own in any company.

Easy routes to the top can be worked out between the crags, which are in abundance. Kettle Crag above Wall End, and Blake Rigg towering over Blea Tarn, are notable. Except for minor runnels near the top of Wrynose Pass, all streams from the fell join ultimately in the River Brathay.

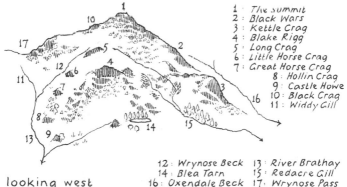

1 : The summit
2 : Black Wars
3 : Kettle Crag
4 : Blake Rigg
5 : Long Crag
6 : Little Horse Crag
7 : Great Horse Crag
8 : Hollin Crag
9 : Castle Howe
10 : Black Crag
11 : Widdy Gill
12 : Wrynose Beck
13 : River Brathay
14 : Blea Tarn
15 : Redacre Gill
16 : Oxendale Beck
17 : Wrynose Pass

looking west

MAP

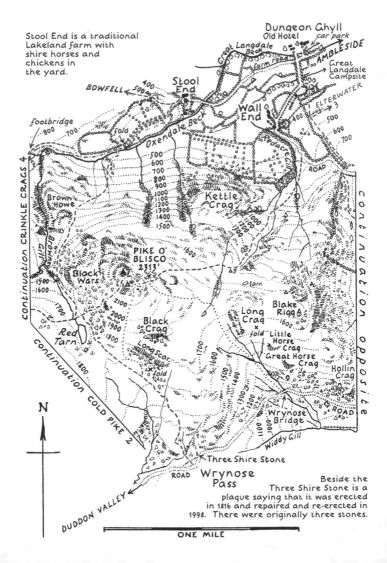

Stool End is a traditional Lakeland farm with shire horses and chickens in the yard.

Beside the Three Shire Stone is a plaque saying that it was erected in 1816 and repaired and re-erected in 1998. There were originally three stones.

ONE MILE

Blea Tarn's once well-wooded western shore is now denuded of many of its trees, although a fringe has been left by the water's edge (including the pines that have graced many a thousand photographs).

Once rhododendrons were rampant in this area, but now most of them have been cut down, leaving only the stumps. Larches and spruces are more recent additions to the scene.

MAP

continuation opposite

ROAD
Bleatarn House
Blea Tarn
car park
Road
fold
1000
800
700
600
Blea Moss Beck
ruin
Castle Howe
500
LITTLE LANGDALE
River Brathay
600
500
Fell Foot
400

Bowfell, from the summit

Fell Foot was once an inn, provided for the benefit of people crossing the passes of Wrynose and Hardknott. In 1958 it was acquired by the National Trust. Behind the house is a Viking 'thing mount' or 'ting mound' where open air meetings took place more than a thousand years ago.

Kettle Crag

ASCENT FROM DUNGEON GHYLL (via WALL END)
2100 feet of ascent : 2¼ miles

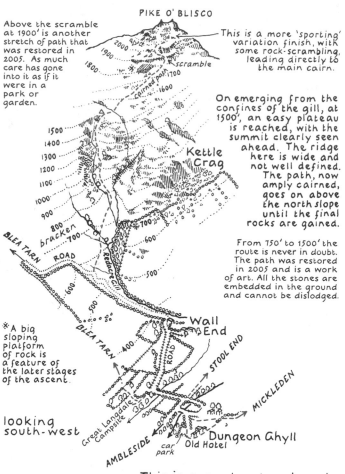

PIKE O' BLISCO

Above the scramble at 1900' is another stretch of path that was restored in 2005. As much care has gone into it as if it were in a park or garden.

This is a more 'sporting' variation finish, with some rock-scrambling, leading directly to the main cairn.

On emerging from the confines of the gill, at 1500', an easy plateau is reached, with the summit clearly seen ahead. The ridge here is wide and not well defined. The path, now amply cairned, goes on above the north slope until the final rocks are gained.

From 750' to 1500' the route is never in doubt. The path was restored in 2005 and is a work of art. All the stones are embedded in the ground and cannot be dislodged.

Kettle Crag

2000
1900
1800
scramble
Cairned path
1700
1600
1500
1400
1300
1200
1100
1000
900
800
bracken
700
700
600
500

BLEA TARN ROAD

Redacre Gill

*A big sloping platform of rock is a feature of the later stages of the ascent.

600
500
400

BLEA TARN ROAD

Wall End

STOOL END

ROAD

MICKLEDEN

looking south-west

Great Langdale Campsite

AMBLESIDE

car park

Dungeon Ghyll Old Hotel

This is a good natural route, much easier than is suggested by the formidable appearance of the objective. The path, although intermittent above 2000', is generally good.

ASCENT FROM DUNGEON GHYLL (via STOOL END)
2100 feet of ascent : 2½ miles

PIKE O' BLISCO

to WRYNOSE PASS

Red Tarn

Black Wars

CRINKLE CRAGS

2000

1900

1800

1700

1600 falls

1700

grass

1200

Isaac Gill

grass

Browney

1500

1400

Brown Howe

1300

CRINKLE CRAGS

1200

1100

footbridge

1000

tarn

800

900

800

Oxendale Beck

700

600

700

600

500

Oxendale

sheepfold

weir

gate

gate

BOWFELL

WALL END

bridge

cattle grid

Stool End

Great Langdale Beck

MICKLEDEN

CAR PARK

Dungeon Ghyll Old Hotel

At 1500' the path passes close to the confluence of two ravines, with another confluence downstream.

The usual route passes through the farmyard of Stool End and crosses Oxendale Beck at the sheepfold by way of a footbridge (rebuilt in 2005). Beyond the sheepfold the route climbs a well-made path (not distinct at the start). Other routes, in use before the bridge at the sheepfold was built, follow the north bank of Oxendale Beck and the west bank of Browney Gill, or keep to the south bank all the way from Stool End Bridge to the sheepfold.

The wide bouldery course of Oxendale Beck testifies to its power in flood. Note that some tributaries are also choked by stones upon reaching the valley.

The subsoil, brown on the climb up from the valley, becomes a rich red as height is gained

looking south-west

An interesting climb, with good rock· and ravine scenery. The section between the beck and Brown Howe, once bumpy and rough, is now well maintained.

ASCENT FROM LITTLE LANGDALE
1800 feet of ascent : 2½ miles from Fell Foot

looking
west-north-west

PIKE O' BLISCO

Black
Crag

2100
2000
1900
1800

WALL END

1700

Wrynose
Pass

grass

small
tarn

1600

Long
Crag

Blake
Rigg

1500

1400

sheepfold

1300

Little
Horse
Crag

1200

ROAD

1100

Great
Horse
Crag

1400

1300

1200

Identify the
gully by its
holly trees
and the
ruin
below it

Wrynose
Bridge

900

1000

800

900

Hollin
Crag

700

holly trees

Widdy Gill

600

bracken

BLEA
TARN

The route from
Wrynose Bridge
takes advantage of
the easiest contours
and affords a simple
passage, avoiding all
contact with crags. There
is no path, however, and the
climbing is tedious until the
final rocks are reached and
the cairned track from Wall
End joined.

500

ROAD

x ruin

fold

500

600

Castle
Howe

x fold

More exciting (and exacting)
is a gully running straight down
from the skyline just to the right
of the craggy shoulder above Hollin
Crag: this gives access to Blake Rigg,
a good viewpoint, whence the flat top
is crossed to join the cairned track from
Wall End. The gully is for scramblers only
and should not be used for descent, being
difficult to locate from above. There is no
path in the gully or on the ridge at the top of it, nor is there
any evidence that human beings have passed this way before.
Bracken on the lower slopes is a hindrance in late summer.

500

River Brathay

Fell
Foot

small
arched bridge

ROAD
BLEA
TARN

grid

LITTLE
LANGDALE

An obvious alternative (not shown on the diagram above —
see next page) is by the broken ridge going up to the summit from
Wrynose Pass, or, more easily, by the Red Tarn path from the Pass,
either of which adds half a mile in distance.

Pike o' Blisco is well worth climbing from any
direction, and, indeed, from all directions. The
approach from Little Langdale by the usual way
leaving Wrynose Bridge, however, is rather dull
in comparison with those from Great Langdale.

ASCENT FROM WRYNOSE PASS
1100 feet of ascent : 1¼ miles
PIKE O' BLISCO

looking north

Incidentally (although this has nothing to do with the ascent) there is a quick and easy crossing (in clear weather) from Wrynose Pass to Redacre Gill (for Great Langdale) over the grass slopes below Black Crag.

2200
2100
2000
grass
Black Crag
1900
.....1800
Long Scar

Red Tarn

Turn off the path here up an easy grass slope to the south-east cairn.
The main path goes on to Oxendale, with a branch turning off for Crinkle Crags 100 yards beyond Red Tarn, to the left; opposite this branch a cairned track climbs to Pike o' Blisco, this being the more usual route.

sheepfold
1700

1600....

If it is desired to visit Black Crag en route (in view of the enthusiastic references to its pinnacle at the foot of the page) leave the path where the beck crosses it at 1550' and follow the beck upwards over easy grass slopes.

This ascent is ideal for motorists who would like to tackle a mild fellwalk (to a grand summit) without venturing too far from their cars.

1500

grass

1400

1300

LITTLE LANGDALE

Three Shire Stone
summit of pass
Wrynose Pass
There is room to park at the top of Wrynose Pass.

DUDDON VALLEY

ROAD

The Needle, Black Crag

This smooth and slender pinnacle, detached from the face of Black Crag, is precariously balanced on a massive plinth of rock, 12 ft. high, the total height to the tip being 35 ft. Well off the beaten track (although only a long half-mile from Wrynose Pass) it may have escaped the notice of cragsmen, there being no evidence of ascent on the pinnacle or in the rock-climbing literature at present available for the area. It seems (to a novice who hasn't tried) that the tip may be gained by 'bridging' the gap with the main crag. He will be a good man who can stand erect on the point of the needle.

The author feels rather proud of this 'discovery' and hopes people will not write to claim (i) a knowledge of the pinnacle (since they were children), (ii) that they have climbed it (blindfolded), and (iii) stood for hours on its point (on their heads).

THE SUMMIT

"see "Some Personal Notes in conclusion"

This is a beautiful 'top', and a colourful one, with pinky-grey rocks outcropping everywhere from dark heather and green mosses. The main cairn is a shapely edifice, gloriously situated on a platform of naked rock at the north-western terminus of a summit-ridge 100 yards long. At the south-east extremity is another cairn, less imposing; this too crowns a craggy pyramid.

BOWFELL

PLAN OF SUMMIT

N

100 yards

2200
2100

GREAT LANGDALE (follow cairns)
WRYNOSE BRIDGE (bear right below top rocks)

RED TARN (cairned path)

WRYNOSE PASS (keep to grass)

DESCENTS: Use the paths when leaving the summit, in fair weather or foul. The north face is terraced with crags, making a direct descent to Oxendale impracticable, nor should streams be followed, many of them plunging into rough and deep ravines.

RIDGE ROUTE

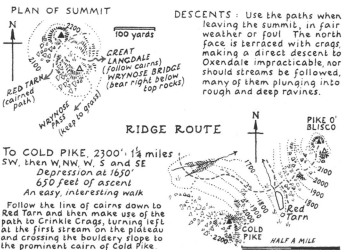

N

PIKE O' BLISCO
2100
2000
1900
1800
Red Tarn
1700
1800
1900
2000
COLD PIKE
2200

HALF A MILE

TO COLD PIKE, 2300' 1¼ miles
SW, then W, NW, W, S and SE
Depression at 1650'
650 feet of ascent
An easy, interesting walk

Follow the line of cairns down to Red Tarn and then make use of the path to Crinkle Crags, turning left at the first stream on the plateau and crossing the bouldery slope to the prominent cairn of Cold Pike.

THE VIEW

As the diagram suggests, most of the detail in the panorama is concentrated between north and east, and here the distant views, from Skiddaw round to the Kentmere fells, are certainly good. At close quarters, however, are Bowfell and Crinkle Crags, displaying their features to such effect that they will win most attention. Wander a few paces (not too many!) from the cairn, in the direction of Great Langdale, for a splendid prospect of that valley.

Principal Fells

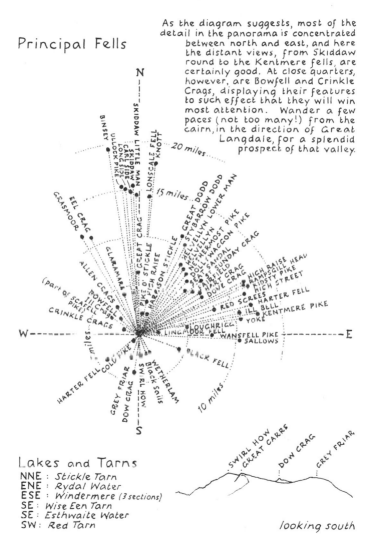

Lakes and Tarns

NNE : *Stickle Tarn*
ENE : *Rydal Water*
ESE : *Windermere (3 sections)*
SE : *Wise Een Tarn*
SE : *Esthwaite Water*
SW : *Red Tarn*

looking south

9 Scafell Pike
from Borrowdale via Esk Hause

All filming in the high mountains is challenging and, generally, the bigger the mountain the bigger the challenge. So Scafell Pike needs a bit of respect. Before each programme I have to fill in a risk assessment form which runs to some pages and is designed to bring comfort to the nervous managers of our risk-averse society. The first time I had to do it I scanned the form's various headings – nuclear war, chemical attack, operating dangerous machinery. None of them seemed to apply to my assault on Scafell Pike. Then I came to the section headed extreme environments. Ah ha! I ticked the box, and in the space where I had to quantify the risk wrote:

'Dangerous. If wet or windy, bloody dangerous.'

Two days later the form was back with a sharp note suggesting I wasn't taking this matter seriously. They were probably right. But I still risked pointing out that we'd been taking film crews onto the hill for more than twenty years and hadn't lost one yet.

It's a military operation getting the camera and sound gear to the top of the hill (and, more important, back again) mainly because the process takes so long. In the Pictorial Guide *The Southern Fells* Wainwright reckons that the approach to Scafell Pike from Borrowdale takes 3½ hours up and 2½ down. If you're filming the trip, it takes at least double that. Sometimes we have to do the whole route twice on consecutive days to be able to get the stuff we need on tape. Now, as Lakeland fell walkers know, the chance of getting the same weather two days running is remote. On more than one occasion, films of some of the bigger walks have started in a sun-drenched valley only to finish on a rain-lashed summit. A tip: you can generally tell it's been a two-day exercise if, part way through, there's a shot of a thunder cloud while the presenter says something like 'Looks as if the weather's on the turn.'

We rarely fail entirely but sometimes it's been touch and go. When we were filming *Wainwright's Remote Lakeland* we had to go back to Grisedale Pike five times because of bad weather and even the final version that appeared in the programme was done in sheeting rain. We were backed into a corner and had to go for it because the programme was being broadcast the following week. But even so we had to miss out three summits and find an escape route off the mountain by way of Gasgale Gill because the conditions were so unsafe. Risk assessment officer please note.

BBC4's *Wainwright Walks* had no such problems when Julia Bradbury set off from Seathwaite in Borrowdale to tackle Scafell Pike – what Wainwright described as 'the toughest proposition the "collector" of summits is called upon to attempt and… the one above all others that, as a patriot, he cannot omit.' I can hear him saying it. And he's right, this is big stuff. The route BBC4 chose stretches over two Wainwright pages. Whatever the weather and even without an attendant film crew, you need to plan it. And while you're planning, don't forget that Seathwaite has the reputation of being the wettest inhabited place in England. Once, that was a fairly dodgy selling point but in the age of the water shortage and the hosepipe ban Seathwaite is rapidly becoming the place to be.

But back to the walk. Wainwright is as close to comprehensive as you can get so far as ascents of the Lakeland summits are concerned. He devotes thirty closely worked pages to Scafell Pike, for example. But once you start to explore the mountains you begin to realise that even the meticulous Mr Wainwright is painting only one part of a broader canvas. Everywhere you look there are humps and hollows, features in a complex landscape, that crowd into the margins of his picture. I'm not accusing A.W. of shirking. Heaven forbid. Each Pictorial Guide would have had to be ten volumes to get all the stories in. But to me fell walking is a means to an end, not an end in itself. It's a way of getting to interesting places where geology or history or human foible left a mark on the map.

A classic example, combining all three, is a few hundred yards from the start of the Scafell Pike ascent at Seathwaite Farm. Most walkers miss it because they're so intent on managing the business of getting to the roof of England. But when you're planning this walk, make time to explore the remains of what's known as the Seathwaite wad. On the face of the fell west of the farm you'll see a tumble of spoil-heaps beside Sour Milk Gill. In the late eighteenth and early nineteenth centuries this was one of the most valuable mineral deposits in the world. It was discovered by accident when a tree blew over on the hillside and the uprooted stump revealed an outcrop of graphite. At a time when lead was worth fifteen pounds a ton, each ton of this black lead was worth as much as five thousand pounds. There were armed guards on the mine. The miners were strip searched after every shift. Anyone caught smuggling the graphite faced transportation. But they still tried and they left us the phrase 'dealing on the black market'. Something to mull over on the long climb out to Esk Hause and, beyond that, the three final summits that, in the days the Seathwaite wad was being worked, were known as the Pikes of Scawfell.

Practical bits
Maps: OL4 and OL6.
Ascent: The *Wainwright Walks* route started at Seathwaite Farm in Borrowdale (NY236122) and approached the mountain by way of Stockley Bridge and Grains Gill to Esk Hause – Scafell Pike 17 in *The Southern Fells*. From there they took a detour from the Wainwright route under Great End to visit Sprinkling Tarn. Then they returned to Wainwright's Scafell Pike 18 to climb over Ill Crag and Broad Crag to the summit. 4 miles and 2,900 feet. (Wainwright says 5½ miles and 3,200 feet but he starts at Seatoller.)

Descent: Wainwright suggests making a circular walk of it by descending via Lingmell Col, Sty Head and Styhead Tarn to Borrowdale – Wainwright's Scafell Pike 15 and 16 in reverse (4½ miles and approximately 2,800 feet back to Seathwaite Farm plus an hour and a half to explore the site of the Seathwaite graphite mines).

If you have benefit of a driver to collect you at the end of the day, you could try what I think is a grander way down and a route with unbeatable views. That's the reverse of Wainwright's Scafell Pike 14 which takes you via Lingmell Col and Piers Gill and finally by the pools and cascades of Lingmell Beck to Burnthwaite in Wasdale. All told, 3¾ miles and 3,000 feet of descent.

Scafell Pike 3210'

the highest mountain in England

formerly 'The Pikes' or 'The Pikes of Scawfell'

from Great Moss,
Upper Eskdale

Scafell Pike

Ill Crag

from the gorge of the Esk

Seathwaite ●

▲ GREAT GABLE

Wasdale Head ●   ▲ GREAT END

▲ SCAFELL PIKE

▲   ▲   ● Dungeon
SCAFELL   BOWFELL   Ghyll

Boot ●

MILES

0   1   2   3   4   5

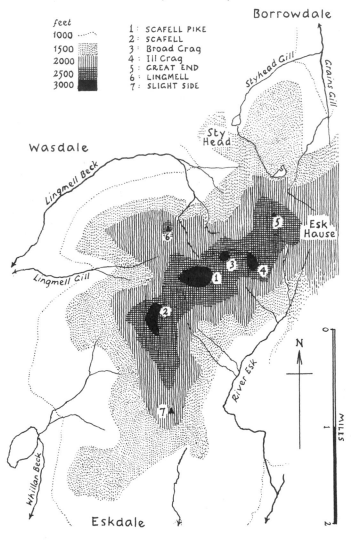

The Scafell Range

Borrowdale

feet	
1000	
1500	
2000	
2500	
3000	

1 : SCAFELL PIKE
2 : SCAFELL
3 : Broad Crag
4 : Ill Crag
5 : GREAT END
6 : LINGMELL
7 : SLIGHT SIDE

Styhead Gill

Grains Gill

Sty Head

Wasdale

Lingmell Beck

Esk Hause

Lingmell Gill

River Esk

Whillan Beck

N

Eskdale

MILES
0
1
2

Scafell Pike's grandest crag:
Dow Crag

Known to climbers
as Esk Buttress, this
400-foot near-vertical
crag rises from the
fellside low down on
the mountain's east
flank, overlooking
the River Esk.

Scafell Pike's best-known crag:
Pulpit Rock

This fine pinnacle (seen
here from Mickledore)
is the best feature of
Pikes Crag, above
Hollow Stones. Its
top (easily reached
from the summit-
to-Mickledore
path) is the
best of all
viewpoints
for Scafell
Crag.

NATURAL FEATURES

The difference between a hill and a mountain depends on *appearance*, not on *altitude* (whatever learned authorities may say to the contrary) and is thus arbitrary and a matter of personal opinion. Grass predominates on a hill, rock on a mountain. A hill is smooth, a mountain rough. In the case of Scafell Pike, opinions must agree that here is a mountain without doubt, and a mountain that is, moreover, every inch a mountain. Roughness and ruggedness are the necessary attributes, and the Pike has these in greater measure than other high ground in the country —— which is just as it should be, for there is no higher ground than this.

Strictly, the name 'Scafell Pike' should be in the plural, there being three principal summits above 3000 feet, the two lesser having the distinguishing titles of Broad Crag and Ill Crag. The main Pike is, however, pre-eminent, towering over the others seemingly to a greater extent than the mere 160 feet or so by which it has superiority in altitude, and in general being a bulkier mass altogether.

The three summits rise from the main spine of an elevated ridge which keeps above 2800 feet to its abrupt termination in the cliffs of Great End, facing north to Borrowdale; lower spurs then run down to that valley. In the opposite direction, southwest, across the deep gulf of Mickledore, is the tremendous rock-wall of the neighbouring and separate mountain of Scafell, which also exceeds 3000 feet: this is the parent mountain in the one sense that its name has been passed on to the Pikes. Scafell's summit-ridge runs south and broadens into foothills, descending ultimately to mid-Eskdale.

continued

This aspect of the Scafell range (well seen from Great Gable) is, in the author's opinion, the finest mountain scene in Lakeland.

The Wasdale flank

NATURAL FEATURES

The flanks of the range are bounded on the west by Wasdale, and by the upper reaches of Eskdale, east. All the waters from the Pikes (and from Scafell) flow into one or other of these two valleys, ultimately to merge in the Ravenglass estuary. Thus it will be seen that Scafell Pike, despite a commanding presence, has not the same importance, geographically, as many other fells in the district. It does not stand at the head of any valley, but between valleys: it is not the hub of a wheel from which watercourses radiate; it is one of the spokes. It is inferior, in this respect, to Great Gable or Bowfell nearby, or even its own Great End.

Another interesting feature of Scafell Pike is that although it towers so mightily above Wasdale it can claim no footing in that valley, its territory tapering quickly to Brown Tongue, at the base of which it is nipped off by the widening lower slopes of Lingmell and Scafell.

Tarns are noticeably absent on the arid, stony surface of the mountain, but there is one sheet of water below the summit to the south, Broadcrag Tarn, which is small and unattractive, but, at 2125 feet, can at least boast the highest standing water in Lakeland.

Crags are in evidence on all sides, and big areas of the upper slopes lie devastated by a covering of piled up boulders, a result not of disintegration but of the volcanic upheavals that laid waste to the mountain during its formation. The landscape is harsh, even savage, and has attracted to itself nothing of romance or historical legend There is no sentiment about Scafell Pike.

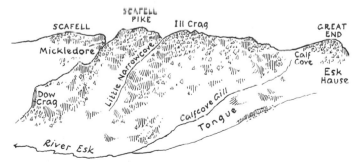

This view is as seen from the south ridge of Esk Pike

The Eskdale flank

MAP

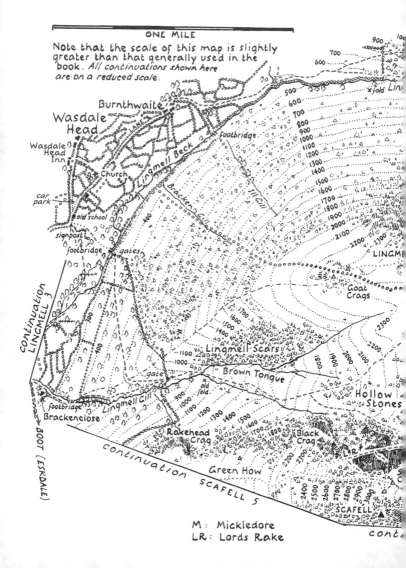

ONE MILE

Note that the scale of this map is slightly greater than that generally used in the book. All continuations shown here are on a reduced scale.

Burnthwaite

Wasdale Head

Wasdale Head Inn

Church

car park

old school

signpost

footbridge   gates

Continuation LINGMELL 3

footbridge

Brackenclose

BOOT (ESKDALE)

Lingmell Beck

Bracken Gill

Lingmell Gill

Ill Gill

footbridge

gate

gate

old fold

Rakehead Crag

continuation SCAFELL 5

Green How

Lingmell Scars

Brown Tongue

Black Crag

LINGME

Goat Crags

Hollow Stones

LR

SCAFELL

cont

M : Mickledore
LR : Lords Rake

MAP

A : to BORROWDALE
B : to GREAT LANGDALE

GABLE TRAVERSE

GREAT GABLE

Sty Head

A

continuation SEATHWAITE FELL 2

Sprinkling Tarn

BORROWDALE

Spouthead Gill

Skew Gill

The Band

Grainy Gill

Stand Crag

Corridor Route

Ruddy Gill

continuation ALLEN CRAGS 3

Greta Gill

Piers Gill

Lambfoot Dub

GREAT END

Long Pike

Round How

Calf Cove

Esk Hause

tarns

Broad Crag

Ill Crag

Tongue

Calf Cove Gill

continuation ESK PIKE 5

Pikes Crag

Crag

SCAFELL PIKE 3210

Cockly Pike

Broadcrag Tarn

Broadcrag

Rough Crag

Little Narrowcove

Broad Crags

Pen

River Esk

N

Dow Crag

C : to ESKDALE (via CAM SPOUT)

C

C

SCAFELL 6

HALF A MILE

BROAD CRAG

ESK HAUSE

ILL CRAG

SCAFELL PIKE

Land over 3000'

Broad Crag, 3054'

Broad Crag is the second of the Scafell Pikes, and a worthy mountain in itself — but it has little fame, is not commonly regarded as a separate fell, and its summit is rarely visited. This latter circumstance appears strange, because the blazed highway between Esk Hause and the main Pike not only climbs over the shoulder of Broad Crag but actually passes within a hundred yards of its summit, which is not greatly elevated above the path. Yet not one person in a thousand passing along here (and thousands do!) turns aside to visit the cairn. The reason for this neglect is more obvious when on the site than it is from a mere study of the map, for the whole of the top is littered deep with piled boulders across which it is quite impossible to walk with any semblance of dignity, the detour involving a desperate and inelegant scramble and the risk of breaking a leg at every stride. Most walkers using the path encounter enough trouble underfoot without seeking more in the virgin jungle of tumbled rock all around. Broad Crag is, in fact, the roughest summit in Lakeland.

The eastern slope descends into Little Narrowcove, and is of small consequence, but the western flank is imposing. On this side the top breaks away in a semi-circle of crags, below which is a shelf traversed by the Corridor Route and bounded lower down a steepening declivity by the great gash of Piers Gill.

Only the proximity of the main Scafell Pike, overtopping the scene, robs Broad Crag of its rightful place as one of the finest of fells.

Broad Crag, and Broad Crag col (right)
from the Corridor Route

Ill Crag, 3068'

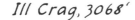

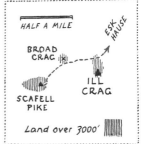

HALF A MILE

BROAD CRAG

SCAFELL PIKE

ILL CRAG

ESK HAUSE

Land over 3000'

Ill Crag is the third of the Scafell Pikes, and the most shapely, appearing as a graceful peak when viewed from upper Eskdale, which it dominates. Like Broad Crag, the summit lies off the path from Esk Hause to the main Pike but is more distant, although in this case too the shoulder of the fell is crossed at a height exceeding 3000', so that the summit is raised but little above it. The detour to the top is simple, only the final short rise being really rougher than the boulder-crossings on the path itself. Ill Crag is prominently seen from the vicinity of Esk Hause, and many wishful (and subsequently disappointed) walkers hereabouts, engaged on their first ascent of Scafell Pike will wrongly assume it to be their objective.

The western slope goes down uneventfully between Broad Crag and Great End to the Corridor Route, and the glory of the fell is its excessively steep and rough fall directly from the cairn eastwards into the wilderness of upper Eskdale: a chaotic and desolate scene set at a precipitous gradient, a frozen avalanche of crags and stones, much of it unexplored and uncharted, wild in the extreme, and offering a safe refuge for escaped convicts or an ideal depository for murdered corpses. Someday, when the regular paths become overcrowded, it may be feasible to track out an exciting and alternative route of ascent for scramblers here, but the author prefers to leave the job to someone with more energy and a lesser love of life.

Ill Crag, from the path above Esk Hause

Pikes Crag

Pulpit Rock

Mickledore
Buttress

Mickledore

Scafell
Crag

from Hollow Stones

Once in a while every keen fellwalker should have a *pre-arranged* night out amongst the mountains. Time drags and the hours of darkness can be bitterly cold, but to be on the tops at dawn is a wonderful experience and much more than recompense for the temporary discomfort.

Hollow Stones is an excellent place for a bivouac, with a wide choice of overhanging boulders for shelter, many of which have been walled-up and made draught-proof by previous occupants. Watch the rising sun flush Scafell Crag and change a black silhouette into a rosy-pink castle! (This doesn't always happen. Sometimes it never stops raining).

Not many readers, not even those who are frequent visitors to Scafell Pike, could give a caption to this picture. It is, in fact, a scene in the unfrequented hollow of Little Narrowcove, looking up towards the summit of the Pike (the top cairn is out of sight). The crags, unsuspected on the usual routes, are a great surprise. Little Narrowcove (reached from Broad Crag col) is a grassy basin sheltered or encircled by cliffs : a good site for a mountain camp.

ASCENTS

The ascent of Scafell Pike is the toughest proposition the 'collector' of summits is called upon to attempt, and it is the one above all others that, as a patriot, he cannot omit. The difficulties are due more to roughness of the ground than to altitude, and to the remoteness of the summit from frequented valleys. From all bases except Wasdale Head the climb is long and arduous, and progress is slow: this is a full-day expedition, and the appropriate preparations should be made. Paths are good, but only in the sense that they are distinct; they are abominably stony, even bouldery — which is no great impediment when ascending but mitigates against quick descent. Ample time should be allowed for getting off the mountain.

In winter especially, when conditions can be Arctic, it is important to select a fine clear day, to start early, and keep moving; reserve three hours of daylight for the return journey. If under deep snow the mountain is better left alone altogether, for progress would then be laborious, and even dangerous across the concealed boulders, with a greater chance of death from exposure than of early rescue if an accident were to occur.

Scafell Pike may be ascended most easily from Wasdale Head, less conveniently from Borrowdale or Great Langdale or Eskdale. But all routes are alike in grandeur of scenery.

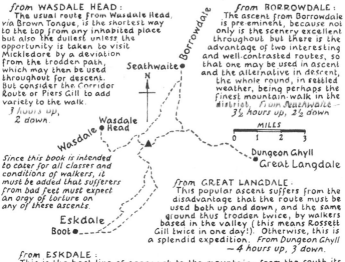

from WASDALE HEAD:
The usual route from Wasdale Head, via Brown Tongue, is the shortest way to the top from any inhabited place but also the dullest unless the opportunity is taken to visit Mickledore by a deviation from the trodden path, which may then be used throughout for descent. But consider the Corridor Route or Piers Gill to add variety to the walk.
3 hours up,
2 down.

Since this book is intended to cater for all classes and conditions of walkers, it must be added that sufferers from bad feet must expect an orgy of torture on any of these ascents.

from BORROWDALE :
The ascent from Borrowdale is pre-eminent, because not only is the scenery excellent throughout but there is the advantage of two interesting and well-contrasted routes, so that one may be used in ascent and the alternative in descent, the whole round, in settled weather, being perhaps the finest mountain-walk in the district. From Seathwaite — 3½ hours up, 2½ down

MILES
0   1   2   3

Dungeon Ghyll
Great Langdale

from GREAT LANGDALE :
This popular ascent suffers from the disadvantage that the route must be used both up and down, and the same ground thus trodden twice, by walkers based in the valley (this means Rossett Gill twice in one day!). Otherwise, this is a splendid expedition. From Dungeon Ghyll — 4 hours up, 3 down.

from ESKDALE :
This is the best line of approach to the mountain: from the south its grandest and most rugged aspect is seen. Variations of route may be adopted, but time is a great enemy : the walk is lengthy (a feature most noticed when returning). From Boot — 4½ hours up, 3½ down.

ASCENT FROM WASDALE HEAD
via BROWN TONGUE

3,000 feet of ascent
3½ miles
(from Wasdale Head Inn)

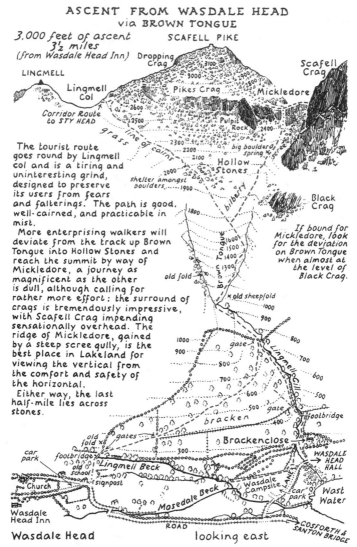

SCAFELL PIKE

LINGMELL

Lingmell Col

Corridor Route to STY HEAD

grass

line of cairns

Dropping Crag

3100
3000
2900
2800
2700

Pikes Crag

Scafell Crag

Mickledore

2600

2500

2400

Pulpit Rock

2300

2200

big boulder & spring

2100

Hollow Stones

shelter amongst boulders

2000

1900

1800

bilberry

Black Crag

Brown Tongue

1600
1500
1400
1300

old fold

× old sheepfold

1000

900

gate

800

1000

900

700

bracken

800

700

600

500

400

Lingmell Gill

700

600

500

footbridge

gate

old fold ×

gates

footbridge

300

gate

Brackenclose

WASDALE HEAD HALL

car park

old school!

Lingmell Beck

signpost

Wasdale Campsite

car park

West Water

Church

Wasdale Head Inn

Mosedale Beck

ROAD

COSFORTH & SANTON BRIDGE

Wasdale Head

looking east

The tourist route goes round by Lingmell col and is a tiring and uninteresting grind, designed to preserve its users from fears and falterings. The path is good, well-cairned, and practicable in mist.

More enterprising walkers will deviate from the track up Brown Tongue into Hollow Stones and reach the summit by way of Mickledore, a journey as magnificent as the other is dull, although calling for rather more effort: the surround of crags is tremendously impressive, with Scafell Crag impending sensationally overhead. The ridge of Mickledore, gained by a steep scree gully, is the best place in Lakeland for viewing the vertical from the comfort and safety of the horizontal.

Either way, the last half-mile lies across stones.

If bound for Mickledore, look for the deviation on Brown Tongue when almost at the level of Black Crag.

ASCENT FROM WASDALE HEAD
via PIERS GILL

3,000 feet of ascent
3¾ miles
(from Wasdale Head Inn)

SCAFELL PIKE

Broad Crag col

Broad Crag

Dropping Crag

3100
2800
2700
2600
2500
2400

LINGMELL

WASDALE

Lingmell Col

At point B, either take the usual path via Lingmell Col, or (a good alternative) follow the stream up to Broad Crag col, there joining the path from Esk Hause

STY HEAD (CORRIDOR ROUTE)

Greta Gill

tarns
grass
old wall

Middleboot Knotts

Criscliffe Knotts

Stand Crag

ravines
grass

1500
1400
1300
1200

A

scree

2000

C

Piers Gill

1600

1300
1400

1300
1200

NOTE WELL THAT THERE IS NO THROUGH WAY ON THE WEST SIDE (true left) OF PIERS GILL, PROGRESS BEING BARRED BY CRAGS. NOR CAN THE GILL BE CROSSED BETWEEN POINTS A AND B. THE BED OF THE GILL IS ALSO IMPASSABLE.

grass

cairn on boulder

1100

wide stony stream-bed

1000

STY HEAD

Spoutdead Gill

a beautiful watersmeet

900

800

looking south

pools and cascades

700

STY HEAD (direct route)

600

Use the Sty Head Valley Route (see Great End 7) and, after crossing at the watersmeet, take advantage of the zig-zags for 250 yards, where a cairn on a boulder indicates the start of an indistinct grassy trod along the east bank. A little doubt is likely to arise at point C, where a steepish wall of broken crag has to be negotiated, but there is easy scrambling only and no real difficulty in finding a way up. The edge of the great ravine may be, and should be, visited at opportune places for the striking views into its depths, but extreme care is necessary, as the sheer walls are badly eroded and dangerously loose.

The tremendous north face of Lingmell, gashed by the great ravine of Piers Gill, is enough justification for essaying this fine and rather adventurous route.
The way is pathless alongside the gill; clear weather is advisable for ascent and essential for descent by this route.

moraines
footbridge

Lingmell Beck

500

Burnthwaite

WASDALE HEAD INN ½

Wasdale Head

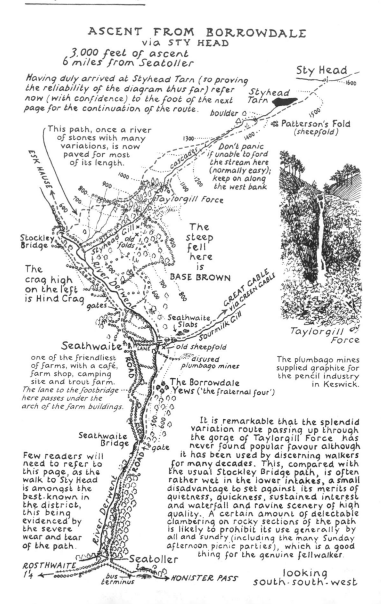

ASCENT FROM BORROWDALE
via STY HEAD
3,000 feet of ascent
6 miles from Seatoller

Having duly arrived at Styhead Tarn (so proving the reliability of the diagram thus far) refer now (with confidence) to the foot of the next page for the continuation of the route.

Sty Head

1600

Styhead Tarn

1500

boulder

Patterson's Fold
(sheepfold)

1400

This path, once a river of stones with many variations, is now paved for most of its length.

1300

cascades

1200

Don't panic if unable to ford the stream here (normally easy); keep on along the west bank

1000

900

800

700

600

ESK HAUSE

Taylorgill Force

The steep fell here is BASE BROWN

Stockley Bridge

Styhead Gill   old folds

River Derwent

The crag high on the left is Hind Crag

gates

GREAT GABLE via GREEN GABLE

Taylorgill Force

Seathwaite Slabs

Sourmilk Gill

Seathwaite

LANE   old sheepfold

disused plumbago mines

one of the friendliest of farms, with a café, farm shop, camping site and trout farm.
The lane to the footbridge here passes under the arch of the farm buildings.

The Borrowdale Yews ('the fraternal four')

The plumbago mines supplied graphite for the pencil industry in Keswick.

ROAD

Seathwaite Bridge

gate

500

400

Few readers will need to refer to this page, as the walk to Sty Head is amongst the best-known in the district, this being evidenced by the severe wear and tear of the path.

It is remarkable that the splendid variation route passing up through the gorge of Taylorgill Force has never found popular favour although it has been used by discerning walkers for many decades. This, compared with the usual Stockley Bridge path, is often rather wet in the lower intakes, a small disadvantage to set against its merits of quietness, quickness, sustained interest and waterfall and ravine scenery of high quality. A certain amount of delectable clambering on rocky sections of the path is likely to prohibit its use generally by all and sundry (including the many Sunday afternoon picnic parties), which is a good thing for the genuine fellwalker.

River Derwent

ROSTHWAITE
14

Seatoller

bus terminus

HONISTER PASS

looking
south-south-west

ASCENT FROM BORROWDALE
via STY HEAD

continued

looking south

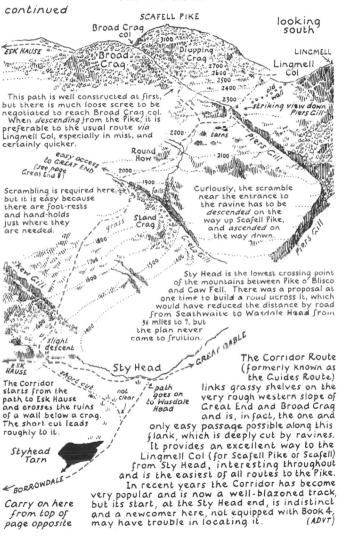

SCAFELL PIKE

Broad Crag col

3100

Broad Crag

Dropping Crag

2700
2600
2500
2400

2300

ESK HAUSE

LINGMELL

Lingmell Col

old wall

striking view down Piers Gill

This path is well constructed at first, but there is much loose scree to be negotiated to reach Broad Crag col. When *descending* from the Pike, it is preferable to the usual route *via* Lingmell Col, especially in mist, and certainly quicker.

2200

tarns

Piers Gill

Round How

2100

easy access to GREAT END (see page Great End 8)

2000

1900

falls

Scrambling is required here, but it is easy because there are foot-rests and hand-holds just where they are needed.

grass

Sand Crag

Greta Gill

Curiously, the scramble near the entrance to the ravine has to be *descended* on the way up Scafell Pike, and *ascended* on the way down.

1800

1700

1500   1400

1600

Kew Gill

Piers Gill

Sty Head is the lowest crossing point of the mountains between Pike o' Blisco and Caw Fell. There was a proposal at one time to build a road across it, which would have reduced the distance by road from Seathwaite to Wasdale Head from 3½ miles to 7, but the plan never came to fruition.

1800

slight descent

ESK HAUSE

Sty Head

GREAT GABLE

The Corridor starts from the path to Esk Hause and crosses the ruins of a wall below a crag. The short cut leads roughly to it.

short cut

not clear

path goes on to Wasdale Head

Styhead Tarn

← BORROWDALE

Carry on here from top of page opposite

The Corridor Route (formerly known as the Guides Route) links grassy shelves on the very rough western slope of Great End and Broad Crag and is, in fact, the one and only easy passage possible along this flank, which is deeply cut by ravines. It provides an excellent way to the Lingmell Col (for Scafell Pike or Scafell) from Sty Head, interesting throughout and is the easiest of all routes to the Pike.

In recent years the Corridor has become very popular and is now a well-blazoned track, but its start, at the Sty Head end, is indistinct and a newcomer here, not equipped with Book 4, may have trouble in locating it.   (ADVT)

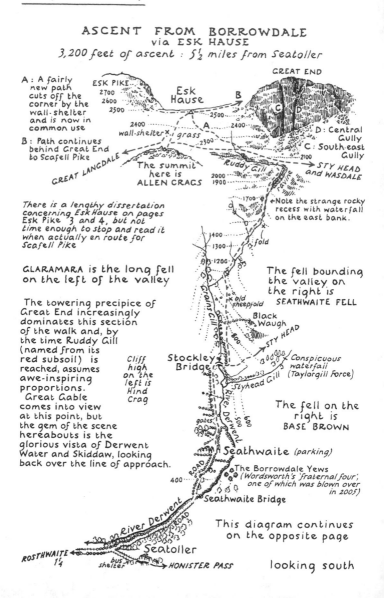

ASCENT FROM BORROWDALE
via ESK HAUSE
3,200 feet of ascent : 5½ miles from Seatoller

GREAT END

ESK PIKE
2700
2600
2500

Esk
Hause

B

A: A fairly new path cuts off the corner by the wall-shelter and is now in common use

2400
wall-shelter ✗ grass

2500

2400

A

2300

C

D

B: Path continues behind Great End to Scafell Pike

GREAT LANGDALE

The summit here is ALLEN CRAGS

Ruddy Gill

D: Central Gully

C: South-east Gully

2100

→ STY HEAD and WASDALE

2000
1900

ravine

There is a lengthy dissertation concerning Esk Hause on pages Esk Pike 3 and 4, but not time enough to stop and read it when actually en route for Scafell Pike

1700

Note the strange rocky recess with waterfall on the east bank.

1400
1300

fold

GLARAMARA is the long fell on the left of the valley

1200

The fell bounding the valley on the right is SEATHWAITE FELL

The towering precipice of Great End increasingly dominates this section of the walk and, by the time Ruddy Gill (named from its red subsoil) is reached, assumes awe-inspiring proportions.

old sheepfold

Black Waugh

STY HEAD

Great Gable comes into view at this point, but the gem of the scene hereabouts is the glorious vista of Derwent Water and Skiddaw, looking back over the line of approach.

Cliff high on the left is Hind Crag

Stockley Bridge

Conspicuous waterfall (Taylorgill Force)

Styhead Gill

The fell on the right is BASE BROWN

gates

River Derwent

500

600

Seathwaite (parking)

400

The Borrowdale Yews (Wordsworth's 'fraternal four'; one of which was blown over in 2005)

ROAD

Seathwaite Bridge

This diagram continues on the opposite page

River Derwent

Seatoller

ROSTHWAITE 1¼

bus shelter

→ HONISTER PASS

looking south

ASCENT FROM BORROWDALE
via ESK HAUSE

continued

This diagram is on a larger scale than that on the opposite page.

SCAFELL PIKE

Dropping Crag

Broad Crag

3100

3000

Broad Crag col (2900')

Ill Crag

3000

2800

3000

Ill Crag col (2900')

gravelly plateau

F

Ill Crag is prominently in view from the section of path between Esk Hause and Calf Cove. It is the highest thing in sight, and wishful thinkers will assume it to be the summit — until the Pike itself is finally revealed, indisputably higher and still far distant across a waste of stones.

summit now in view for the first time

E

2900

Ill Crag col is wide. Broad Crag col is narrow and steepsided

Upper Eskdale

grass

D

2800

watershed reached

2800

steep slopes on this side go down to Wasdale

C

GREAT END

Calf Cove

Calfcove Gill

B

wall-shelter
last running water

2600

Esk Hause

ESK PIKE

A

2500

grass

ROUTE OF APPROACH FROM GRAINS GILL

2400

wall-shelter ×

STY HEAD and WASDALE

GREAT LANGDALE

looking south-west

The path is distinct and well-cairned but in places is formed of nail scratches on boulders.

A – B : easy; gradient slight.

B – C : stony, rising path

C – D : easy.

D – E : rough; 150 yards of big stones to cross.

E – F : easy.

F onwards : excessively rough — inescapable boulders, stones and scree.

Of the many routes of approach to Scafell Pike, this, from Borrowdale *via* Esk Hause, is the finest. The transition from the quiet beauty of the valley pastures and woods to the rugged wildness of the mountain·top is complete, but comes gradually as height is gained and after passing through varied scenery, both nearby and distant, that sustains interest throughout the long march.

ASCENT FROM GREAT LANGDALE
3,400 feet of ascent : 5½ miles (from Dungeon Ghyll, Old Hotel)

From Esk Hause onwards the route coincides with that from Borrowdale. Please see the previous page for a description.

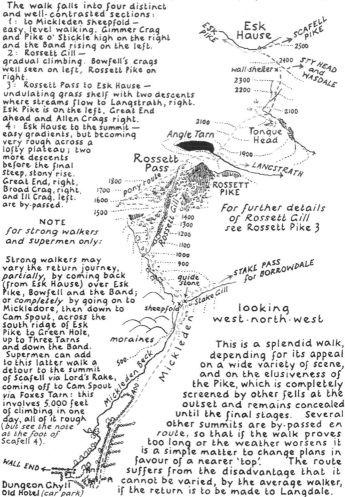

The walk falls into four distinct and well-contrasted sections:

1: to Mickleden sheepfold — easy, level walking. Gimmer Crag and Pike o' Stickle high on the right and the Band rising on the left.

2: Rossett Gill — gradual climbing. Bowfell's crags well seen on left, Rossett Pike on right.

3: Rossett Pass to Esk Hause — undulating grass shelf with two descents where streams flow to Langstrath, right. Esk Pike is on the left. Great End ahead and Allen Crags right.

4: Esk Hause to the summit — easy gradients, but becoming very rough across a lofty plateau; two more descents before the final steep, stony rise. Great End, right, Broad Crag, right, and Ill Crag, left, are by-passed.

NOTE
for strong walkers and supermen only:

Strong walkers may vary the return journey, partially, by coming back (from Esk Hause) over Esk Pike, Bowfell and the Band; or completely by going on to Mickledore, then down to Cam Spout, across the south ridge of Esk Pike to Green Hole, up to Three Tarns and down the Band. Supermen can add to this latter walk a detour to the summit of Scafell via Lord's Rake, coming off to Cam Spout via Foxes Tarn: this involves 5,000 feet of climbing in one day, all of it rough (but see the note at the foot of Scafell 4).

Esk Pike
Esk Hause
SCAFELL PIKE
2500
2400
STY HEAD and WASDALE
wall-shelter ×
2300
2200
2100
2100
Angle Tarn
Tongue Head
1900
LANGSTRATH
Rossett Pass
ROSSETT PIKE
1800
1700
pony route
1600
1500

For further details of Rossett Gill see Rossett Pike 3

1400
1300
1200
1100
1000
900

guide stone
STAKE PASS for BORROWDALE

Stake Gill
sheepfold
× × ×

looking
west · north · west

moraines
Mickleden
Mickleden Beck
500

WALL END ←

Dungeon Ghyll
Old Hotel (car park)

This is a splendid walk, depending for its appeal on a wide variety of scene, and on the elusiveness of the Pike, which is completely screened by other fells at the outset and remains concealed until the final stages. Several other summits are by-passed en route, so that if the walk proves too long or the weather worsens it is a simple matter to change plans in favour of a nearer 'top'. The route suffers from the disadvantage that it cannot be varied, by the average walker, if the return is to be made to Langdale.

Two views on the walk from Esk Hause to the summit

Many hearts have sunk into many boots as this scene unfolds. Here, on the shoulder of Ill Crag, the summit comes into sight, at last; not almost within reach as confidently expected by walkers who feel they have already done quite enough to deserve success, but still a rough half-mile distant, with two considerable descents (Ill Crag col and Broad Crag col) and much climbing yet to be faced before the goal is reached.

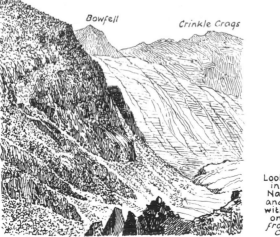

Bowfell

Crinkle Crags

Looking down into Little Narrowcove and Eskdale, with Ill Crag on the left, from Broad Crag col

ASCENT FROM ESKDALE
3100 feet of ascent : 7½ miles from Boot

continued on following page

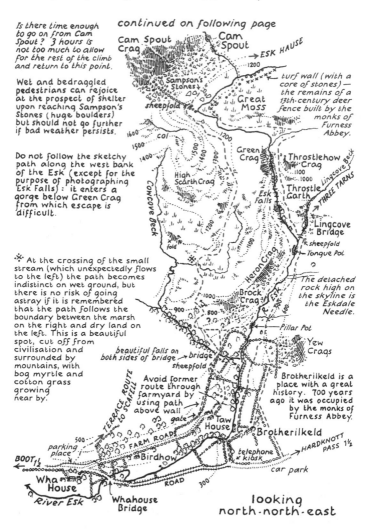

Is there time enough to go on from Cam Spout? 3 hours is not too much to allow for the rest of the climb and return to this point.

Wet and bedraggled pedestrians can rejoice at the prospect of shelter upon reaching Sampson's Stones (huge boulders) but should not go further if bad weather persists.

Do not follow the sketchy path along the west bank of the Esk (except for the purpose of photographing Esk Falls): it enters a gorge below Green Crag from which escape is difficult.

✳ At the crossing of the small stream (which unexpectedly flows to the left) the path becomes indistinct on wet ground, but there is no risk of going astray if it is remembered that the path follows the boundary between the marsh on the right and dry land on the left. This is a beautiful spot, cut off from civilisation and surrounded by mountains, with bog myrtle and cotton grass growing near by.

Cam Spout Crag
Cam Spout
⟶ ESK HAUSE
1200

turf wall (with a core of stones) — the remains of a 13th-century deer fence built by the monks of Furness Abbey.

Sampson's Stones
sheepfold
Great Moss

col
1600
1500
1400
1200
1500
1400
1700
Green Crag
Throstlehow Crag
1100
1000
Three Tarns
Lingcove Beck

High Scarth Crag
Esk Falls
Throstle Garth

Concove Beck
1200
1100
Lingcove Bridge
sheepfold
Tongue Pot

1000
Heron Crag
Brock Crag
900
800
ESK
The detached rock high on the skyline is the Eskdale Needle.

Pillar Pot
Yew Crags

beautiful falls on both sides of bridge
bridge
sheepfold

Avoid former route through farmyard by using path above wall
gate

Brotherilkeld is a place with a great history. 700 years ago it was occupied by the monks of Furness Abbey.

TERRACE ROUTE TO SCAFELL
500
parking place
Taw House
Brotherilkeld
⟶ HARDKNOTT PASS 1½

BOOT 1½
FARM ROAD
Birdhow
telephone kiosk
car park

Wha House House
ROAD
300

River Esk
Whahouse Bridge

looking north-north-east

ASCENT FROM ESKDALE

continued

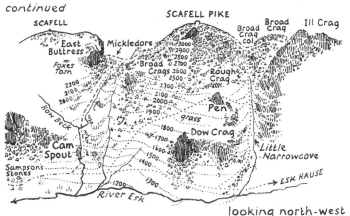

looking north-west

TO CAM SPOUT:

There is no time for dawdling when bound for Scafell Pike, and the fine high-level approach by way of Taw House and the Cowcove zigzags is recommended as the quickest route to Cam Spout. The path from Brotherilkeld *via* Lingcove Bridge has too many distractions and temptations to halt and provides a final problem in crossing Great Moss dryshod.

FROM CAM SPOUT ONWARDS:

The usual route from Cam Spout goes up steeply by the waterfalls and proceeds thereafter on a good path, becoming a river of stones, to the ridge of Mickledore, where a well-blazed track climbs across boulders to the summit. The rock-scenery on the last stages of the struggle to Mickledore is good, Scafell East Buttress being extremely impressive, but conditions underfoot are abominable. The variation just below Mickledore that cuts off a corner and gains the ridge at its lowest point is rather easier. This route can be done in mist.

A secluded but circuitous and no less rough alternative is offered by Little Narrowcove, reached by passing below the imposing buttress of Dow Crag and completely dominated by the tremendous cliff of Ill Crag. Note the dotted line on the diagram indicating a shorter way that skirts the left edge of Dow Crag, crosses a col near the rocky peak of Pen and enters Little Narrowcove at mid-height; by careful observation it is possible, on this variation, to keep to grass all the way across the breast of the Pike. Clear weather is needed here.

It seems remarkable that England's highest mountain has no direct path to its summit on this, its finest side. It is not merely steepness that has kept walkers away from it, but rather the unavoidable, inescapable shawl of boulders covering the final 500 feet, where progress is not only painfully slow but carries a risk of displacing stones that have never before been trodden and may be balanced precariously and easily disturbed. There is no fun in pioneering routes over such rough terrain, which is safest left in virgin state.

THE SUMMIT

This is it: the Mecca of all weary pilgrims in Lakeland; the place of many ceremonies and celebrations, of bonfires and birthday parties; the ultimate; the supreme; the one objective above all others; the highest ground in England; the top of Scafell Pike.

It is a magnet, not because of its beauty for this is not a place of beauty, not because of the exhilaration of the climb for there is no exhilaration in toiling upwards over endless stones, not because of its view for although this is good there are others better. It is a magnet simply because it is the highest ground in England.

There is a huge cairn that from afar looks like a hotel: a well-built circular edifice with steps leading up to its flat top from the west. Set into the vertical nine-foot north wall of the cairn is a tablet commemorating the gift of the summit to the nation.   A few yards distant, to the west, is a triangulation column of the Ordnance Survey; a visitor in doubt and seeking confirmation of his whereabouts should consult the number on the front plate of the column: if it is anything other than S.1537 he has good cause for doubt — heaven knows where his erring steps have led him, but it is certainly not to the summit of Scafell Pike.

The surrounding area is barren, a tumbled wilderness of stones of all shapes and sizes, but it is not true, as has oft been written and may be thought, that the top is entirely devoid of vegetation: there is, indeed, a patch of grass on the south side of the cairn sufficient to provide a couch for a few hundredweights of exhausted flesh.

Yet this rough and desolate summit is, after all, just as it should be, and none of us would really want it different. A smooth green promenade here would be wrong. This is the summit of England, and it is fitting that it should be sturdy and rugged and strong.

THE SUMMIT

DESCENTS: It is an exaggeration to describe walkers' routes across the top of Scafell Pike as *paths*, because they make an uneasy pavement of angular boulders that are too unyielding ever to be trodden into subjection; nevertheless the routes are quite distinct, the particular boulders selected for their feet by the pioneers having, in the past century or so, become so extensively scratched by bootnails that they now appear as white ribbons across the grey waste of stones. Thus there is no difficulty in following them, even in mist.

The only place in descent where a walker might go astray is in going down by the Wasdale Head path to join the Corridor Route for Sty Head, the bifurcation above Lingmell Col being surprisingly vague: in mist a walker might find himself well down Brown Tongue before discovering his error. It is actually safer for a stranger seeking the Corridor Route, particularly in mist, to use the Esk Hause path as far as the first col, at this point turning off *left* down into a hollow; a stream rises here and is a certain guide to the Corridor, which is reached exactly and unmistakably at the head of Piers Gill.

PLAN OF SUMMIT

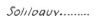

Soliloquy.........

In summertime the cairn often becomes over-run with tourists, and a seeker after solitary contemplation may then be recommended to go across to the south peak, where, after enjoying the splendid view of Eskdale, he can observe the visitors to the summit from this distance. He may find himself wondering what impulse had driven these good folk to leave the comforts of the valley and make the weary ascent to this inhospitable place.

Why does a man climb mountains? Why has he forced his tired and sweating body up here when he might instead have been sitting at his ease in a deckchair at the seaside, looking at girls in bikinis, or fast asleep, or sucking ice-cream, according to his fancy. On the face of it the thing doesn't make sense.

Yet more and more people are turning to the hills; they find something in these wild places that can be found nowhere else. It may be solace for some, satisfaction for others: the joy of exercising muscles that modern ways of living have cramped, perhaps; or a balm for jangled nerves in the solitude and silence of the peaks; or escape from the clamour and tumult of everyday existence. It may have something to do with a man's subconscious search for beauty, growing keener as so much in the world grows uglier. It may be a need to readjust his sights, to get out of his own narrow groove and climb above it to see wider horizons and truer perspectives. In a few cases, it may even be a curiosity inspired by ~~awainwright~~'s Pictorial Guides. Or it may be, and for most walkers it *will* be, quite simply, a deep love of the hills, a love that has grown over the years, whatever motive first took them there: a feeling that these hills are friends, tried and trusted friends, always there when needed.

It is a question every man must answer for himself.

THE VIEW

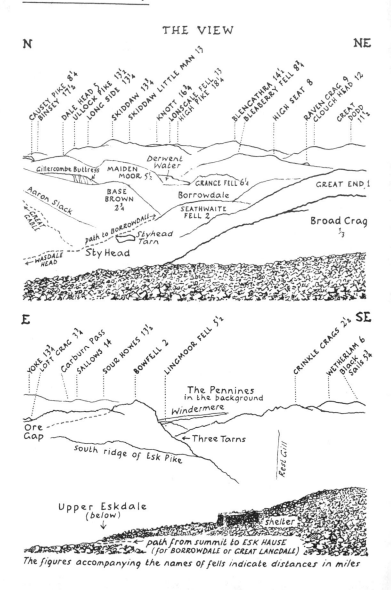

N   NE

CAUSEY PIKE 8¼
BINSEY 17½
DALE HEAD 5
ULLOCK PIKE 13½
LONG SIDE 13¾
SKIDDAW 13¾
SKIDDAW LITTLE MAN 13
KNOTT 16¾
LONSCALE FELL 13
HIGH PIKE 18¼
BLENCATHRA 14½
BLEABERRY FELL 8¾
HIGH SEAT 8
RAVEN CRAG 9
CLOUGH HEAD 12
GREAT DODD 11½

Gillercombe Buttress
MAIDEN MOOR 5½
Derwent Water
BASE BROWN 2¾
Borrowdale
GRANGE FELL 6¼
GREAT END 1

Aaron Slack
SEATHWAITE FELL 2
GREAT GABLE
path to BORROWDALE
Styhead Tarn
Sty Head
Broad Crag ⅓
← WASDALE HEAD

E   SE

YOKE 13¾
LOFT CRAG 3¾
Garburn Pass
SALLOWS 14
SOUR HOWES 13½
BOWFELL 2
LINGMOOR FELL 5½
CRINKLE CRAGS 2½
WETHERLAM 6
Black Sails 5¾

The Pennines
in the background

Ore Gap
Windermere
← Three Tarns
Rest Gill
south ridge of Esk Pike

Upper Eskdale
(below)
shelter
← path from summit to ESK HAUSE
(for BORROWDALE or GREAT LANGDALE)

The figures accompanying the names of fells indicate distances in miles

THE VIEW

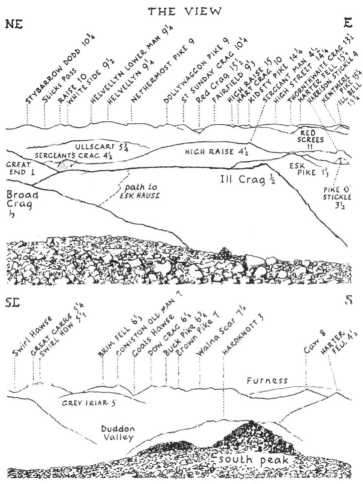

This being the highest ground in England the view is the most extensive, although not appreciably more so than those seen from many nearby fells. There is much interesting detail in every direction, and no denying the superiority of altitude, for all else is below eye-level, with old favourites like Great Gable and Bowfell seeming, if not humbled, less proud than they usually do (Scafell, across Mickledore, often looks of equal or greater height). Despite the wide variety of landscape, however, this is not the most pleasing of summit views, none of the valleys or lakes in view being seen really well.

THE VIEW

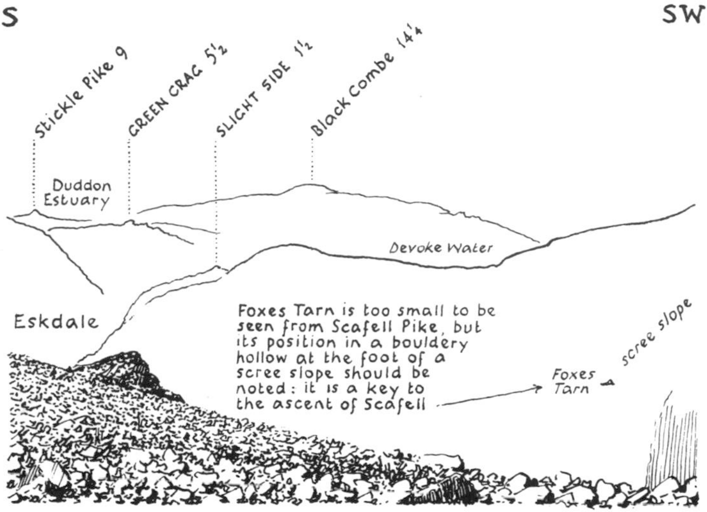

S   SW

Stickle Pike 9
GREEN CRAG 5½
SLIGHT SIDE 5½
Black Combe 14¼

Duddon
Estuary

Devoke Water

Eskdale

scree slope

Foxes Tarn is too small to be
seen from Scafell Pike, but
its position in a bouldery
hollow at the foot of a
scree slope should be
noted: it is a key to
the ascent of Scafell

Foxes
Tarn

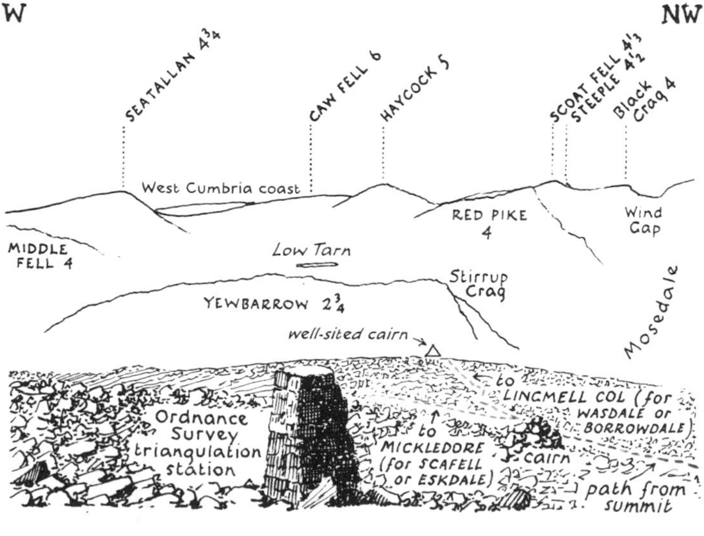

W   NW

SEATALLAN 4¾
CAW FELL 6
HAYCOCK 5
SCOAT FELL 4⅓
STEEPLE 4½
Black
Crag 4

West Cumbria coast

RED PIKE
4

Wind
Gap

MIDDLE
FELL 4

Low Tarn

YEWBARROW 2¾

Stirrup
Crag

Mosedale

well-sited cairn

Ordnance
Survey
triangulation
station

to
LINGMELL COL (for
WASDALE or
BORROWDALE)

to
MICKLEDORE
(for SCAFELL
or ESKDALE)

cairn

path from
summit

THE VIEW

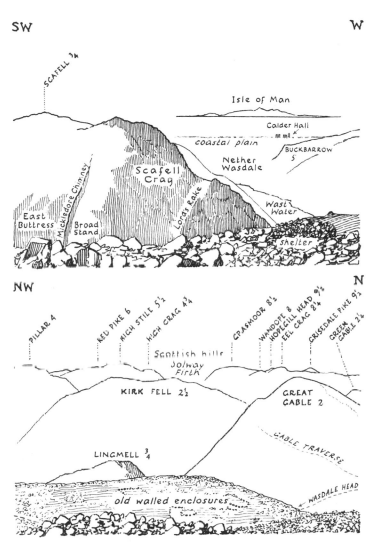

RIDGE ROUTES

To GREAT END, 2984': 1⅓ miles
NE, then N

Three depressions (Broad Crag col, 2900',
Ill Crag col, 2900', Calf Cove col, 2830')
350 feet of ascent
Rough ground; slow progress.

This route makes use of the popular path to Esk Hause, much trodden but never smoothed, this being left when easier ground is reached above Calf Cove. Great End is then straight ahead, and gained up a gentle grass slope between boulders.

To LINGMELL, 2649': ⅞ mile : NNW
Depression (Lingmell Col) at 2370'
280 feet of ascent

Use the distinct Wasdale path and when it swings away to the left go on ahead across the grassy col and straight up the other side to the fine cairn.

To SCAFELL, 3162': 1¼ miles

SW to Mickledore; then compass useless.
Many depressions (especially of the spirits)
700 feet of ascent (850 via Foxes Tarn)

Medals have been won for lesser deeds

This is a walk not to be undertaken lightly, and not at all if time is short or if limbs are already tired. It is the one ridge-route on these hills where direct progress is barred completely to the walker, a considerable detour being necessary to circumvent the difficulties. (*If Langdale is the evening's destination, this journey is too much for the average walker*).

The most interesting traverse in Lakeland, the rock scenery being superb and the route ingenious.

The problem can be studied from the summit of the Pike and on the initial descent to Mickledore. (*See the diagram but also see the warning on page 30.*)

LR : Lord's Rake
FT : Foxes Tarn
M : Mickledore Ridge

continued

RIDGE ROUTES

To SCAFELL (continued)

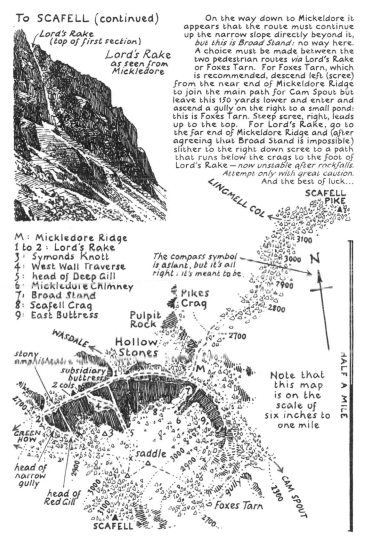

*Lord's Rake
(top of first section)*

*Lord's Rake
as seen from
Mickledore*

*Lord's Rake
as seen from
Mickledore*

On the way down to Mickledore it appears that the route must continue up the narrow slope directly beyond it, *but this is Broad Stand: no way here.* A choice must be made between the two pedestrian routes *via* Lord's Rake or Foxes Tarn. For Foxes Tarn, which is recommended, descend left (scree) from the near end of Mickledore Ridge to join the main path for Cam Spout but leave this 150 yards lower and enter and ascend a gully on the right to a small pond: this is Foxes Tarn. Steep scree, right, leads up to the top. For Lord's Rake, go to the far end of Mickledore Ridge and (after agreeing that Broad Stand is impossible) slither to the right down scree to a path that runs below the crags to the foot of Lord's Rake — *now unstable after rockfalls. Attempt only with great caution.*
And the best of luck...

M : Mickledore Ridge
1 to 2 : Lord's Rake
3 : Symonds Knott
4 : West Wall Traverse
5 : head of Deep Gill
6 : Mickledore Chimney
7 : Broad Stand
8 : Scafell Crag
9 : East Buttress

The compass symbol is aslant, but it's all right : it's meant to be.

N

SCAFELL PIKE

LINGMELL COL

3100

3000

2900

2800

2700

Pikes Crag

Pulpit Rock

Hollow Stones

WASDALE

stony amphitheatre

subsidiary buttress

2 cols

M

2700

GREEN HOW

head of narrow gully

head of Red Gill

saddle

Note that this map is on the scale of six inches to one mile

HALF A MILE

CAM SPOUT

Foxes Tarn

gully

SCAFELL

2300

2700

2900

3000

3100

10 Blencathra
from Scales via Sharp Edge

Blencathra was one of Wainwright's six favourite mountains and the Sharp Edge approach was one of his six favourite places that aren't summits. His first contact with the mountain wasn't auspicious. Planning his first trip to the Lakes in 1930, studying the Bartholomew maps spread out on his bedroom floor in Blackburn, he decided to tackle Blencathra after tea on a day when he and his mates had already done something like seventeen miles and any number of summits. He didn't make it. But he did many times later. He devoted more pages to the mountain than any other in the Pictorial Guides.

When we filmed the ascent for *Wainwright's Memorial Walk*, our version of the 1930s adventure, I confess to feeling a jot nervous. No, that's a lie. I was terrified. Sharp Edge's reputation is fearsome with tales of people being blown off or losing their footing on the ridge and sliding into the abyss. And I don't have a head for heights. The researcher on our mountain filming, David Powell-Thompson, *does* have a head for heights: he's like a mountain goat, forever balancing on improbable bits of rock. But even he warned that Sharp Edge would be a challenge.

It was. I lived to tell this tale but the pictures of me feeling my way across – the ruptured crab manoeuvre, I called it at the time – weren't going to win me points for technical presentation. But there were plenty of compensations. When the steepest bit is past and the nerves settle and you're beginning to convince yourself that it was nothing really, you raise your eyes to the view around you and realise you're in one of the world's very special places. As Wainwright put it, you're standing on 'a breaking wave carved in stone ... The crest itself is sharp enough for shaving (the former name was Razor Edge) and can be traversed only *à cheval* at some risk of damage to tender parts.' Many people must have read that because the day I did the traverse I saw at least three walkers stop and check their tender parts before walking on to the summit.

When Julia Bradbury tackled the ascent for *Wainwright Walks*, her producers sensibly hired David to take her across as well. He'd counted me out and counted me back and hopefully would be able to do the same for her. In the event she coped with Sharp Edge considerably more gracefully than me.

After the programme Jan Ostrowski, the cameraman who'd filmed both crossings, rubbed it in by saying that youth was a wonderful thing and Julia at least added to the picturesque surroundings, unlike some people he could mention. Crews can be so hurtful. But to be fair to them – and I am in moments of weakness – they're doing the real work. Capturing the exposure of Sharp Edge on tape isn't easy. While the presenter is concentrating on the proximity of tender bits to sharp rock the cameraman is perched on a razor edge holding 30 lbs of high-priced electronics on his shoulder and relating the shuffling body in front of him to the dizzying drops below. If he gets it wrong it can look to the viewer as if the presenter is making an almighty fuss about nothing. And that would never do.

Practical bits

Map: OL5

Ascent: Both *Wainwright Walks* and *Memorial Walk* started this route at the White Horse pub in Scales on the A66 (NY344269) and approached Sharp Edge via Scales Fell and the path above the River Glenderamackin to Scales Tarn, the route on Blencathra 25 in *The Northern Fells*, (2¾ miles, 2250 feet).

Descent: For my money, the best way down is the reverse of the route on Blencathra 17, by Hall's Fell. It's not as exposed as Sharp Edge but you wouldn't want that twice in a day. The first half mile is over a ridge called Narrow Edge. Like Sharp Edge, it's not a place to be in ice or snow but in good weather its rocky gateways and soaring towers of rock are grand. Wainwright describes this route as positively the finest way to any mountain top in the district. With respect, Sharp Edge is that. But this is positively the finest way down.

Blencathra

2847'

MUNGRISDALE 2
HESKET NEWMARKET 9

from
Mungrisdale road end

better known,
until recently,
as Saddleback

BOWSCALE FELL ▲
Mungrisdale ●
SKIDDAW
▲ ● Skiddaw
House
SOUTHER FELL ▲
▲ BLENCATHRA
LONSCALE
FELL ▲
● Scales
● Threlkeld

MILES
0 1 2 3 4

NATURAL FEATURES

Blencathra is one of the grandest objects in Lakeland. And one of the best known. Seen from the south-west, the popular aspect, the mountain rises steeply and in isolation above the broad green fields of Threlkeld, a feature being the great sweeping curve leaping out of the depths to a lofty summit-ridge, where the skyline then proceeds in a succession of waves to a sharp peak before descending, again in a graceful curve, to the valley pastures far to the east.

This is a mountain that compels attention, even from those dull people whose eyes are not habitually lifted to the hills. To artists and photographers it is an obvious subject for their craft; to sightseers passing along the main road or former railway between Keswick and Penrith, its influence is magnetic; to the dalesfolk it is the eternal background to their lives, there at birth, there at death. But most of all it is a mountaineers' mountain.

continued

from Castlerigg Stone Circle

NATURAL FEATURES

continued

The supreme feature of Blencathra, the one that invests the mountain with special grandeur, is the imposing southern front, a remarkable example of the effect of elemental natural forces. It forms a tremendous facade above the valley, and makes a dark, towering backcloth to a stage of farmsteads and cottages, of emerald pastures and meadows and woodlands along its base. There is nothing inviting in these shattered cliffs and petrified rivers of stone that seem to hold a perpetual threat over the little community below: the scene arrests attention, but intimidates and repels. Few who gaze upon these desolate walls are likely to feel any inclination and inspiration to scramble up through their arid, stony wildernesses to the contorted skyline so high above. Consequently the area has remained a no-man's-land for walkers, even though closely within sight of road and railway travellers. Blencathra is ascended thousands of times a year but rarely by ways up the southern front. This is a pity. Here is the greatness of the mountain. Its detail is a fascinating study.

west   east

THE SOUTHERN FRONT
3¼ miles

The outer slopes, rising on the west and east flanks from valley level to the uppermost escarpment below the summit ridge, are smoothly curved, massive and yet so symmetrical that they might well have been designed by a master architect to supply a perfect balance to the structure. These two outlyers are Blease Fell and Scales Fell.

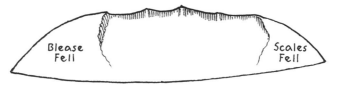

Blease
Fell

Scales
Fell

continued

NATURAL FEATURES

continued

From their extremities the slopes of Blease Fell and Scales Fell extend uneventfully towards each other across the front until, suddenly and dramatically, they are halted at the edge of a scene of devastation, the wreckage of what appears to have been, in ages past, a tremendous convulsion that tore the heart out of the mountain and left the ruins seemingly in a state of tottering collapse. The picture is chaotic: a great upheaval of ridges and pinnacles rising out of dead wastes of scree and penetrated by choked gullies and ravines, the whole crazily tilted through 2000' of altitude. Even in this area of confusion and disorder, however, Nature has sculptured a distinct pattern.

Four watercourses emerge from surrounding debris to escape to the valley:

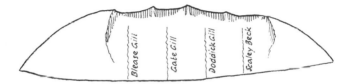

Between the four ravines, three lofty spurs, alike in main characteristics, thrust far out; narrow and frail where they leave the solid mass of the mountain, they widen into substantial buttresses as they descend to the valley. It is as though a giant hand had clawed at the mountain, each finger scooping out a deep hollow, with narrow strips of ground left undisturbed between.

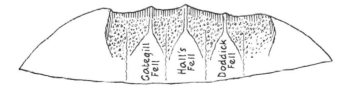

There are thus five buttresses on the southern front, each named as a separate fell. The two outer are grassy, with flat tops; the three in the middle are heathery and rise to distinct peaks, the central one being Blencathra's summit. Such is the pattern of the southern front.

continued

NATURAL FEATURES

continued

The other flanks of the mountain are mainly smooth and rounded, although on the east side Scales Fell breaks its curve to form the hollow of Mousthwaite Comb. But, from the summit, high ground continues north across a slight depression (the Saddle) to the prominent top of Foule Crag, this being the outline from which the alternative name, Saddleback, derives. A distinct ridge curves away to the Glenderamackin col from Foule Crag, while a rocky spur goes off to the east, this latter being the well-known Sharp Edge, second in fame to Striding Edge on Helvellyn as a test for walkers. Deepset in the hollow between Sharp Edge and the main ridge is one of the most characteristic mountain tarns in the district, Scales Tarn.

It is interesting to note that although Blencathra lies well to the east of the axis of Lakeland, approximately 99% of its drainage joins the Derwent in the west, only a few drops being gathered by the Eden catchment.

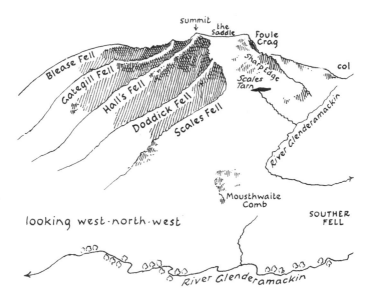

looking west·north·west

Blencathra joins Bowfell in the author's best half-dozen.

The summit escarpment

looking
west

from
Scales Fell
to the
summit

from
the summit
to Gategill
Fell Top

from
Gategill
Fell Top
to
Blease Fell

MAP

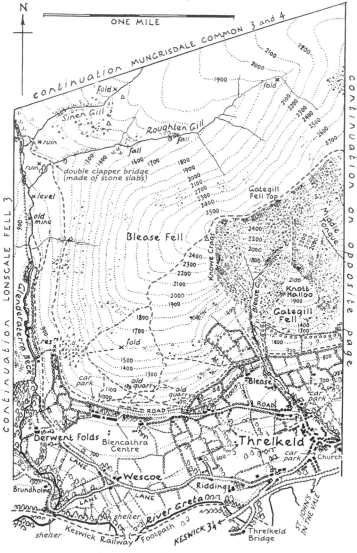

MAP

When this book was first published road widening and improvement schemes were in progress and a bypass for Threlkeld was contemplated, a policy that the author deplored, stating his preference for fragrant lanes and narrow winding highways. Now the changes have been completed, but the country lanes are still there, some of them having even benefitted by being relieved of through traffic.

Another major change that has taken place since that time is the closure of the railway from Keswick to Threlkeld and its conversion to the Keswick Railway Footpath. This is broad and well-surfaced throughout its length and provided with shelters and notices giving information about the railway and the surrounding countryside. The path starts at the back of the swimming pool in Keswick (see Latrigg 3), and forms part of the best route of ascent of Blencathra from Keswick. The route leaves the railway at the shelter in the vicinity of Brundholme. Then it continues through beautiful unspoilt countryside to the former farmhouse of Derwent Folds with its lovely old porch, and hence to the Blencathra Centre. The length from the town centre to the summit is 5 miles. This route was not possible in 1962.

ASCENT FROM THRELKELD
via ROUGHTEN GILL
2400 feet of ascent : 5 miles

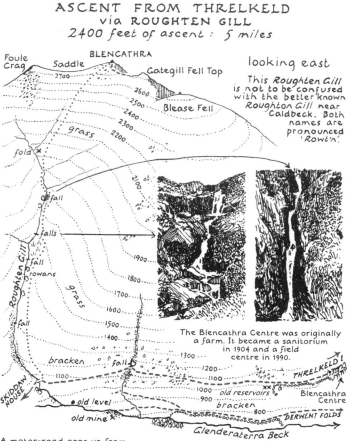

BLENCATHRA

Foule Crag

Saddle — 2700

Gategill Fell Top

2600

Blease Fell

2500

2400

2300

grass — 2200

fold ×

2100

fall

falls

1900

fall — Rowans

1800

Roughten Gill

grass

1700

1600

fall — 1500

1400

bracken — fall — 1300

1100 — 1200

1100

SKIDDAW HOUSE

old level — 1000 — old reservoirs

old mine × — 900 — bracken — 800

Glenderaterra Beck

THRELKELD

Blencathra Centre

DERWENT FOLDS

looking east

This *Roughten Gill* is not to be confused with the better known *Roughton Gill* near Caldbeck. Both names are pronounced 'Rowt'n'.

The Blencathra Centre was originally a farm. It became a sanitorium in 1904 and a field centre in 1990.

A motor-road goes up from Threlkeld to the car park at the Blencathra Centre and ends there. Its direction is continued by a public bridleway along the side of a wall. Use this.

For walkers who panic at the proximity of precipices and cannot face steep slopes, the roundabout route by Roughten Gill, which holds no terrors at all, is a good way to the top, but most people will find it unexciting and dreary. The best thing about it is delayed until the very end : the sudden thrilling view of Lakeland, which has been hidden during the climb.

ASCENT FROM THRELKELD
via BLEASE FELL
2450 feet of ascent : 2½ miles

looking north

Blease Fell

Gategill Fell Top

BLENCATHRA

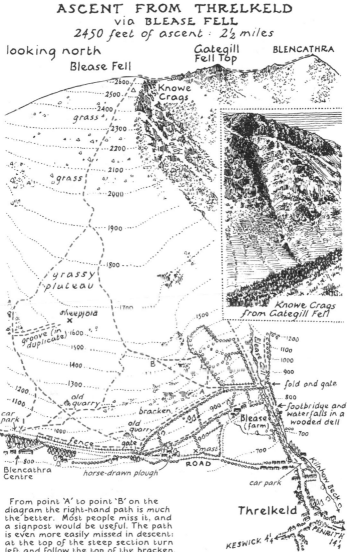

2600
2500
2400
grass
2300
2200
2100
grass
2000
1900
1800
grassy plateau
1700
sheepfold ×
groove (in duplicate)
1600
1500
1400
1300
old quarry
1200
1100
car park
1000
fence
800
Blencathra Centre
horse-drawn plough
ROAD
× mast

Knowe Crags

1500

B

A

bracken

old quarry

gate

Blease (farm)

Blease Gill

1200
1100
1000
900
← fold and gate
800
← footbridge and waterfalls in a wooded dell
700

700

car park

Kilnhow Beck

Threlkeld

KESWICK 4¼

PENRITH 14¼

Knowe Crags from Gategill Fell

From point 'A' to point 'B' on the diagram the right-hand path is much the better. Most people miss it, and a signpost would be useful. The path is even more easily missed in descent: at the top of the steep section turn left and follow the top of the bracken.

Blease Gill

ASCENT FROM THRELKELD
via BLEASE GILL
2400 feet of ascent : 2 miles

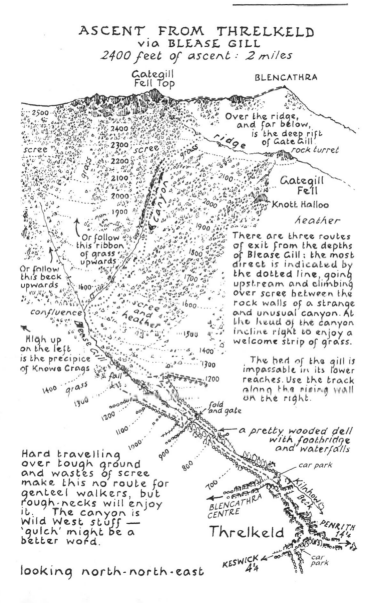

Gategill Fell Top

BLENCATHRA

2500

2400
2300
2200
2100
2000
1900

scree

grass

scree

grass

canyon

ridge

Over the ridge, and far below, is the deep rift of Gate Gill

rock turret

2100

2000

Gategill Fell

Knott Halloo

heather

Or follow this ribbon of grass upwards

Or follow this beck upwards

1900

1800

1600

1700

confluence

1600

scree and heather

1500

High up on the left is the precipice of Knowe Crags

1400

1400

1300

grass

fall

1300

1200

1200

1100

There are three routes of exit from the depths of Blease Gill: the most direct is indicated by the dotted line, going upstream and climbing over scree between the rock walls of a strange and unusual canyon. At the head of the canyon incline right to enjoy a welcome strip of grass.

The bed of the gill is impassable in its lower reaches. Use the track along the rising wall on the right.

fold and gate

1000

a pretty wooded dell with foothbridge and waterfalls

900

car park

800

Kilnhow Beck

Hard travelling over tough ground and wastes of scree make this no route for genteel walkers, but rough-necks will enjoy it. The canyon is Wild West stuff — 'gulch' might be a better word.

700

BLENCATHRA CENTRE

Threlkeld

PENRITH 14¼

KESWICK 4¼

car park

looking north-north-east

ASCENT FROM THRELKELD
via GATEGILL FELL
2450 feet of ascent : 2 miles

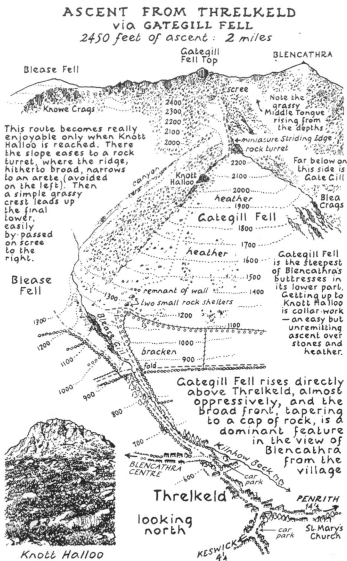

Blease Fell

Gategill Fell Top

BLENCATHRA

Knowe Crags

scree

Note the grassy Middle Tongue rising from the depths

2400
2300
2200
2100
2000

miniature Striding Edge rock turret

This route becomes really enjoyable only when Knott Halloo is reached. There the slope eases to a rock turret, where the ridge, hitherto broad, narrows to an arete (avoided on the left). Then a simple grassy crest leads up the final tower, easily by-passed on scree to the right.

canyon

Knott Halloo

2200

Far below on this side is Gate Gill

2100

2000

heather

1900

Blea Crags

Gategill Fell

1800

Blease Fell

heather

1700

1600

Gategill Fell is the steepest of Blencathra's buttresses in its lower part. Getting up to Knott Halloo is collar-work — an easy but unremitting ascent over stones and heather.

1500

remnant of wall

1400

two small rock shelters

1300

1200

1100

1300

1200

1000

bracken

900

1100

fold

1000

900

Gategill Fell rises directly above Threlkeld, almost oppressively, and the broad front, tapering to a cap of rock, is a dominant feature in the view of Blencathra from the village

800

700

Kinhow Beck (↓)

BLENCATHRA CENTRE

car park

600

Threlkeld

looking north

car park

PENRITH 14¼

St. Mary's Church

Knott Halloo

KESWICK 4¼

looking up to Gategill Fell Top
from just above Knott Halloo,
with the rock turret
on the right

Gategill Fell

looking up the
ridge from the
rock turret

looking down the ridge
from Gategill Fell Top

The rock turret is at the far end of
the shadow; to the right is Knott
Halloo, the furthest point in view.

Gate Gill

Blencathra's summit is directly ahead.
Gategill Fell rises on the left, and
Hall's Fell on the right.

ASCENT FROM THRELKELD
via MIDDLE TONGUE
2400 feet of ascent : 2 miles

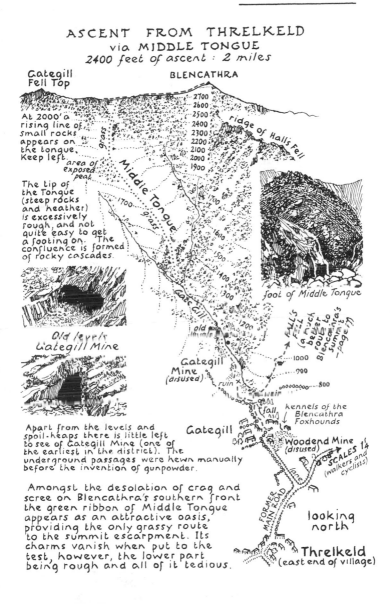

Gategill
Fell Top

BLENCATHRA

2700
2600
2500
2400
2300
2200
2100
2000
1900

ridge of Halls Fell

At 2000'a rising line of small rocks appears on the tongue. Keep left

area of exposed peat

grass

Middle Tongue

grass

1700

The tip of the Tongue (steep rocks and heather) is excessively rough, and not quite easy to get a footing on. The confluence is formed of rocky cascades.

1600
1500
1400
1300

foot of Middle Tongue

Old levels
Gategill Mine

Gate Gill

1200

old

1100

Gategill
Mine
(disused)

ruin ×

FALLS
FELL
(a much better route to Blencathra's summit — page 11)

1000

900

800

kennels of the Blencathra Foxhounds

Apart from the levels and spoil-heaps there is little left to see of Gategill Mine (one of the earliest in the district). The underground passages were hewn manually before the invention of gunpowder.

fall

Gategill

Woodend Mine
(disused)

SCALES 1¼ (walkers and cyclists)

Amongst the desolation of crag and scree on Blencathra's southern front the green ribbon of Middle Tongue appears as an attractive oasis, providing the only grassy route to the summit escarpment. Its charms vanish when put to the test, however, the lower part being rough and all of it tedious.

lane

FORMER MAIN ROAD

looking north

Threlkeld
(east end of village)

ASCENT FROM THRELKELD
via HALL'S FELL
2400 feet of ascent : 2 miles

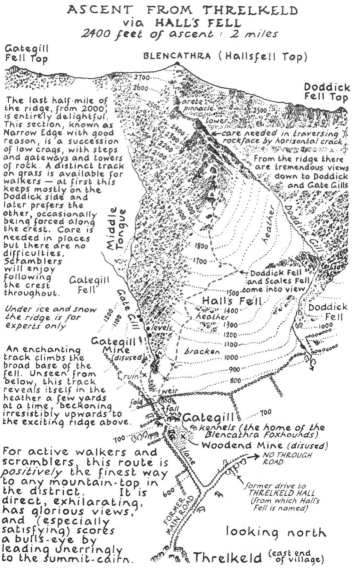

Gategill
Fell Top

BLENCATHRA (Hallsfell Top)

Doddick
Fell Top

2700
2600
2500
arete
pinnacle
lower

The last half-mile of the ridge, from 2000, is entirely delightful. This section, known as Narrow Edge with good reason, is a succession of low crags, with steps and gateways and towers of rock. A distinct track on grass is available for walkers — at first this keeps mostly on the Doddick side and later prefers the other, occasionally being forced along the crest. Care is needed in places but there are no difficulties. Scramblers will enjoy following the crest throughout.

Under ice and snow the ridge is for experts only

An enchanting track climbs the broad base of the fell. Unseen from below, this track reveals itself in the heather a few yards at a time, beckoning irresistibly upwards to the exciting ridge above.

2400
2300
2200
2100

← care needed in traversing rockface by horizontal crack

From the ridge there are tremendous views down to Doddick and Gate Gills

Middle Tongue

Gategill
Fell

2000
1900

1800

1700

Heather

Doddick Gill

← Doddick Fell and Scales Fell come into view

Hall's Fell

1500
heather 1400
1300
1200
1100
1000
900
800

Doddick
Fell

1200
1100

Gate Gill

•levels

Gategill
Mine (disused)

bracken

1000

ruin ×

weir

fold
fall

Gategill

700

← kennels (the home of the Blencathra Foxhounds)

→ Woodend Mine (disused)

For active walkers and scramblers, this route is positively the finest way to any mountain-top in the district. It is direct, exhilarating, has glorious views, and (especially satisfying) scores a bull's-eye by leading unerringly to the summit-cairn.

700

lane

NO THROUGH ROAD

former drive to THRELKELD HALL (from which Hall's Fell is named)

600

FORMER MAIN ROAD

looking north

Threlkeld (east end of village)

looking down
the ridge
from the
summit

Hall's Fell

the middle
section

the curve in
the ridge

looking up the ridge
to the summit

Doddick Gill from 1350' on Doddick Fell. On the left is Hall's Fell, rising to Hall's Fell Top (the summit of Blencathra).

ASCENT FROM THRELKELD
via DODDICK GILL
2150 feet of ascent : 2¾ miles

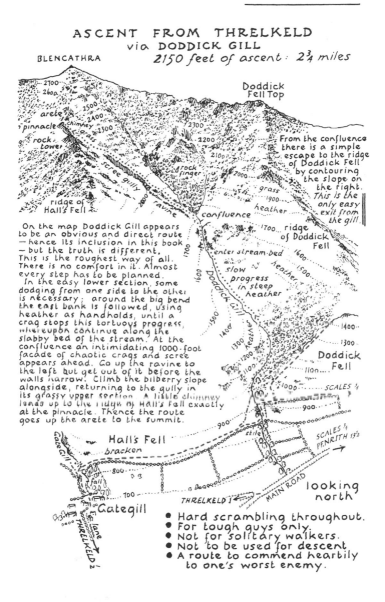

BLENCATHRA

2700
2600

arête
pinnacle
rock tower

2500
2400
2300
chimney
grass

scree gully

ridge of Hall's Fell

ravine

Doddick Fell Top

2300
2200
2100
rock finger
2000

confluence

From the confluence there is a simple escape to the ridge of Doddick Fell by contouring the slope on the right. *This is the only easy exit from the gill.*

1900
heather
grass

1700   ridge of Doddick Fell

enter stream bed
slow progress in steep heather

1600
1500
heather

Doddick Gill

1800
1700
1600
1500
1400
1300   heather
1200
1100
1000

1400
1300

Doddick Fell

1100
SCALES ¾

On the map Doddick Gill appears to be an obvious and direct route — hence its inclusion in this book — but the truth is different. This is the roughest way of all. There is no comfort in it. Almost every step has to be planned.
In the easy lower section, some dodging from one side to the other is necessary; around the big bend the east bank is followed, using heather as handholds, until a crag stops this tortuous progress, whereupon continue along the slabby bed of the stream. At the confluence an intimidating 1000-foot façade of chaotic crags and scree appears ahead. Go up the ravine to the left but get out of it before the walls narrow. Climb the bilberry slope alongside, returning to the gully in its grassy upper section. A little chimney lands up to the ridge of Hall's Fell exactly at the pinnacle. Thence the route goes up the arête to the summit.

900

Hall's Fell
bracken

stile

900

SCALES ¾
PENRITH 13½

Gate Gill

800
fall

700

Gategill

lane
THRELKELD 2

THRELKELD 1   MAIN ROAD

looking north

- Hard scrambling throughout.
- For tough guys only.
- Not for solitary walkers.
- Not to be used for descent
- A route to commend heartily to one's worst enemy.

ASCENT FROM SCALES
via DODDICK FELL
2150 feet of ascent : 1¼ miles

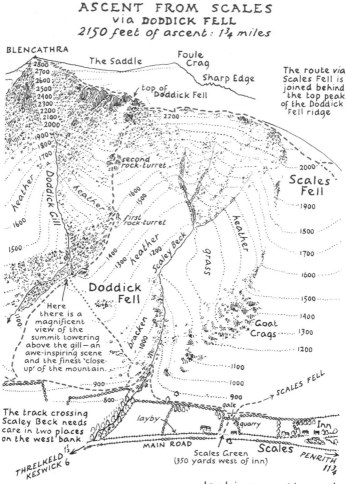

BLENCATHRA

The Saddle
Foule Crag
Sharp Edge

2800
2700
2600
2500
2400
2300
2200
2100
2000
1900
1800
1700

top of Doddick Fell

The route via Scales Fell is joined behind the top peak of the Doddick Fell ridge

2200

second rock-turret

2000

Scales Fell

1900

1600
1500

1800

first rock-turret

1700

1400

heather

1600

1300

Scaley Beck

grass

1500

heather

1200

Doddick Gill

Doddick Fell

Here there is a magnificent view of the summit towering above the gill—an awe-inspiring scene and the finest 'close-up' of the mountain.

1500

1400

1300

Goat Crags

1200

bracken

1100

1000

SCALES FELL

900

gate

800

The track crossing Scaley Beck needs care in two places on the west bank.

layby

900

quarry

Inn

MAIN ROAD

Scales Green (350 yards west of inn)

Scales

THRELKELD 1½
KESWICK 6

PENRITH 11¾

looking north-west

It is usual, from Scales, to ascend by way of Scales Fell, a very popular route, but better by far is the more direct ridge of Doddick Fell, a grand climb, quite easy, with striking views of the objective. This is a splendid way to the top of Blencathra.

looking up to Doddick Fell Top from 1450'

Doddick Fell

looking down the ridge from Doddick Fell Top

Scaley Beck

Doddick Fell is on the left, rising to the peak of Doddick Fell Top. Blencathra's summit is seen in the top left corner.

ASCENT FROM SCALES
via SCALEY BECK
2150 feet of ascent : 2 miles

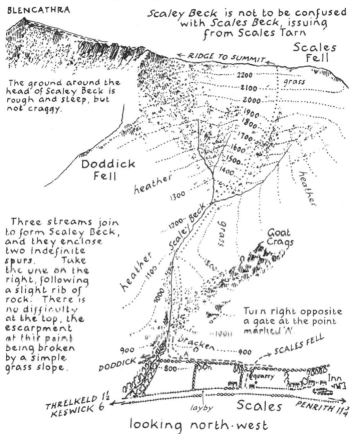

BLENCATHRA

Scaley Beck is not to be confused with Scales Beck, issuing from Scales Tarn

Scales Fell

RIDGE TO SUMMIT

The ground around the head of Scaley Beck is rough and steep, but not craggy.

Doddick Fell

heather

heather

2200 grass
2100
2000
1900
1800
1700
1600
1500
1400
1300
1200
Scaley Beck

grass

Goat Crags

Three streams join to form Scaley Beck, and they enclose two indefinite spurs. Take the one on the right, following a slight rib of rock. There is no difficulty at the top, the escarpment at this point being broken by a simple grass slope.

heather

1100

1000

Turn right opposite a gate at the point marked 'A'

900

bracken

900   SCALES FELL

A

DODDICK

800

SCALES FELL

quarry

Inn

THRELKELD 1½
KESWICK 6

layby

Scales

PENRITH 11¾

looking north-west

Of the various watercourses on the south front Scaley Beck is the most practicable as a route of ascent, being nowhere too rough to stop progress; the exit, too, is easy. There is little of interest, however, and the route falls far short of that via the adjacent ridge of Doddick Fell.

ASCENT FROM SCALES
via SHARP EDGE
2250 feet of ascent : 2¾ miles

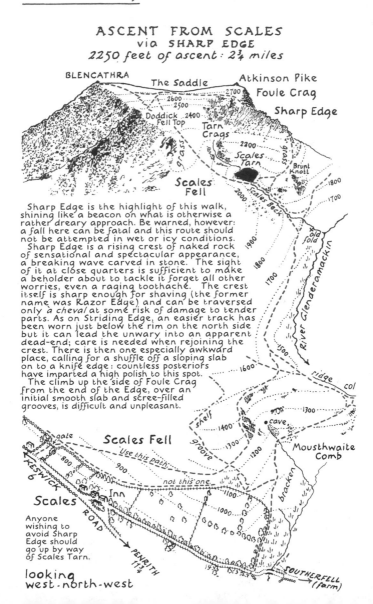

BLENCATHRA
The Saddle
Atkinson Pike
Foule Crag
Sharp Edge
2600
2500
2700
Doddick Fell Top
2400
Tarn Crags
2200
Scales Tarn
grass
Brunt Knott
1800
Scales Fell
2000
1700
Scale Beck
1900
old fold
1800
1700
River Glenderamackin
1600
ridge
col
shelf groove
1400
1300
1300
cave
Mousthwaite Comb
1500
1200
bracken
Scales Fell
gate
800
Use this path
900
not this one
1100
1000
KESWICK 6
Scales
Inn
ROAD
PENRITH 11¾
SOUTHERFELL (farm)

Sharp Edge is the highlight of this walk, shining like a beacon on what is otherwise a rather dreary approach. Be warned, however: a fall here can be fatal and this route should not be attempted in wet or icy conditions.

Sharp Edge is a rising crest of naked rock of sensational and spectacular appearance, a breaking wave carved in stone. The sight of it at close quarters is sufficient to make a beholder about to tackle it forget all other worries, even a raging toothache. The crest itself is sharp enough for shaving (the former name was Razor Edge) and can be traversed only *a cheval* at some risk of damage to tender parts. As on Striding Edge, an easier track has been worn just below the rim on the north side but it can lead the unwary into an apparent dead-end; care is needed when rejoining the crest. There is then one especially awkward place, calling for a shuffle off a sloping slab on to a knife edge: countless posteriors have imparted a high polish to this spot.

The climb up the side of Foule Crag from the end of the Edge, over an initial smooth slab and scree-filled grooves, is difficult and unpleasant.

Anyone wishing to avoid Sharp Edge should go up by way of Scales Tarn.

looking west-north-west

looking down from
Foule Crag

looking east
along the Edge
(the 'awkward
place' in the
foreground)

Sharp Edge

the approach from
Scales Tarn

from Scales Tarn

Foule Crag
Sharp Edge
Brunt Knott

the path from Scales

ASCENT FROM SCALES
via SCALES FELL
2150 feet of ascent : 2¼ miles

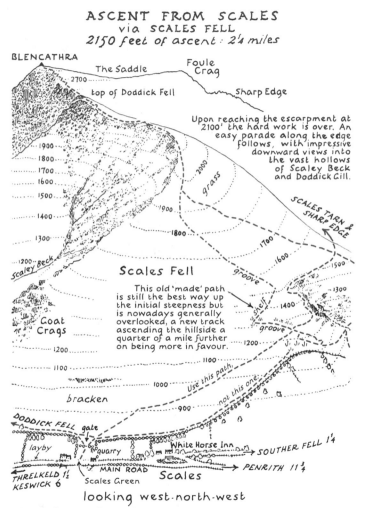

BLENCATHRA

The Saddle

Foule Crag

2700

top of Doddick Fell

Sharp Edge

Upon reaching the escarpment at 2100' the hard work is over. An easy parade along the edge follows, with impressive downward views into the vast hollows of Scaley Beck and Doddick Gill.

1900
1800
1700
1600
1500
1400
1300
1200

Scaley Beck

2000

grass

1900

1800

1700

1600

1500

SCALES TARN & SHARP EDGE

Scales Fell

This old 'made' path is still the best way up the initial steepness but is nowadays generally overlooked, a new track ascending the hillside a quarter of a mile further on being more in favour.

groove

shelf

1400

1300

groove

1200

Coat Crags

1200

1100

1100

1000

Use this path

not this one:

bracken

900

DODDICK FELL gate

White Horse Inn

SOUTHER FELL 1¼

layby

quarry

MAIN ROAD

PENRITH 11¾

THRELKELD 1½
KESWICK 6

Scales Green

Scales

looking west·north·west

This is the best-known route up Blencathra, and has been in common use for over a century. Until recently, the tough grass of Scales Fell resisted the formation of a continuous track. The climb, tedious up to 2000', becomes excellent in its later stages.

ASCENT FROM MUNGRISDALE
2250 feet of ascent : 4 miles

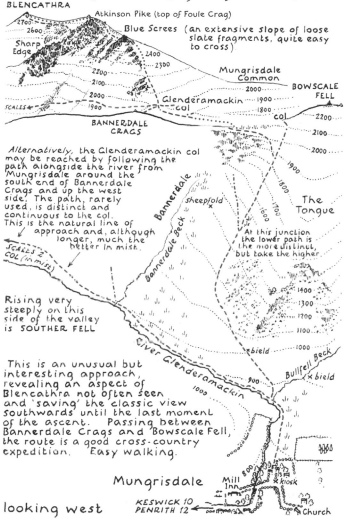

BLENCATHRA

Atkinson Pike (top of Foule Crag)

2700
2600

Blue Screes (an extensive slope of loose slate fragments, quite easy to cross)

Sharp Edge

2400
2300

Mungrisdale Common

BOWSCALE FELL

2200
2100
2000
1900

2000
1900
1800

Glenderamackin col

col

2200
2100
2000

SCALES

BANNERDALE CRAGS

1900

The Tongue

Alternatively, the Glenderamackin col may be reached by following the path alongside the river from Mungrisdale around the south end of Bannerdale Crags and up the west side. The path, rarely used, is distinct and continuous to the col. This is the natural line of approach and, although longer, much the better in mist.

Bannerdale

Bannerdale Beck

sheepfold

1600

1800
1900

At this junction the lower path is the more distinct, but take the higher.

SCALES 2 COL (in mist)

1400
1300
1200
1100

Rising very steeply on this side of the valley is SOUTHER FELL

bield

1000

River Glenderamackin

Bullfell Beck

× bield

This is an unusual but interesting approach, revealing an aspect of Blencathra not often seen and 'saving' the classic view southwards until the last moment of the ascent. Passing between Bannerdale Crags and Bowscale Fell, the route is a good cross-country expedition. Easy walking.

900
1000

Mungrisdale

Mill Inn

× kiosk

800

Church

looking west

KESWICK 10
PENRITH 12

THE VIEW

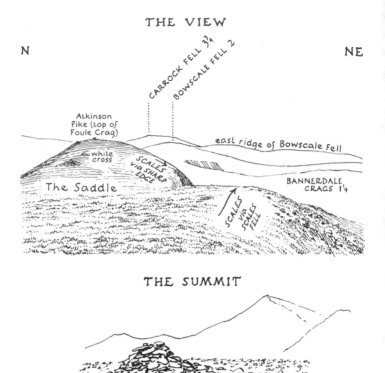

N   NE

CARROCK FELL 3¾

BOWSCALE FELL 2

Atkinson
Pike (top of
Foule Crag)

white
cross

SCALES via SHARP EDGE

east ridge of Bowscale Fell

The Saddle

BANNERDALE
CRAGS 1¼

SCALES VIA SCALES FELL

THE SUMMIT

The summit is effectively poised above the abyss, precisely at the point where the ridge of Hall's Fell comes up out of the depths to a jutting headland. The summit is, in fact, known as Hallsfell Top. At ground level on the highest point there is an Ordnance Survey trigonometrical station, apparently disused. Otherwise nothing marks the summit but a poor untidy heap of rubble. Much slaty stone is lying exposed here, but it is unsuitable for building cairns, and until somebody carries up a few decent-sized blocks the cairn will continue to disappoint.

The summit is windswept and shelterless and lacks a natural seat, but a few yards down Hall's Fell on the left the lee-side of a small outcrop usually cuts off the prevailing wind.

The excellent turf along the top deserves special mention.

continued

THE VIEW

NE   E

The Pennines in the background   Cross
                                        Fell
The Eden Valley   Penrith
                          SOUTHER
                          FELL 2
Mungrisdale

       south ridge of
       Bannerdale Crags

← SCALES TARN

continued

Descents:

The best *ascents* are by the narrow ridges —— Hall's Fell,
Sharp Edge, Doddick Fell and Gategill Fell, *in that order* ——
but the best routes of *descent* are those tedious in ascent:
Blease Fell, Scales Fell, Glenderamackin col and Roughten
Gill, *in that order.* The latter two are roundabout and not
suitable in mist, but Blease Fell and Scales Fell, lying at
opposite ends of the well-defined summit escarpment, are
simple ways off in any weather. The narrow ridges will be
found bumpy going down, although Hall's Fell and Doddick
Fell are quite practicable and enjoyable, but all may become
dangerous under ice and snow.   The gills and ravines on
the southern front are much too rough to be considered for
descent no matter how good the weather.

11 Great Calva
via Whitewater Dash

Most visitors to the northern Lake District will have seen Great Calva — the properly mountain-shaped mountain between Skiddaw and Blencathra — but a lot less would be able to put a name to it and even fewer will have been to its summit. Which is a great shame because it is one of the really great viewing platforms of Lakeland.

When we filmed here as part of the *Remote Lakeland* walk, we approached over the rather boring summit of Knott. It's a mountain for which A.W. reserved a particular scorn. He said the top was so flat and featureless that it was a perfect place to stage a cricket match. At the time I suggested it was the perfect place to send the England team to practice until they learned the difference between cricket and surrender. Little has happened to change that view in the intervening years.

This time, though, for Granada's *Wainwright Country*, we're taking a route that's a delight from start to finish. We're also taking a liberty for the first time in this book by varying one of Wainwright's routes. I'm sure he wouldn't mind. He always used to say that his ascents were just suggestions. The mountains were there for everyone to explore in their own way. Well, yes, but with most summits Wainwright so filleted the ground that, in truth, there are very few new ways to discover. But, as it happens, there are on this walk. The Cumbria Way footpath wasn't around when he surveyed these northern fells but it allows us an approach that captures the very best of the landscape.

We're going to begin from the minor road at Peter House Farm and follow the footpath up under Dead Crags to the waterfall at Whitewater Dash (Wainwright uses its local name, Dash Falls). It's a really special place – even better in wild weather. If you do end up taking this stroll in the pouring rain the falls will take the edge off your misery. The water plunges off a rocky ledge and tumbles in a carefree

234

sort of way five hundred feet to the valley floor. You can almost hear it shouting 'YaHee' as it goes. We join the Wainwright route beyond Dead Beck and strike for the summit.

The view from Great Calva will make your day. It's perfectly placed to show off the great rift of Lakeland. South over Thirlmere and the Vale of Grasmere, Rydal and, in the far distance, a glimpse of Windermere. Or was I just imagining that in the iron grey mist? As our cameraman said to me the last time we were there, 'If this view doesn't get you excited, you're dead.'

Practical bits
Map: OL4.
Ascent: Start at Peter House Farm (NY249324), where car parking is now available and where the Cumbria Way is signposted off the minor road. Follow the rough track under Dead Crags to the falls and then over Candlescaves Bog (not as horrible as it sounds) until you cross Dead Beck. Then pick up the left-hand route shown on Great Calva 6 in *The Northern Fells* (approximately 3 miles and 1500 feet).
Descent: I'd suggest you use the reverse of Wainwright's Great Calva 5 which will take you down to the road south of Orthwaite. Turn left and it's a short walk back along the road to the start point. Again, that will be about 1500 feet of descent over 3¾ miles

Great Calva

2265'

*from the path to
Skiddaw House*

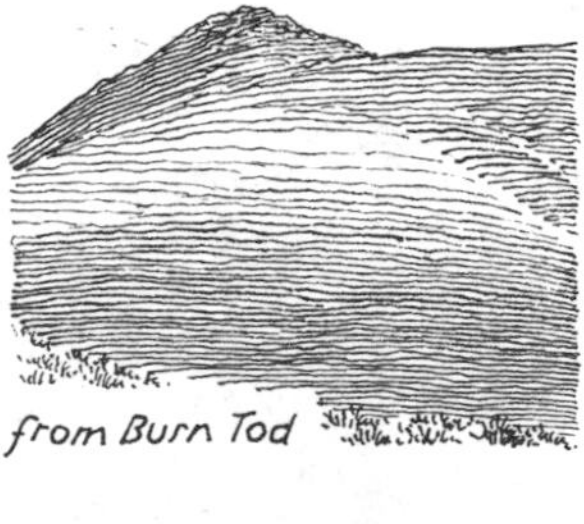

from Burn Tod

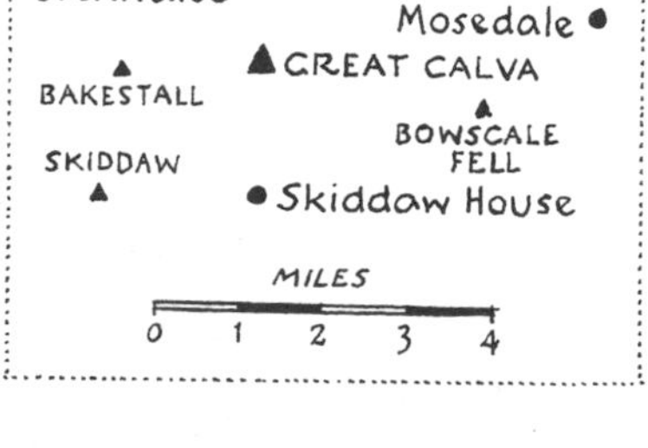

Orthwaite   ▲ KNOTT
                    Mosedale ●
       ▲   ▲ GREAT CALVA
BAKESTALL
                    BOWSCALE
SKIDDAW   FELL ▲
       ▲   ● Skiddaw House

MILES

0   1   2   3   4

NATURAL FEATURES

Most regular visitors to Lakeland will be familiar with the outline of Great Calva even though they may never in their wanderings have been within miles of it, because its symmetrical pyramid neatly fills in the head of the valley opening south between the Skiddaw and Blencathra massifs and is conspicuously seen from many points on the busy road approaching Keswick from Grasmere.

It occupies a splendid position overlooking the broad depression of Skiddaw Forest, with which it seems to be inseparably associated, more so even than Skiddaw itself. Calva dominates the Forest, rising from it in a strange patchwork of colours indicative of areas of heather, its principal covering, that have been burnt off, are newly shooting up or are long established, giving odd contrasts in appearance.

The actual top, which is stony, is a fine belvedere, but behind is an extensive plateau without an irrigation system and so forming a morass across which one can step gingerly to the solid ground of Little Calva, a place of little interest; and, beyond, the fell drops away steeply in a series of spiky aretes to the magnificent Dash Falls. This is Calva's best aspect; nevertheless the fell's appeal is more likely to depend upon its unique function as the watchtower of Skiddaw Forest.

Bridge on the road to Skiddaw House, above Dash Falls

Great Calva 3

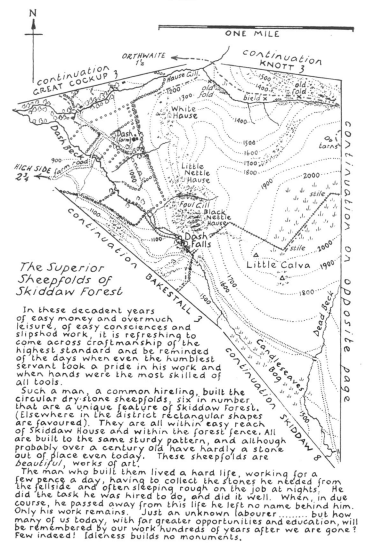

MAP

ONE MILE

N

ORTHWAITE 1½ →

continuation KNOTT 3

continuation GREAT COCKUP 3

Hause Gill

old fold

1700

1300

old fold

1500

1400

bield ×

White House

1400

Dash (farm)

Dash Beck

1500

1600

1700

1800

1900

2000

continuation on opposite page

tarns

900

HIGH SIDE (farm) 2¾ →

1000

Little Nettle House

1100

Foul Gill

Black Nettle House

stile

1100

2000

Dash Falls

stile

Little Calva

1900

1800

The Superior Sheepfolds of Skiddaw Forest

continuation BAKESTALL 3

1600

1700

1500

Dead Beck

Candleseaves Bog

continuation SKIDDAW 8

1500

In these decadent years of easy money and overmuch leisure, of easy consciences and slipshod work, it is refreshing to come across craftsmanship of the highest standard and be reminded of the days when even the humblest servant took a pride in his work and when hands were the most skilled of all tools.

Such a man, a common hireling, built the circular dry-stone sheepfolds, six in number, that are a unique feature of Skiddaw Forest. (Elsewhere in the district rectangular shapes are favoured). They are all within easy reach of Skiddaw House and within the forest fence. All are built to the same sturdy pattern, and although probably over a century old have hardly a stone out of place even today. These sheepfolds are beautiful, works of art.

The man who built them lived a hard life, working for a few pence a day, having to collect the stones he needed from the fellside and often sleeping rough on the job at nights. He did the task he was hired to do, and did it well. When, in due course, he passed away from this life he left no name behind him. Only his work remains. Just an unknown labourer .... but how many of us today, with far greater opportunities and education, will be remembered by our work hundreds of years after we are gone? Few indeed! Idleness builds no monuments.

MAP

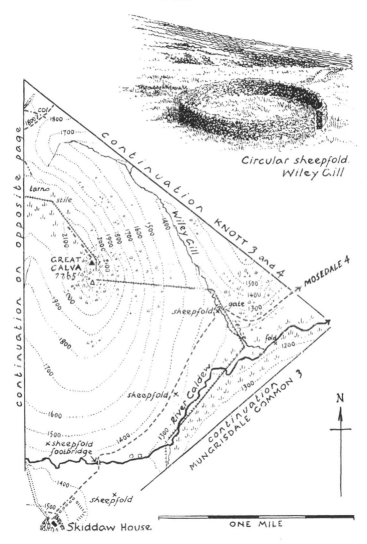

Circular sheepfold.
Wiley Gill

continuation on opposite page

col
1800
1800
1700
tarns
stile
2100
1600
1500
1400
2000
1900
1700
1600
1500
GREAT
CALVA
2265'
1900
1800
1700
1600
1500
sheepfold ×
sheepfold ×
1400
1300
footbridge
× sheepfold
1400
1500
× sheepfold

Skiddaw House

continuation KNOTT 3 and 4

Wiley Gill

MOSEDALE 4

1500
1400
gate
1300
fold
1200
1300

River Calder

continuation MUNGRISDALE COMMON 3

N

ONE MILE

ASCENT FROM ORTHWAITE
1500 feet of ascent : 3¾ miles

GREAT CALVA

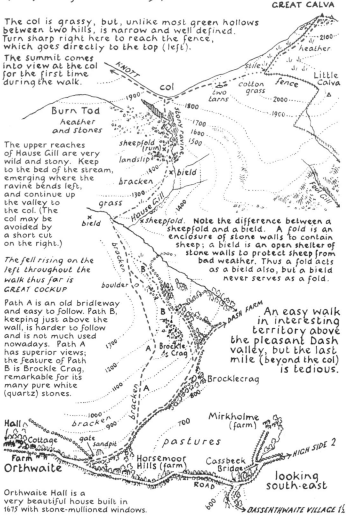

The col is grassy, but, unlike most green hollows between two hills, is narrow and well defined. Turn sharp right here to reach the fence, which goes directly to the top (left).

The summit comes into view at the col for the first time during the walk.

KNOTT

col

heather

2100

stile

Little Calva

cotton grass

fence

two tarns

2000

1900

1900

1800

1700

1600

1500

Burn Tod
heather and stones

stony ravine

sheepfold (ruin)

landslip

1400

bield

bracken

1300

grass

House Gill

1400

Coot Gill

The upper reaches of Hause Gill are very wild and stony. Keep to the bed of the stream, emerging where the ravine bends left, and continue up the valley to the col. (The col may be avoided by a short cut on the right.)

bield

sheepfold. Note the difference between a sheepfold and a bield. A fold is an enclosure of stone walls to contain sheep; a bield is an open shelter of stone walls to protect sheep from bad weather. Thus a fold acts as a bield also, but a bield never serves as a fold.

The fell rising on the left throughout the walk thus far is GREAT COCKUP

bracken

boulder

B

B

2000

Path A is an old bridleway and easy to follow. Path B, keeping just above the wall, is harder to follow and is not much used nowadays. Path A has superior views; the feature of Path B is Brockle Crag, remarkable for its many pure white (quartz) stones.

1700

A

Brockle Crag

1200

1100

DASH FARM

An easy walk in interesting territory above the pleasant Dash valley, but the last mile (beyond the col) is tedious.

A

Brocklecrag

1000

bracken

900

800

700

Mirkholme (farm)

Hall

Cottage

gate

sandpit

Farm

Orthwaite

Horsemoor Hills (farm)

pastures

Cassbeck Bridge

HIGH SIDE 2

ROAD

600

looking south-east

BASSENTHWAITE VILLAGE 1½

Orthwaite Hall is a very beautiful house built in 1675 with stone-mullioned windows.

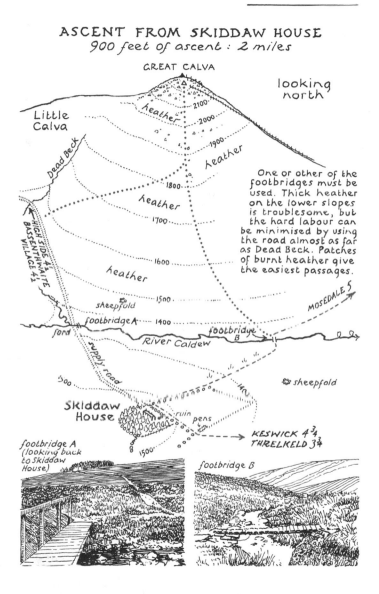

ASCENT FROM SKIDDAW HOUSE
900 feet of ascent : 2 miles

GREAT CALVA

looking north

Little Calva

heather — 2100
— 2000
— 1900

heather

Dead Beck

— 1800

heather

— 1700

HIGH SIDE 4½
BASSENTHWAITE VILLAGE 4½

One or other of the footbridges must be used. Thick heather on the lower slopes is troublesome, but the hard labour can be minimised by using the road almost as far as Dead Beck. Patches of burnt heather give the easiest passages.

— 1600

heather

— 1500

sheepfold

footbridge A — 1400

MOSEDALE 5

ford

River Caldew

footbridge B

supply road

— 500

sheepfold

Skidaw House

ruin pens

KESWICK 4¾
THRELKELD 3¾

— 1500

footbridge A (looking back to Skidaw House)

footbridge B

THE SUMMIT

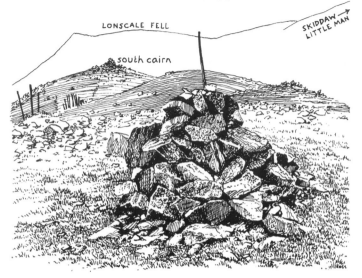

LONSCALE FELL

SKIDDAW LITTLE MAN →

south cairn

What appears to be the obvious top of the symmetrical pyramid of Great Calva, as seen on the climb up from Skiddaw Forest, is found on investigation not to be the true summit at all, and the prominent cairn overlooking this approach is succeeded by one at a greater elevation 130 yards further along a gentle incline. The top of the fell is made interesting by a scattering of stones and is given added distinction by a wire fence, which is ineffectual because of a gap of fifty yards near the summit. *In mist*, note that the *right*-angle in the fence occurs at the lower (south) cairn.

DESCENTS : The fence is a guide to the Caldew Valley, descending east from the south cairn; and, starting north-west from the top cairn, it leads safely down, after many changes of direction and a traverse of Little Calva, to the Skiddaw House road just above Dash Falls.   For Threlkeld or Keswick, via Skiddaw House, go straight down the south slope but incline to the right when the steepness and stoniness have subsided, gaining the Skiddaw House road at the footbridge. (A beeline might be halted by the River Caldew, which, although only a mile and a half from its source, is already lusty.)

LONSCALE FELL

Skiddaw House

The south cairn

THE SUMMIT

continued

There is no need to sit shivering in the lee of the cairn. A few yards down the east slope, across the fence, is a splendidly-constructed windproof shelter.

summit shelter

RIDGE ROUTE

To KNOTT, 2329' : 1½ miles : NW, then NE

Depression at 1810'
550 feet of ascent

Walkers whose boots let water in will soon be cognisant of the fact.

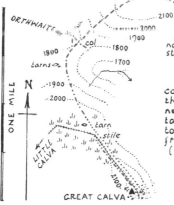

It matters not which side of the fence is taken; it is slightly easier to avoid the bogs on the east side. Proceed to the accompaniment of loud squelches as far as the angle of the fence, where turning down to the col, which is neat and narrow. The pull up on to Knott is steep initially, becoming easy.

To SKIDDAW there is no convenient ridge, a descent to the Skiddaw House road being necessary whichever route is taken. The best plan is to go up to Skiddaw House and ascend from there (see Skiddaw page 21). (As a point of interest, it may be mentioned that the fence, if followed closely and starting northwest, will lead almost to the top of Skiddaw, after many changes of direction)

THE VIEW

An observation of particular interest is mentioned on the next page following.

From the lower cairn there is the best of all prospects of Skiddaw Forest — a strange, silent wilderness irrigated by the infant Caldew. The neighbouring fells are not well presented, but there is a distant view of the Solway Firth bisected by the Sandale television mast, which isn't a very inspiring sight either.

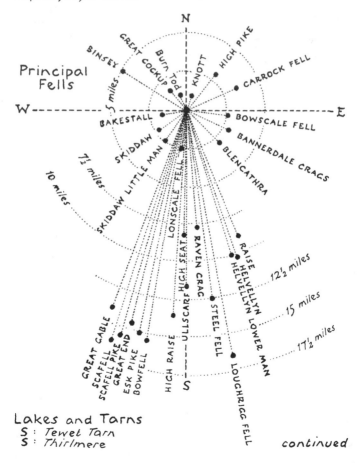

Principal
Fells

Lakes and Tarns
S : *Tewet Tarn*
S : *Thirlmere*

continued

THE VIEW

continued

GREAT CALVA
← Skiddaw Forest

← Glenderaterra Valley

Vale of St. John's

CENTRAL FELLS

The Helvellyn Range

EASTERN FELLS

Thirlmere

Ullscarf

Dunmail Raise →

N

Vale of Grasmere

Grasmere
Rydal Water
Rothay Valley

Land over 1500'

Windermere

FIVE MILES

THE GREAT CENTRAL FAULT

Lakeland is severed by a great geological fault: a deep trough running north and south across the district. The lakes of Windermere, Rydal Water, Grasmere and Thirlmere lie in this trough and the main road north of Ambleside takes advantage of the simple passage it affords, Dunmail Raise at 782' being the highest point. The rift continues through the Vale of St. John's and the Glenderaterra valley to Skiddaw Forest, where, situated exactly at its head, there rises the graceful cone of Great Calva. The trough is steeply bounded by high hills on both sides, notably the Helvellyn range. Great Calva's unique position provides it with a view along the direct line of the fault, so that, despite the mountains crowding into the scene, there is a remarkable vista, like looking along the sights of a gun, through the heart of the district to the low Windermere fells in the extreme south.

Carrock Fell from the top of Great Calva

12 Knott Rigg and Ard Crags
from Newlands Hause

The last time we filmed at Newlands Hause was with some-one emitting clouds of smoke and wheezing disconcertingly. No, the chap in question was Stuart Harrison and the smoke and sound effects were coming from his traction engine Western Star, which we were taking across the high passes just to prove it could be done. Wainwright would have loved to see it, this link with the early opening up of the Lake District. He was fascinated by and immersed in the history of man's connections with the Lakeland mountains. He knew that steam-powered road-engines and road-rollers broke out many of the Lakeland passes, the traction engines anchored to precarious summits and hauling road-rollers up and down the hairpin tracks.

A.W. had strangely conflicting views about development in his beloved Lake District. For example, he thoroughly disap-proved of the water boards – particularly the aldermanic van-dals of Manchester Corporation – who had flooded valleys like Mardale. The Forestry Commission ran a close second in the public enemy stakes for what they'd done to places like Ennerdale. But he had an altogether more forgiving view of the quarrymen and miners who carved out a hard living from the Lakeland fellsides. They were somehow real. Locals in the best sense who, like the fell farmers, were an integral part of the landscape. When we were filming with him and passed old workings and adits in the mountains, he would talk about them as if they were honourable memorials to a disappeared age, not evidence of human insensitivity.

If he could have been standing at Newlands Hause that day, watching Western Star struggle up the last few hundred yards out of Keskadale, he would have had mixed feelings. The old-fashionedness of the scene would have struck a chord. Stuart with his unrivalled knowledge of the machine and its quirky ways would have appealed. Wainwright admired people who were masters of their job. On the other hand the driving of roads to places like Newlands Hause had led to an influx of cars that he hated and he never missed an opportunity to complain about them.

So we'll leave him there, adding up the two sides of this rather troublesome balance sheet, while we head for Knott Rigg. In fact, this walk gives you two for the price of one. The climb out from the Hause is a comfortable stroll – at least it is if you've sorted out 'certain functions' before you set off, as you'll note in Wainwright's text. Knott Rigg gives you great high level views of some of the hard mountains – Wandope and Eel Crag, Hindscarth and Robinson. And the ridge walk to Ard Crags is a bonus.

Wainwright reckoned this was the place to come to avoid the masses. 'Save a visit here for a warm, still day in August, and envy not the crowds heading for Great Gable.' Lie back in the heather and enjoy the solitude. We did when we filmed the route for Granada. We also wholeheartedly agreed with the great man that, even though it's only 1800 feet or so, it's a place where you can find a personal heaven in a busy world.

Practical bits
Map: OL4.
Ascent: Start from the car park at Newlands Hause (NY 194 176) and take the route Wainwright shows on Knott Rigg 3 in *The North Western Fells* (just 720 feet to the summit and 1 mile). Then follow the ridge route to Ard Crags from Knott Rigg 6.
Descent: If your car is parked at Newlands Hause you may well want to return the way you've come but there's a more varied descent to Rigg Beck, the reverse of Wainwright's Ard Crags 3. It descends 1350 feet in 1½ miles. The downside of this route is that you will end up with a 2½ mile walk back to your car along the valley road.

Knott Rigg

1824'

from Buttermere

Keskadale is the long arm of Newlands extending southwest and providing the only outlet for vehicles from the head of the valley. The road is accommodated for two long miles along the side of a narrow and steepsided ridge of moderate height before climbing over a pass, Newlands Hause, formed by the gentle termination of the ridge; lovely Buttermere is beyond. This ridge has two distinct summits: the higher, overlooking Newlands, is Ard Crags; the lower, overlooking Buttermere, is Knott Rigg.

Sail Beck, coming down from the Eel Crag *massif*, of which Knott Rigg is an offshooting spur, very sharply marks the western boundary of the fell.

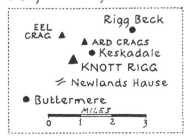

EEL CRAG ▲

Rigg Beck ●

▲ ARD CRAGS

● Keskadale

▲

KNOTT RIGG

⚞ Newlands Hause

● Buttermere

MILES

0   1   2   3

MAP

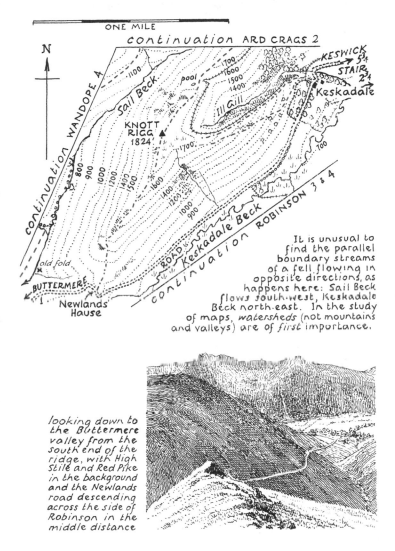

ONE MILE

N

continuation ARD CRAGS 2

KESWICK 5¼

STAIR 2¼

Keskadale

continuation WANDOPE A

Sail Beck

pool

1700
1600
1500
1400

Ill Gill

KNOTT RIGG 1824

1700

1400
1200
1000
900

100

continuation ROBINSON 3 & 4

Keskadale Beck

ROAD

800
900
1000
1200
1400
1500
1600

old fold

BUTTERMERE 1

Newlands Hause

It is unusual to find the parallel boundary streams of a fell flowing in opposite directions, as happens here: Sail Beck flows south-west, Keskadale Beck north-east. In the study of maps, *watersheds* (not mountains and valleys) are of *first* importance.

looking down to the Buttermere valley from the south end of the ridge, with High Stile and Red Pike in the background and the Newlands road descending across the side of Robinson in the middle distance

ASCENT FROM NEWLANDS HAUSE
720 feet of ascent : 1 mile

Upon reaching the ridge there is at once a fine view down the other side to Sail Beck and across it to the tremendous scarred wall of Wandope, Eel Crag and Sail.

Beyond the last outcrop the excellent turf of the ridge gives place to tougher grass, the summit being reached across a marshy plateau.

An advantage of solitary travel on the fells, greatly appreciated by all lone walkers, is the freedom to perform a certain function as and where one wishes, without any of the consultations and subterfuges necessitated by party travel. The narrow crest of the Knott Rigg ridge is no place for indulging the practice, however, whether alone or accompanied, walkers here being clearly outlined against the sky and in full view from two valleys. This comment is intended for males particularly. Women (according to an informant) have a different way of doing it.

Newlands Hause is commonly but wrongly referred to as Buttermere Hause

KNOTT RIGG

pools

summit now comes into view

outcrop astride ridge

grass

pleasant grey rocks

1500

1400

the ridge is reached between two small outcrops

1300

Leave the pass at the waist-high signpost adjoining the parking area and follow the thin track that can be seen ahead climbing up to the ridge.

This is one of the few paths in Lakeland owing their existence very largely to motorists exercising their legs from cars left at the Hause, where the verges provide plenty of space for parking.

1200

grass

1100

bracken

depression

bracken

BUTTERMERE

Newlands Hause 1096'

parking area

ROAD

1000

Moss Beck

looking north

NEWLANDS KESWICK

This is a simple and straightforward climb on the sunny side of the Hause, requiring an absence of one hour only from a car parked there. It affords a pleasant exercise, very suitable for persons up to 7 years of age or over 70.

ASCENT FROM KESKADALE
1000 feet of ascent : 1¼ miles

Upland marshes occur on almost all fells : on flat summits and plateaux, in hollows and on grassy shelves. They act as reservoirs for the streams, draining very slowly and holding back moisture to ensure continuous supplies independent of present prevailing weather. It is because of the marshes that the streams seldom lack water. They are safe to walk upon and cause little discomfort.
Bogs are not functional. They are infrequent in Lakeland; there are no places bad enough to trap walkers, but some are a danger to sheep.

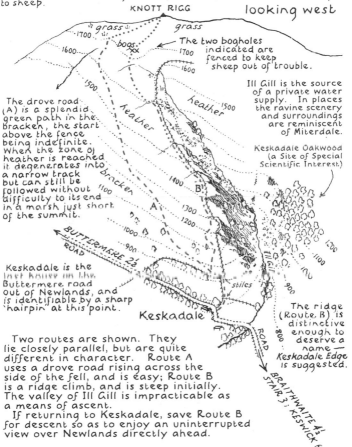

KNOTT RIGG

looking west

grass   grass

1700

bogs   The two bogholes
xx   indicated are
1700   fenced to keep
1600   sheep out of trouble.

1600

1500   heather   Ill Gill is the source
of a private water
supply. In places
the ravine scenery
and surroundings
are reminiscent
of Miterdale.

The drove road
(A) is a splendid
green path in the
bracken, the start
above the fence
being indefinite.
When the zone of
heather is reached
it degenerates into
a narrow track
but can still be
followed without
difficulty to its end
in a marsh just short
of the summit.

heather

Keskadale Oakwood
(a Site of Special
Scientific Interest)

bracken

1400   B

1100

1300

A   1200

1000   Ill Gill

BUTTERMERE 2½
ROAD

900

Keskadale is the
last house on the
Buttermere road
out of Newlands, and
is identifiable by a sharp
hairpin at this point.

stiles

Keskadale

ROAD

800

The ridge
(Route B) is
distinctive
enough to
deserve a
name —
Keskadale Edge
is suggested.

BRAITHWAITE 4½
STAIR 3; KESWICK 6

Two routes are shown. They lie closely parallel, but are quite different in character. Route A uses a drove road rising across the side of the fell, and is easy; Route B is a ridge climb, and is steep initially. The valley of Ill Gill is impracticable as a means of ascent.
If returning to Keskadale, save Route B for descent so as to enjoy an uninterrupted view over Newlands directly ahead.

THE SUMMIT

There are two summits at about the same altitude and about thirty yards apart. The more southerly has two tiny cairns.

DESCENTS:
The simplest way off the fell is south to Newlands Hause, and the finest is via Keskadale Edge, but between these routes (assuming they cannot be located in mist) there should not be any trouble in going straight down to the road at the base of the fell. Sail Beck is rougher to approach and saves nothing.

Considering that it is clearly in view to travellers along the Buttermere road and conveniently near, the side valley of Ill Gill is rarely entered. It has many charming features beyond its rather hostile portals and is worth a visit as far as a waterslide a quarter-mile in.

Keskadale Edge and Ill Gill

THE VIEW

Knott Rigg is so tightly sandwiched between the impending masses of Robinson and the Eel Crag range that an extensive view is not to be expected. The distant scene is not completely restricted, however, and eastwards there is a glorious outlook across the valley of Newlands to the lofty skyline of Helvellyn and the Dodds.

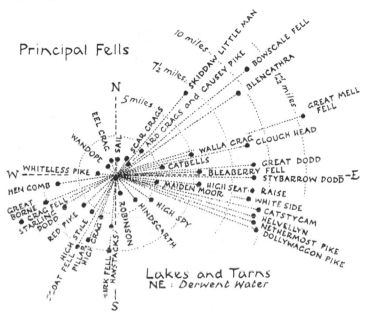

Principal Fells

Lakes and Tarns
NE : Derwent Water

RIDGE ROUTE

To ARD CRAGS, 1906': 1 mile: NE
Depression at 1660'
200 feet of ascent

There is little fall in height for a furlong or so, then follows a gradual descent to a hollow occupied by a patch of gravel and a pond (sometimes dry). Thereon a better path rises through heather to Ard Crags.

HALF A MILE

Ard Crags

from Rigg Beck

Rigg Beck •

EEL
CRAG ▲ ▲ ARD CRAGS

KNOTT ▲ • Keskadale
RIGG

✦ Newlands Hause

• Buttermere

MILES

0   1   2   3

There is one point on the path alongside Rigg Beck where the defile ahead is occupied by the shapely pyramid of Ard Crags, its appearance suggesting a complete isolation from other fells. At the top of Rigg Beck, however, a high pass forms a bridge with the greater mass of the Eel Crag range; nevertheless, a clear identity is maintained by the ridge of Ard Crags as it runs southwest over Knott Rigg to Newlands Hause.

Both flanks are rough and exceedingly steep. Erosion on the south side — facing Newlands — has been halted by a plantation to protect the road and farmstead of Keskadale at its foot.

MAP

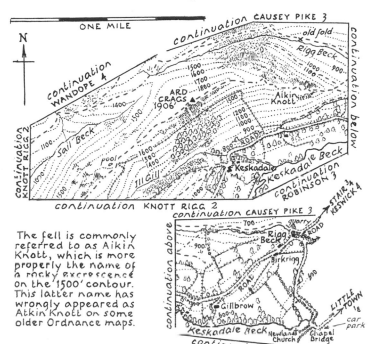

continuation CAUSEY PIKE 3

continuation WANDOPE 4

continuation KNOTT RIGG 2

old fold

Rigg Beck

continuation below

ARD CRAGS 1906'

Aikin Knott

Sail Beck

poor

Till Gill

ROAD

Keskadale

Keskadale Beck

continuation ROBINSON 3

continuation KNOTT RIGG 2

continuation CAUSEY PIKE 3

STAIR 3½
KESWICK 4

quarry

Rigg Beck

ROAD

Birkrigg

continuation above

ROAD

Gillbrow

LITTLE TOWN 1½

car park

Keskadale Beck

Newlands Church

Chapel Bridge

continuation ROBINSON 3

The fell is commonly referred to as Aikin Knott, which is more properly the name of a rocky excrescence on the 1500' contour. This latter name has wrongly appeared as Atkin Knott on some older Ordnance maps.

Rigg Beck

The sharp bend carrying the road over Rigg Beck is *comparatively* new. Formerly the road crossed at a ford lower down (still to be seen). Nearby, but now vanished, was a place of call, the Mill Dam Inn. Rest and refreshment for travellers are now to be found at Birkrigg, Gillbrow and Keskadale.

Higher up the road than the Rigg Beck crossing, at a wooded bend west of Gillbrow, is Bawd Hall, which was for many years in ruins, and Aikin, which was formerly a barn. Both are now occupied dwellings.

ASCENT FROM RIGG BECK
1350 feet of ascent : 1½ miles

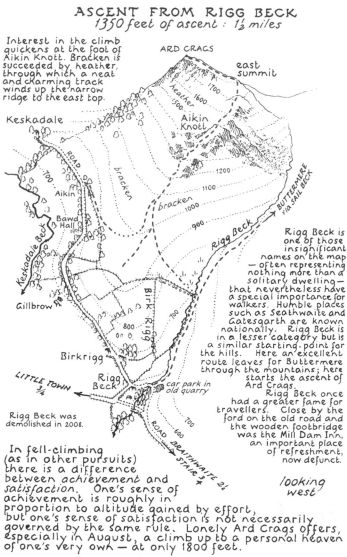

Interest in the climb quickens at the foot of Aikin Knott. Bracken is succeeded by heather, through which a neat and charming track winds up the narrow ridge to the east top.

ARD CRAGS

east summit

heather

Aikin Knott

Keskadale

ROAD

Aikin

Bawd Hall

bracken

bracken

1700
1600
1500
1200
1100
1000
900

Rigg Beck

BUTTERMERE VIA SAIL BECK

Gillbrow

Keskadale Beck

Birk Rigg

800

Rigg Beck is one of those insignificant names on the map — often representing nothing more than a solitary dwelling — that nevertheless have a special importance for walkers. Humble places such as Seathwaite and Gatesgarth are known nationally. Rigg Beck is in a lesser category but is a similar starting-point for the hills. Here an excellent route leaves for Buttermere through the mountains; here starts the ascent of Ard Crags.

Birkrigg

Rigg Beck

car park in old quarry

LITTLE TOWN 3/4

Rigg Beck was demolished in 2008.

Rigg Beck once had a greater fame for travellers. Close by the ford on the old road and the wooden footbridge was the Mill Dam Inn, an important place of refreshment, now defunct.

ROAD

BRAITHWAITE 2½
STAIR 2½

700
600

looking west

In fell-climbing (as in other pursuits) there is a difference between achievement and satisfaction. One's sense of achievement is roughly in proportion to altitude gained by effort, but one's sense of satisfaction is not necessarily governed by the same rule. Lonely Ard Crags offers, especially in August, a climb up to a personal heaven of one's very own — at only 1800 feet.

THE SUMMIT

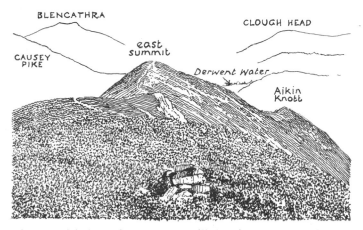

BLENCATHRA
CLOUGH HEAD
CAUSEY PIKE
east summit
Derwent Water
Aikin Knott

Save a visit here for a warm still day in August, and envy not the crowds heading for Great Gable. This is easier, more rewarding, and *solitary*. The narrow crest is a dense carpet of short springy heather, delightful to walk upon and even better as a couch for rest and meditation. But slumber is a hazard, for crags fall away sharply below one's boots to Keskadale. The highest point is marked by a pile of stones.

DESCENTS : *For Newlands,* follow the ridge over the east summit and Aikin Knott. *For Buttermere,* traverse Knott Rigg and aim for Newlands Hause. *The flanks of the fell are too rough for descent.*

The summit crags

looking down to Keskadale from the summit

THE VIEW

The highlight of the view is the beautiful detail of Newlands, a picture of bright pastures intermingled with heathery ridges, backed by the Helvellyn range, which is seen end to end in the distance. In other directions, nearby higher fells seriously curtail the view, and this is especially so between west and north, where the massive wall of the Eel Crag range towers above, impressively close. Eel Crag itself impends on the scene overpoweringly. Also of interest is the regular pattern of aretes descending from the long summit of Scar Crags just across the deep valley of Rigg Beck.

Principal Fells

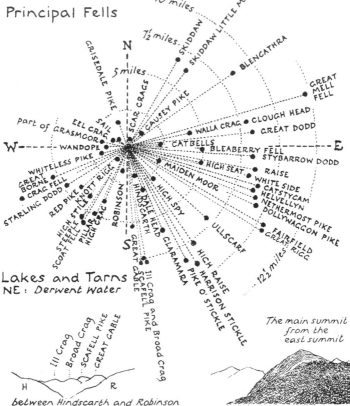

10 miles · 7½ miles · 5 miles · 12½ miles

GRISEDALE PIKE · SKIDDAW · SKIDDAW LITTLE MAN · BLENCATHRA · GREAT MELL FELL · SCAR CRAGS · CAUSEY PIKE · WALLA CRAG · CLOUGH HEAD · GREAT DODD · SAIL · EEL CRAG · part of GRASMOOR · CATBELLS · BLEABERRY FELL · STYBARROW DODD · WANDOPE · HIGH SEAT · RAISE · WHITELESS PIKE · MAIDEN MOOR · WHITE SIDE · GREAT BORNE · CATSTYCAM · CRAG FELL · HELVELLYN · STARLING DODD · RED PIKE · KNOTT RIGG · HIGH SPY · NETHERMOST PIKE · HIGH STILE · DOLLYWAGGON PIKE · SCOAT FELL · ROBINSON · STEEPLE · PILLAR · HINDSCARTH · ULLSCAR · FAIRFIELD · HIGH CRAG · GREAT RIGG · DALE HEAD · CLARAMARA · GREAT GABLE · HIGH RAISE · PIKE O' STICKLE · HARRISON STICKLE · Ill Crag and Broad Crag · SCAFELL PIKE

W — E · N · S

Lakes and Tarns

NE : Derwent Water

Ill Crag · Broad Crag · Scafell Pike · Great Gable

H · R

between Hindscarth and Robinson

The main summit from the east summit

RIDGE ROUTE

To KNOTT RIGG, 1824': 1 mile : SW
Depression at 1660'
130 feet of ascent

This is the natural continuation of the line of ascent over Aikin Knott.
From the cairn a thin track in heather skirts the rim of a gully with a view downwards to Keskadale, and goes on to a depression. The heather is here left behind and a short climb up the facing grass slope leads to a definite ridge with Knott Rigg's cairn at the end of it.

looking southwest along the ridge to Knott Rigg

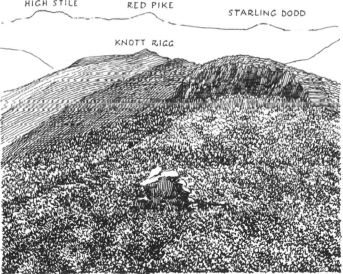

13 Castle Crag
from Borrowdale

Castle Crag is the gobstopper in the Jaws of Borrowdale. Less than a thousand feet, easy walking and a doorway to a lost world. I suggested it to the BBC4 production team because it's a walk that wraps up so many of Wainwright's passions. Borrowdale was his favourite valley – 'a pageant of beauty from end to end'. Castle Crag itself was his choice for any Lakeland visitor with just has a couple of hours to spare but who desperately wants to get to a summit. And everywhere there's a vibrant history, the voices of the past that echoed out of the landscape and spoke to Wainwright down the centuries.

We spent some happy days together in Borrowdale filming the *Wainwright's Lakeland* series for the BBC in the 1980s. We didn't mind the steady drizzle but A.W.'s memories of the time he spent there in the winter of 1962/63 sparkled through our conversation. The wintery grip was so strong that year that the mountains were out of bounds. 'Every Sunday I walked alone in a fairyland of glittering jewels under blue skies... Derwent Water was frozen from shore to shore and had the awesome stillness of a polar icecap... I was nearer to heaven that winter than I am ever likely to be.'

Wainwright's fascination with the fingerprints that man has left on the landscape is satisfied everywhere in Borrowdale. Grange, where we start this walk, gets its name from the days when it was a sheep grange, an outlying farm owned by the monks of Furness Abbey. And Castle Crag was once an industrial factory floor rattling to the clogs and shovels of generations of slate workers. The route to the summit is on zig-zag paths through slate spoil-heaps that nature is slowly taking back as its own.

The crag was also home to someone who was more than a match for Wainwright in the eccentricity stakes. Millican Dalton, professor of adventure, lived in caves on the crag. He offered mountain rapid shooting, rafting and hair's breadth escapes. He was a London insurance agent who'd gone native. He was teetotal, vegetarian, a socialist and a pacifist. What a shame he was long dead by the time Wainwright and I wandered down Borrowdale. It would have been just wonderful to sit at the mouth of the cave and listen to them going at it hammer and tongs.

So when you visit Castle Crag take the detour to the caves that are marked on the Wainwright map, imagine Millican Dalton in his bushman's hat and home-made clothes and look for his slogan carved by the cave entrance: 'Don't waste words – jump to conclusions'. M.D. and A.W. would probably have agreed about at least part of that statement.

Practical bits

Map: OL4.

Ascent: The *Wainwright Walks* route starts at Grange in Borrowdale (NY254175), tracks the River Derwent and joins the old quarry road under the crag before making a sharp ascent through the old slate workings. It's the route Wainwright shows on Castle Crag 5 in *The North Western Fells* (1½ miles and 700 feet of ascent).

Descent: If you're pushed for time, go back the way you came. Alternatively you can walk down to the hamlet of Rosthwaite using the reverse of Castle Crag 6 and then stroll back to Grange along the valley road. Again, 1¼ miles and 700 feet of descent.

Castle Crag

951'

Grange
●

CASTLE
▲ CRAG

Rosthwaite
●

ONE MILE

from the south

NATURAL FEATURES

Perhaps, to be strictly correct, Castle Crag should be regarded not as a separate fell but as a protuberance on the rough breast of Low Scawdel, occurring almost at the foot of the slope and remote from the ultimate summit of High Spy far above and out of sight. Castle Crag has no major geographical function — it is not a watershed, does not persuade the streams of Scawdel from their predestined purpose of joining the Derwent and interrupts only slightly the natural fall of the fell to Borrowdale: on the general scale of the surrounding heights it is of little significance.

Yet Castle Crag is so magnificently independent, so ruggedly individual, so aggressively unashamed of its lack of inches, that less than justice would be done by relegating it to a paragraph in the High Spy chapter. Its top is below 1000 feet (its 'official' height in 2008 being 951 feet), which makes it the only fell below 1000 feet in this series of books that is awarded the 'full treatment', a distinction well earned.

Castle Crag conforms to no pattern. It is an obstruction in the throat of Borrowdale, confining passage therein to the width of a river and a road, hiding what lies beyond, defying cultivation. Its abrupt pyramid, richly wooded from base almost to summit but bare at the top, is a wild tangle of rough steep ground, a place of crags and scree and tumbled boulders, of quarry holes and spoil dumps, of confusion and disorder. But such is the artistry of nature, such is the mellowing influence of the passing years, that the scars of disarray and decay have been transformed in a romantic harmony, cloaked by a canopy of trees and a carpet of leaves. There are lovely copses of silver birch by the crystal clear river, magnificent specimens of Scots pine higher up. Naked of trees, Castle Crag would be ugly; with them, it has a sylvan beauty unsurpassed, unique.

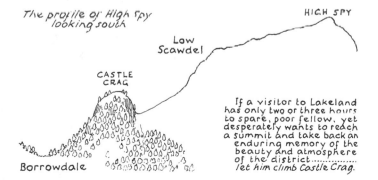

The profile of High Spy looking south

HIGH SPY

Low Scawdel

CASTLE CRAG

Borrowdale

If a visitor to Lakeland has only two or three hours to spare, poor fellow, yet desperately wants to reach a summit and take back an enduring memory of the beauty and atmosphere of the district..............
let him climb Castle Crag.

Castle Crag 3

The summit-quarry

The pedestrian path to the
top goes up the grass
on the right

summit

Quarries and caves of Castle Crag

In addition to the summit-quarry, which is open to the sky
and obvious to all who climb the fell, the steep flank above the
Derwent is pitted with cuttings and caverns and levels, every
hole having its tell-tale spoilheap, but the scars of this former
industrial activity are largely concealed by a screen of trees
and not generally noticed. Much of this flank is precipitous,
the ground everywhere is very rough, and the vertically-hewn
walls of naked stone are dangerous traps for novice explorers.

Of these quarries the best known
is High Hows, the debris of which is
passed on the riverside walk from
Grange to Rosthwaite. A detour up
the quarry road leads to a series of
caverns of special interest because
in one of them Millican Dalton,
a mountaineering adventurer
and a familiar character in the
district between the wars (died
1947, aged 80), furnished a home
for his summer residence, using
an adjacent cave at a higher
level (the 'Attic') as sleeping
quarters. *Note here his lettering
(though now difficult to read) cut
in the rock at the entrance —
'Don't!! Waste words, jump to conclusions'*

The Attic

Millican's Cave

MAP

The thick line forming a square has a special significance. It encloses one mile of country containing no high mountain, no lake, no famous crag, no tarn,

But, in the author's humble submission, it encloses the loveliest square mile in Lakeland — the Jaws of Borrowdale.

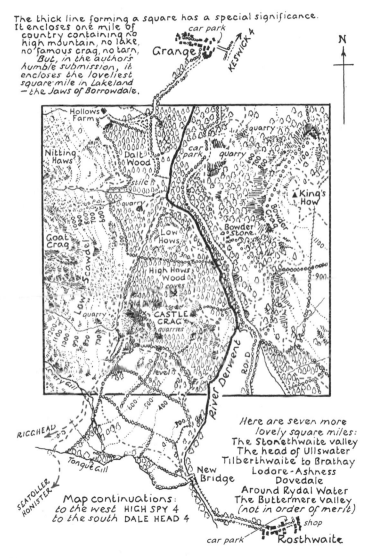

Here are seven more lovely square miles:
The Stonethwaite valley
The head of Ullswater
Tilberthwaite to Brathay
Lodore-Ashness
Dovedale
Around Rydal Water
The Buttermere valley
(not in order of merit)

Map continuations:
to the west   HIGH SPY 4
to the south   DALE HEAD 4

ASCENT FROM GRANGE

700 feet of ascent
1½ miles

CASTLE CRAG

900
800
700
600
col
stile
500
caves
quarry
folds
old road
400
gate
Low Hows
quarry

The old road formerly served Rigghead Quarry and is now in bad condition, the surface having been scoured away from the foundations. It is an excellent route for walkers, however, bound for Seatoller or Honister and avoids the main road entirely.

The ascent proper starts at point A, where a wooden stile is seen on a wall to the left. The detail is given below.

Whether time permits or not, on no account miss the little riverside walk below Low Hows. Here are the most beautiful reaches of the Derwent. (This walk may be followed through to Millican Dalton's caves, and on to Rosthwaite) This is an area of charming campsites: permission only from Hollows Farm.

River Derwent

ROAD

Dalt Wood
campsite
campsite
HOLLOWS FARM →

quarry
spoil heap
900
800
stile
700
seat
stile (at the top of a little rocky ridge)
stream
GRANGE
600
A
old road

Turn up where the stream crosses the old road from the left.

As far as the big bend of the Derwent all is level walking.

car park

Grange

Church

looking south

In the 1960s Cockermouth Rural District Council lapsed from their usual good taste by operating a refuse tip on land adjoining this route. The blight on the landscape was only temporary, however, since the tip has now disappeared without trace.

Leave Grange by a lane (signposted to Hollows Farm) almost opposite the church.

ASCENT FROM ROSTHWAITE

700 feet of ascent
1½ miles

From the ridge, the old Rigghead–Grange 'road' can be seen ahead and below in a wild setting.

There are magnificent Scots pines near the wall at the top of the wood.

A quarry path ascends the big enclosure (A). A detour of 50 yards to the old level and stone shelter, which are typical evidences of former quarrying operations, is recommended. Near the top corner of the enclosure the original path crossed the wall and proceeded on the far side to the ridge. This route is not now used, and it is more usual to pass through the gate in the cross-wall to enclosure B (note another level here in the corner) and, upon reaching the ridge, cross the wall to join the original route: a stile is provided here. Now the spoil-heap ahead is climbed by a zig-zag path carved in the naked stones, after which the way to the summit is clear.

Leave Rosthwaite by the lane opposite the village shop, bearing right at the farm buildings.

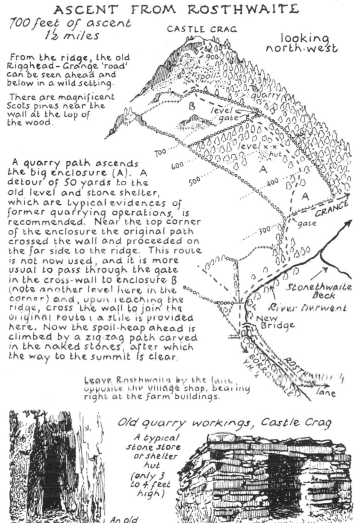

CASTLE CRAG

looking north-west

Old quarry workings, Castle Crag

A typical stone store or shelter hut (only 3 to 4 feet high)

An old level

THE SUMMIT

The summit is circular in plan, about 60 yards in diameter, and a perfect natural stronghold. Even today, one man in possession, armed with a stick, could prevent its occupation by others whatever their number, there being one strategic point (the place of access to the top) where passage upward is restricted to single-file traffic. Authorities agree that there was once a fort here, probably early British, but it needs a trained eye to trace any earthworks—which, in any case, must have been severely disturbed by an old quarry that has cut a big slice out of the summit and, be it noted, constitutes an unprotected danger. Photographers (who have a habit of taking backward steps when composing their pictures) should take care lest they suddenly vanish.

The highest point is a boss of rock, and this is crowned by a low horseshoe-shaped wall, below which, set in the rock, is a commemorative tablet: a war memorial to the men of Borrowdale, effective and imaginative. Immediately to the west of the summit is a larch tree that blocks out much of High Spy, and other specimens surround the perimeter.

DESCENTS: For the ordinary walker there is only one way on and off, and this is on the south side, by a clump of larch, where a clear track descends between the edge of the quarry (right) and a cutting (left) to the flat top of the spoil-heap, at the end of which a ramp on the right inclines in zigzags to the grass below. Here, if bound for Rosthwaite, cross the wall on the left; for Grange the way continues down, crossing two walls by stiles, to the old Rigghead road.

ENVIRONS
OF THE SUMMIT

THE SUMMIT

When this guide was first published, the altitude of the summit (now officially 951 feet) had yet to be determined. It was frequently quoted as 900 feet, but the following reasoning demonstrated that it must actually be in excess of this figure.

From High Doat (927'; 1 mile south) the summit appears to be above the horizontal plane of Latrigg (1203'; 6½ miles), giving a height of not less than 970', and probably 980' or 990'.

Look at High Doat from Castle Crag : it is obviously lower.

THE VIEW

The view is circumscribed but is open to the north, where Derwent Water, backed by Skiddaw, makes a fine scene. The steep fall from the summit on all sides provides an aerial study of the beautiful detail of mid-Borrowdale.

Principal Fells

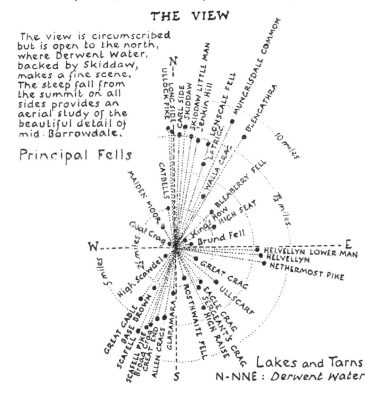

Lakes and Tarns
N–NNE: Derwent Water

14 Catbells
from Hawse End

When you read Wainwright recommending this as the perfect place for grandmothers and infants, what's your first thought?

I can guess.

Unless you're a fit and fearless grandmother who's about to tick off the last of the 214 Wainwrights, or a particularly precocious infant who reads the Pictorial Guides rather than regular picturebooks, you probably think it's a mountain you'll avoid.

I have for years.

I've seen Catbells from afar. From Latrigg and Dodd and Skiddaw. From Robinson and Causey Pike. From a launch on Derwentwater and a bar in Keswick. But I'd never really been tempted by what I confess I thought of as its tabloid charms until Julia Bradbury tackled it for the BBC4 series of Wainwright walks.

Having seen it, I'm sold on it. It may be the high-level family stroll of choice and a bit too busy in high season, but it isn't anywhere near as ordinary as my preconceptions had suggested. It may be popular but it isn't common. It may be relatively easy of access but it also has a bite. As well as grassy slopes it has craggy flanks, and even a smattering of industrial archaeology which draws me to mountain landscapes. Catbells is becoming more broadsheet by the minute.

And its views are nothing short of exotic – Borrowdale and Newlands, Hindscarth and Robinson. Causey Pike in your face. But as Wainwright says (and I should have taken more notice of years ago), the eye is constantly drawn back to Borrowdale and the expanses of Derwent Water.

Catbells has been at the heart of Lakeland's many lives. From its summit you can look across to the stone circle at Castlerigg, built a thousand years before Stonehenge. Below is the island where the friend of Cuthbert of Lindisfarne, St. Herbert set up his monastic cell. Across the lake is another island where one of the first Lakeland entrepreneurs, Joseph Pocklington (a retired banker with a monstrous lack of taste), built druidical ruins while early tourists hired the Duke of Portland's yacht and sailed past firing off a cannon and marvelling at the echoes from the mountains.

Wordsworth, Coleridge, Ruskin and J. M. W. Turner all came to admire the scene and to capture it in gentler reverberations that would captivate audiences across the world.

Of course, if all this isn't enough you can walk on from Catbells. It's the perfect place from which to venture across Maiden Moor to High Spy and Dale Head. But as one convert to another, give Catbells a chance first.

Practical bits

Map: OL 4.

Ascent: For *Wainwright Walks* BBC4 took the tourist route, crossing Derwent Water by launch from Keswick Pier to Hawse End (NY264227). From there the route is the one Wainwright shows on Catbells 5 in *The North Western Fells* (1750 feet of ascent in 1½ miles).

Descent: There are any number of varied ways off but let me suggest just two. To get you back to Derwent Water, you could try the easy descent to Grange in Borrowdale – the reverse of the route on Catbells 6. A short walk along the valley will get you to the Lodore landing stage and a launch back to Keswick.

If you want to make a more strenuous day of it, try the long march to Dale Head. From there you can drop in to the Honister Pass and catch the Honister Rambler bus back to Keswick instead.

Catbells

1481'

Cat Bells
(two words)
on Ordnance maps

from Derwent Water

● Portinscale
● Keswick

● Stair

▲ CATBELLS
● Little Town
▲ MAIDEN MOOR
● Grange
MILES

0   1   2   3   4

from the Portinscale path

NATURAL FEATURES

Catbells is one of the great favourites, a family fell where grandmothers and infants can climb the heights together, a place beloved. Its popularity is well deserved: its shapely topknot attracts the eye, offering a steep but obviously simple scramble to the small summit; its slopes are smooth, sunny and sleek; its position overlooking Derwent Water is superb. Moreover, for stronger walkers it is the first step on a glorious ridge that bounds Borrowdale on the west throughout its length with Newlands down on the other side. There is beauty everywhere — and nothing but beauty. Its ascent from Keswick may conveniently, in the holiday season, be coupled with a sail on the lake, making the expedition rewarding out of all proportion to the small effort needed. Even the name has a magic challenge.

Yet this fell is not quite so innocuous as is usually thought, and grandmothers and infants should have a care as they romp around. There are some natural hazards in the form of a line of crags that starts at the summit and slants down to Newlands, and steep outcrops elsewhere. More dangerous are the levels and open shafts that pierce the fell on both flanks: the once-prosperous Yewthwaite Mine despoils a wide area in the combe above Little Town in Newlands, to the east the debris of the ill-starred Brandley Mine is lapped by the water of the lake, and the workings of the Old Brandley Mine, high on the side of the fell at Skelgill Bank, are in view on the ascent of the ridge from the north. A tragic death in one of the open Yewthwaite shafts in 1962 serves as a warning.

Words cannot adequately describe the rare charm of Catbells, nor its ravishing view. But no publicity is necessary: its mere presence in the Derwent Water scene is enough. It has a bold 'come hither' look that compels one's steps, and no suitor ever returns disappointed, but only looking back often. It has only to be seen from Friar's Crag — and a spell is cast. No Keswick holiday is consummated without a visit to Catbells.

from Yewthwaite Comb

Crags and Caverns of Catbells

left: The crags of Mart Bield, below the summit on the Newlands side of the fell

right: A dangerous hole at Yewthwaite Mine.
At the end of a rock cutting the adit suggests a level (horizontal tunnel) but in fact is the opening of a vertical shaft.

below: Workings at the Old Brandley Mine.
A shaft with twin entrances, overhung by a tree, *left,* and a nearby level, *right.*

MAP

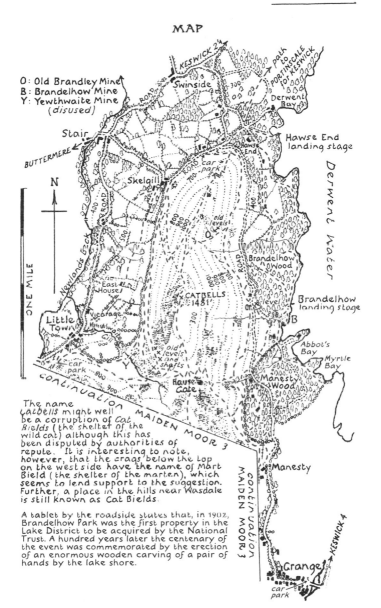

O: Old Brandley Mine
B: Brandelhow Mine
Y: Yewthwaite Mine
(disused)

KESWICK 2½

PATH to PORTINSCALE for KESWICK

Swinside

Derwent Bay

Stair

BUTTERMERE

Hawse End landing stage

Hawse End

ROAD car park

Skelgill

Derwent Water

N
ONE MILE

old levels

Brandelhow Wood

CATBELLS 1481

Brandelhow landing stage

East House

Vicarage

old level

B

Little Town

car park

old levels and shafts

Abbot's Bay

Myrtle Bay

Y

Newlands Beck

Hause Gate

Manest Wood

continuation MAIDEN MOOR 3

continuation MAIDEN MOOR 3

Manesty

KESWICK 4

The name *Catbells* might well be a corruption of *Cat Bields* (the shelter of the wild cat) although this has been disputed by authorities of repute. It is interesting to note, however, that the crags below the top on the west side have the name of Mart Bield (the shelter of the marten), which seems to lend support to the suggestion. Further, a place in the hills near Wasdale is still known as Cat Bields.

A tablet by the roadside states that, in 1902, Brandelhow Park was the first property in the Lake District to be acquired by the National Trust. A hundred years later the centenary of the event was commemorated by the erection of an enormous wooden carving of a pair of hands by the lake shore.

Grange

car park

ASCENT FROM HAWSE END
1250 feet of ascent : 1½ miles

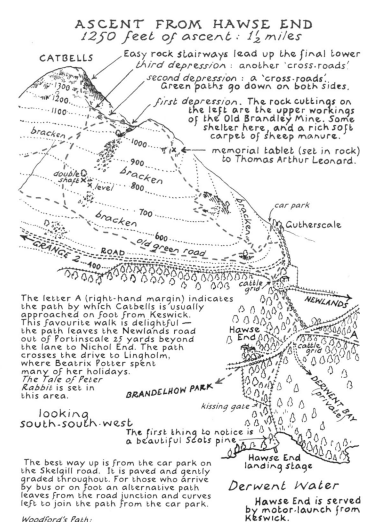

CATBELLS

Easy rock stairways lead up the final tower
third depression : another 'cross-roads'

second depression : a 'cross-roads'.
Green paths go down on both sides.

first depression. The rock cuttings on
the left are the upper workings
of the Old Brandley Mine. Some
shelter here, and a rich soft
carpet of sheep manure.

memorial tablet (set in rock)
to Thomas Arthur Leonard.

1300
1200
1100
1000
900
double
shaft
level
800
700
600

bracken

bracken

bracken

bracken

car park

Gutherscale

old green road

GRANGE 2
ROAD

cattle
grid

NEWLANDS

Hawse
End

cattle
grid

A

The letter A (right-hand margin) indicates
the path by which Catbells is usually
approached on foot from Keswick.
This favourite walk is delightful —
the path leaves the Newlands road
out of Portinscale 25 yards beyond
the lane to Nichol End. The path
crosses the drive to Lingholm,
where Beatrix Potter spent
many of her holidays.
*The Tale of Peter
Rabbit* is set in
this area.

BRANDELHOW PARK

DERWENT BAY (private)

kissing gate

looking
south·south·west

The first thing to notice is
a beautiful Scots pine

Hawse End
landing stage

Derwent Water

The best way up is from the car park on
the Skelgill road. It is paved and gently
graded throughout. For those who arrive
by bus or on foot an alternative path
leaves from the road junction and curves
left to join the path from the car park.

Hawse End is served
by motor·launch from
Keswick.

Woodford's Path:
This series of zigzags was engineered
by a Sir John Woodford, who lived near,
and his name deserves to be remembered
by those who use his enchanting stairway.
It starts 80 yards along the old green road.

One of the very best
of the shorter climbs.
A truly lovely walk.

ASCENT FROM GRANGE
1250 feet of ascent : 2 miles

Of course there is no gate at Hause Gate, just as there is no door at Mickledoor. 'Gate' and 'door' are local geographical terms for a way or opening through the hills or across a ridge. 'Hause' is another good Lakeland name for a pass. 'Hause Gate' is therefore really a tautological name. 'Hawse End' (with a 'w') is not a mis-spelling, 'hause' being inappropriate to the place.

Except for the zigzags below Hause Gate, the whole climb is set at an easy gradient, making it ideal for a gentle stroll on a fine evening after a big meal. The view opens beautifully as height is gained on a wide grass path, the start of which, near Manesty Farm, is the old road to Hawse End, now part of the long-distance footpath, the Allerdale Ramble.

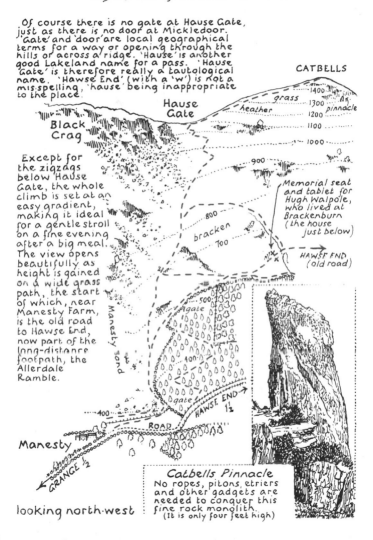

CATBELLS

Hause Gate

Black Crag

1400
1300 — grass — pinnacle
heather — 1200
1100
1000
900

Memorial seat and tablet for Hugh Walpole, who lived at Brackenburn (the house just below)

bracken
700
800

HAWSE END (old road)

Manesty Road

500 — gate
400
gate
gate
HAWSE END 1½

400

Manesty

GRANGE ½

ROAD

looking north-west

Catbells Pinnacle
No ropes, pitons, etriers and other gadgets are needed to conquer this fine rock monolith.
(It is only four feet high)

ASCENT FROM NEWLANDS

via SKELGILL
1200 feet of ascent : 1⅓ miles from Stair

via LITTLE TOWN
950 feet of ascent : 1⅓ miles from Little Town

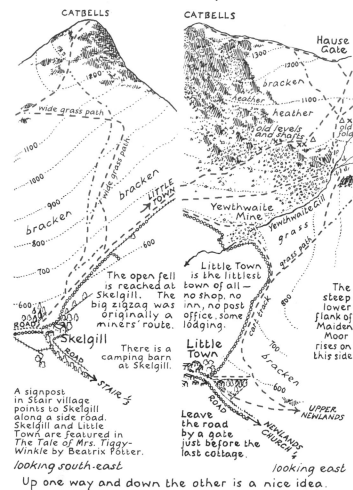

CATBELLS

1200

wide grass path

1100

1000

wide grass path

900

bracken

800

700

600

bracken

600

LITTLE TOWN

600

ROAD

Skelgill

ROAD

STAIR ⅓

A signpost in Stair village points to Skelgill along a side road. Skelgill and Little Town are featured in *The Tale of Mrs. Tiggy-Winkle* by Beatrix Potter.

looking south-east

The open fell is reached at Skelgill. The big zigzag was originally a miners' route.

There is a camping barn at Skelgill.

CATBELLS

Hause Gate

1300

1200

bracken

heather

1100

heather

old levels and shafts

old fold

Yewthwaite Mine

Yewthwaite Gill

grass

grass path

Little Town is the littlest town of all — no shop, no inn, no post office, some lodging.

cart track

600

700

Little Town

bracken

600

ROAD

NEWLANDS CHURCH ⅓

UPPER NEWLANDS

Leave the road by a gate just before the last cottage.

The steep lower flank of Maiden Moor rises on this side

looking east

Up one way and down the other is a nice idea.

THE SUMMIT

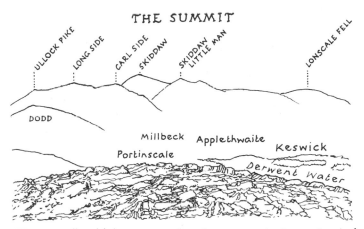

The summit, which has no cairn, is a small platform of naked rock, light brown in colour and seamed and pitted with many tiny hollows and crevices that collect and hold rainwater — so that, long after the skies have cleared, glittering diamonds adorn the crown. Almost all the native vegetation has been scoured away by the varied footgear of countless visitors; so popular is this fine viewpoint that often it is difficult to find a vacant perch. In summer this is not a place to seek quietness.

DESCENTS: Leave the top only by the ridge; lower down there is a wealth of choice. Keep clear of the craggy Newlands face.

RIDGE ROUTE

To MAIDEN MOOR, 1887'
1½ miles : S. then SW
Depression (Hause Gate) at 1180'
700 feet of ascent

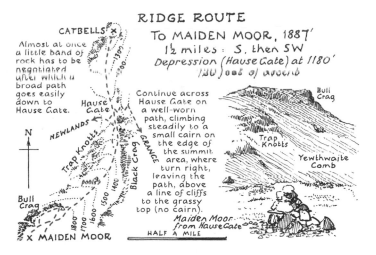

CATBELLS x
Almost at once a little band of rock has to be negotiated after which a broad path goes easily down to Hause Gate.

Hause Gate

NEWLANDS

Trap Knotts

Black Crag

GRANGE

Bull Crag

x MAIDEN MOOR

Continue across Hause Gate on a well-worn path, climbing steadily to a small cairn on the edge of the summit area, where turn right, leaving the path, above a line of cliffs to the grassy top (no cairn).

Maiden Moor from Hause Gate

HALF A MILE

Bull Crag

Trap Knotts

Yewthwaite Comb

THE VIEW

Scenes of great beauty unfold on all sides, and they are scenes in depth to a degree not usual, the narrow summit permitting downward views of Borrowdale and Newlands within a few paces. Nearby valley and lake attract the eye more than the distant mountain surround, although Hindscarth and Robinson are particularly prominent at the head of Newlands and Causey Pike towers up almost grotesquely directly opposite. On this side the hamlet of Little Town is well seen down below, a charming picture, but it is to Derwent Water and mid-Borrowdale that the captivated gaze returns again and again.

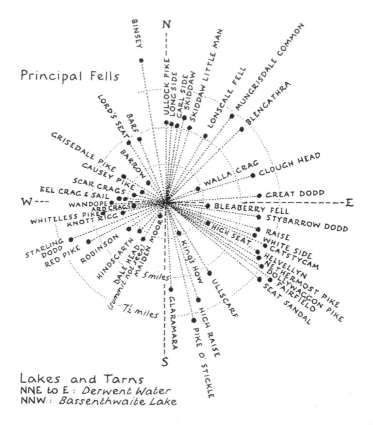

Principal Fells

Lakes and Tarns
NNE to E : Derwent Water
NNW : Bassenthwaite Lake

Hindscarth and Robinson from Catbells

15 Haystacks
from Gatesgarth via Scarth Gap

On my first visit to Haystacks the noise was deafening and the rock field above the Honister quarry road bone-shattering. We were approaching the mountain with all the pomp of an imperial expedition. Sitting like a Nawab in the centre of the roaring, diesel-powered palanquin was the Wainwright.

We had to go to Haystacks. It was his favourite mountain. It was where he wanted his ashes scattered when the time came. But we didn't think he'd make it unassisted so we hired a tracked vehicle to take him up through the quarry workings.

Then the Nawab raised his hand. In response to the command the vehicle rocked for a moment before sliding off the boulder and coming to a crashing halt.

'Enough. It's an insult to the mountain and to my back. I'll take my chance on foot.'

His loyal retainers dutifully shouldered their packs and the caravan moved off through the driving rain. It was slow going but we made it, with many rests. You may have seen the results in the BBC series *Wainwright's Lakeland*. The old lad dressed in a grey/green plastic coat that wouldn't have been out of place on the deck of a trawler in Icelandic waters. Him sitting by his last resting place at Innominate Tarn and musing about a lifetime in the mountains.

Later that day we almost lost him. We'd agreed to meet at a particular viewpoint but on that visit the word 'viewpoint' meant a rock in a mist from which we could see all of ten feet. Anyhow, he set off. We set off and got lost. I remember saying to Richard Else, the producer, that it would be fairly bad PR for the series if Wainwright had stumbled off the edge. Yes, he wanted to end up on Haystacks, but not quite yet. And then we found the appointed rock with Wainwright sitting on it and he said 'What kept you?'

He looked out into the mist and explained that he carried the whole panorama in his mind's eye – from Great Gable in the south east round to Grike in the west. I'd never even heard of Grike and I couldn't see it that day (although it became part of my exploration of *Remote Lakeland* many years later). There was a poignant moment just before we set off on our slow progress back to the quarry road: Wainwright said he didn't mind this weather because he looked out through a wall of mist all the time. Even with his glasses perched on his forehead and his face three inches from the page he could scarcely read his own Pictorial Guides, let alone see a mountain that, in youth, he'd identified on a far horizon.

Practical bits

Map: OL4.

Ascent: When BBC4 came to Haystacks as part of *Wainwright Walks*, Julia Bradbury missed out on the delights of caterpillar vehicles. They approached the mountain from Gatesgarth Farm (NY195150) outside Buttermere, following the route on Haystacks 5 from *The Western Fells*. Up the graded zig-zag path across the breast of Buttermere Fell. Between the rocky outcrops of Low and High Wax Knott. And then by way of the saddle at Scarth Gap to the summit (1¾ miles and 1550 feet).

Descent: The choice is yours. Wainwright himself gives a rare recommendation on Haystacks, suggesting making it a circular route by returning via Warnscale Bottom – Haystacks 6 in reverse. If you can get someone to pick you up in a car, though, there are other, more varied ways. By retracing your steps to Scarth Gap you can drop down to the Black Sail Hut and the road in Ennerdale – Haystacks 8 backwards. That's the easy way, with less than a thousand feet of descent over 1¼ miles. A more exciting and demanding route starts on the ridge route described on Haystacks 12. Skirt Brandreth and head for Green Gable – a lovely, undervalued mountain – and then climb over the galumphing Great Gable before dropping in by the Beck Head descent to Wasdale Head and a deserved pint of Great Gable bitter brewed at the Wasdale Head Inn's micro brewery. (A.W. would only have had a half.)

Haystacks

1959'

properly
Hay Stacks
(two words)
as on
Ordnance maps

from Gamlin End, High Crag

Gatesgarth
●
HIGH
CRAG
▲
HAYSTACKS
▲
Black ●Sail Y.H.
MILES
0   1   2

NATURAL FEATURES

Haystacks stands unabashed and unashamed in the midst of a circle of much loftier fells, like a shaggy terrier in the company of foxhounds, some of them known internationally, but not one of this distinguished group of mountains around Ennerdale and Buttermere can show a greater variety and a more fascinating arrangement of interesting features. Here are sharp peaks in profusion, tarns with islands and tarns without islands, crags, screes, rocks for climbing and rocks not for climbing, heather tracts, marshes, serpentine trails, tarns with streams and tarns with no streams.   All these, with a background of magnificent landscapes, await every visitor to Haystacks but they will be appreciated most by those who go there to linger and explore.   It is a place of surprises around corners, and there are many corners. For a man trying to get a persistent worry out of his mind, the top of Haystacks is a wonderful cure.

The fell rises between the deep hollow of Warnscale Bottom near Gatesgarth, and Ennerdale: between a valley familiar to summer motorists and a valley reached only on foot. It is bounded on the west by Scarth Gap, a pass linking the two. The Buttermere aspect is the better known, although this side is often dark in shadow and seen only as a silhouette against the sky: here, above Warnscale, is a great wall of crags. The Ennerdale flank, open to the sun, is friendlier but steep and rough nevertheless.

Eastwards, beyond the tangle of tors and outcrops forming the boundary of Haystacks on this side, a broad grass slope rises easily and unattractively to Brandreth on the edge of the Borrowdale watershed; beyond is Derwent country.

The spelling of Haystacks as one word is a personal preference of the author (and others), and probably arises from a belief that the name originated from the resemblance of the scattered tors on the summit to stacks of hay in a field. If this were so, the one word *Haystacks* would be correct (as it is in *Haycock*).
But learned authorities state that the name derives from the Icelandic 'stack', meaning 'a columnar rock' and that the true interpretation is *High Rocks* This is logical and appropriate. *High Rocks* is a name of two words and would be wrongly written as *Highrocks*.

The summit tarn

Big Stack,
looking east from a point
near the path to the
summit from
Scarth Gap.

In the picture below
Big Stack appears on
the extreme right.

The north crags,
looking west from the
slopes of Green Crag.

The path is seen
skirting the cliff
on the left.

MAP

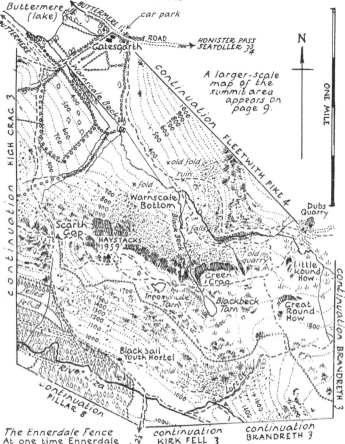

The Ennerdale Fence
At one time Ennerdale was enclosed by a fence nearly twenty miles in length, running along both watersheds and around the head of the valley. The fence was mainly of post and wire, and in most places only the posts survive. On Haystacks the fence has been restored, but it comes to a curiously abrupt end at Scarth Gap. In general, the line of the fence followed parish boundaries but on Haystacks there is considerable deviation. Here the series of iron stakes embedded in rock (erected to mark the boundary of the Lonsdale estate) coincides with the parish boundary, but the fence keeps well to the south of this line.

ASCENT FROM GATESGARTH
1550 feet of ascent : 1¼ miles

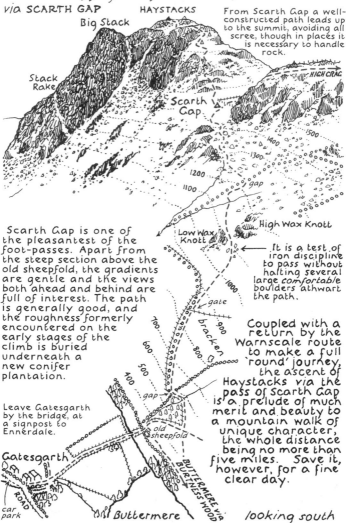

via SCARTH GAP   HAYSTACKS

Big Stack

Stack Rake

HIGH CRAG

Scarth Gap

1500
1400
1300
1200
1100

From Scarth Gap a well-constructed path leads up to the summit, avoiding all scree, though in places it is necessary to handle rock.

gap

High Wax Knott

Low Wax Knott

It is a test of iron discipline to pass without halting several large *comfortable* boulders athwart the path.

Scarth Gap is one of the pleasantest of the foot-passes. Apart from the steep section above the old sheepfold, the gradients are gentle and the views both ahead and behind are full of interest. The path is generally good, and the roughness formerly encountered on the early stages of the climb is buried underneath a new conifer plantation.

1000

gate

900

bracken

700

800

600

500

400

gap

old sheepfold

Leave Gatesgarth by the bridge, at a signpost to Ennerdale.

Coupled with a return by the Warnscale route to make a full 'round' journey, the ascent of Haystacks *via* the pass of Scarth Gap is a prelude of much merit and beauty to a mountain walk of unique character, the whole distance being no more than five miles. Save it, however, for a fine clear day.

Gatesgarth

ROAD

car park

BUTTERMERE via BURTNESS WOOD

Buttermere

looking south

ASCENT FROM GATESGARTH
via WARNSCALE
1600 feet of ascent : 2¾ miles

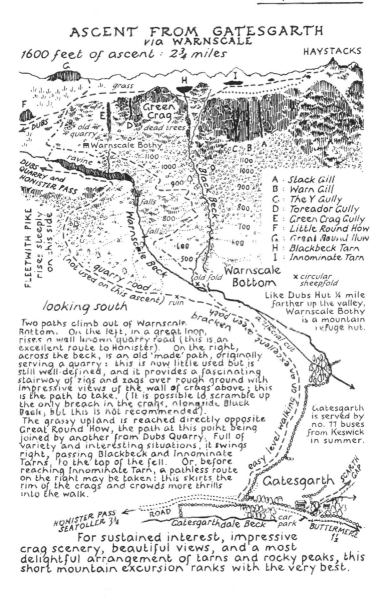

HAYSTACKS

A · Slack Gill
B · Warn Gill
C · The Y Gully
D · Toreador Gully
E · Green Crag Gully
F · Little Round How
G · Great Round How
H · Blackbeck Tarn
I · Innominate Tarn

x circular sheepfold

Like Dubs Hut ¼ mile farther up the valley, Warnscale Bothy is a mountain refuge hut.

looking south

Two paths climb out of Warnscale Bottom. On the left, in a great loop, rises a well known quarry road (this is an excellent route to Honister). On the right, across the beck, is an old 'made' path, originally serving a quarry: this is now little used but is still well-defined, and it provides a fascinating stairway of zigs and zags over rough ground with impressive views of the wall of crags above; this is the path to take. (It is possible to scramble up the only breach in the crags, alongside Black Beck, but this is not recommended).
The grassy upland is reached directly opposite Great Round How, the path at this point being joined by another from Dubs Quarry. Full of variety and interesting situations, it swings right, passing Blackbeck and Innominate Tarns, to the top of the fell. Or, before reaching Innominate Tarn, a pathless route on the right may be taken: this skirts the rim of the crags and crowds more thrills into the walk.

Gatesgarth is served by no. 77 buses from Keswick in summer.

For sustained interest, impressive crag scenery, beautiful views, and a most delightful arrangement of tarns and rocky peaks, this short mountain excursion ranks with the very best.

ASCENT FROM HONISTER PASS
1050 feet of ascent : 2¼ miles

A note of explanation is required.   This ascent-route does not conform to the usual pattern, being more in the nature of an upland cross-country walk than a mountain climb : there are two pronounced descents before foot is set on Haystacks. The wide variety of scene and the fascinating intricacies of the path are justification for the inclusion of the route in this book.

HAYSTACKS

If returning to Honister, note the path to Brandreth just below Innominate Tarn. It is marked by a cairn, but it is very difficult to follow. By using this until it joins the Great Gable path and then swinging left around Dubs Bottom, the Drum House can be regained without extra effort or time.

After traversing the back of Green Crag the path drops to the outlet of Blackbeck Tarn, rising stonily therefrom with a profound abyss on the right. This section is the highlight of the walk.

tarn *1800*

Innominate Tarn

BRANDRETH

Blackbeck Tarn

Green Crag

Great Round How *1600*

Little Round How

grass

WARNSCALE BOTTOM

Dubs Bottom ← stepping stones

1500

1400

WARNSCALE BOTTOM

1500

1600

Dubs Quarry (disused)

BRANDRETH
GREAT GABLE

1700

looking west

foundations of Drum House

1700

1600

old tramway

1500

1400 rock cutting

1300

1200

quarry road

Honister Slate Mine

BUTTERMERE

Honister Pass 1190'

From the hut at Dubs Quarry leave the road and go down to the stream, crossing it (by stepping stones) where its silent meanderings through the Dubs marshes assume a noisy urgency.

From the top of Honister Pass Haystacks is nowhere in sight, and even when it comes into view, after crossing the shoulder of Fleetwith Pike at the Drum House, it is insignificant against the towering background of Pillar, being little higher in altitude and seemingly remote across the wide depression of Dubs Bottom. But, although the route here described is not a natural approach, the elevation of Honister Pass, its car-parking facilities, and the unerring pointer of the tramway make access to Haystacks particularly convenient from this point.

ASCENT FROM ENNERDALE
(BLACK SAIL YOUTH HOSTEL)
970 feet of ascent
1¼ miles

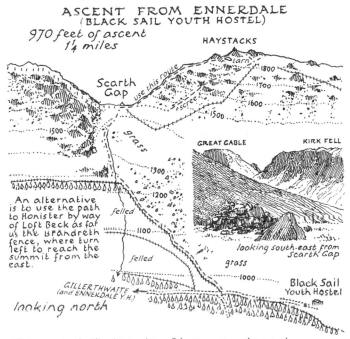

HAYSTACKS

use this route

Scarth Gap

Tarn

1800
1700
1600
1500

scree

grass

1500

1300

GREAT GABLE   KIRK FELL

1200

felled

1100

An alternative
is to use the path
to Honister by way
of Loft Beck as far
as the Brandreth
fence, where turn
left to reach the
summit from the
east.

felled

grass

looking south-east from Scarth Gap

1000

Black Sail
Youth Hostel

GILLERTHWAITE
(and ENNERDALE Y.H.)

looking north

This route is likely to be of interest only to those
staying at the magnificently situated Black Sail
Youth Hostel. This hostel is open to everyone, but those
intending to use it are advised to book well in advance.

formerly a
shepherd's
hut......

Black Sail Youth Hostel

THE SUMMIT

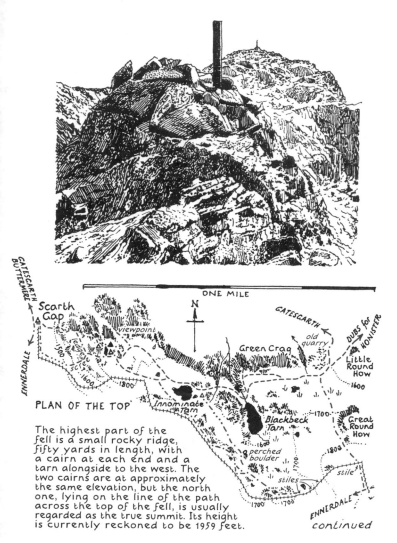

PLAN OF THE TOP

The highest part of the
fell is a small rocky ridge,
fifty yards in length, with
a cairn at each end and a
tarn alongside to the west. The
two cairns are at approximately
the same elevation, but the north
one, lying on the line of the path
across the top of the fell, is usually
regarded as the true summit. Its height
is currently reckoned to be 1959 feet.

continued

THE SUMMIT

continued

Haystacks fails to qualify for inclusion in the author's "best half-dozen" only because of inferior height, a deficiency in vertical measurement. Another thousand feet would have made all the difference.

But for beauty, variety and interesting detail, for sheer fascination and unique individuality, the summit-area of Haystacks is supreme. This is in fact the best fell-top of all — a place of great charm and fairyland attractiveness. Seen from a distance, these qualities are not suspected: indeed, on the contrary, the appearance of Haystacks is almost repellent when viewed from the higher surrounding peaks: black are its bones and black is its flesh. With its thick covering of heather it is dark and sombre even when the sun sparkles the waters of its many tarns, gloomy and mysterious even under a blue sky. There are fierce crags and rough screes and outcrops that will be grittier still when the author's ashes are scattered here. ✕

Yet the combination of features, of tarn and tor, of cliff and cove, the labyrinth of corners and recesses, the maze of old sheepwalks and paths, form a design, or a lack of design, of singular appeal and absorbing interest. One can forget even a raging toothache on Haystacks.

✕ *After his death in 1991, Wainwright's ashes were duly scattered on Haystacks.*

perched boulder on a rock platform

Note the profile in shadow. Some women have faces like that.

On a first visit, learn thoroughly the details of the mile-long main path across the top, a magnificent traverse, because this serves as the best introduction to the geography of the fell.

Having memorised this, several interesting deviations may be made: the parallel alternative above the rim of the north face, the scramble onto Big Stack, the 'cross-country' route around the basin of Blackbeck Tarn, the walk alongside the fence, and so on.

typical summit tors

DESCENTS: A well-made path starts just west of the summit and leads down to Scarth Gap. An alternative path farther south is marred by loose stones and should be avoided. It is advisable to regard the whole of the north edge as highly dangerous. The only advice that can be given to a novice lost on Haystacks *in mist* is that he should kneel down and pray for safe deliverance.

THE VIEW

This is not a case of distance lending enchantment to the view, because apart from a glimpse of Skiddaw above the Robinson-Hindscarth depression and a slice of the Helvellyn range over Honister, the scene is predominantly one of high mountains within a five-mile radius. And really good they look — the enchantment is close at hand. Set in a tight surround, they are seen in revealing detail: a rewarding study deserving leisurely appreciation.

Principal Fells

N

SKIDDAW
SKIDDAW LITTLE MAN

10 miles

FELLBARROW
FELLBARROW
Darling Fell
Low Fell
WHITELESS PIKE
KNOTTS
CRASMOOR
EEL CRAG
WANDOPE
SAIL RIGG
ROBINSON
HINDSCARTH
FLEETWITH PIKE
DALE HEAD

GREAT DODD
STYBARROW DODD
RAISE
WHITE SIDE
HELVELLYN LOWER MAN
HELVELLYN
NETHERMOST PIKE
DOLLYWACCON PIKE
FAIRFIELD

MELLBREAK
(summit not seen)
HIGH STILE
HIGH CRAG

Bowness Knott
Latterbarrow
CRAG FELL
GRIKE

W

CAW FELL
(summit not seen)

ULLSCARF
GREY KNOTTS

E

PILLAR
BRANDRETH
GREEN GABLE
GREAT GABLE
GREAT END
SCAFELL CRAG
SCAFELL PIKE

YEWBARROW
KIRK FELL

5 miles

S

Lakes and Tarns

SE : *Innominate Tarn*
WNW: *Ennerdale Water*
NW : *Crummock Water*
NNW: *Buttermere*

CRASMOOR   WANDOPE   EEL CRAG   SAIL   ROBINSON
WHITELESS PIKE   KNOTT RIGG
High Snockrigg

looking north

RIDGE ROUTES

(map showing HAYSTACKS, Green Crag, GATESCARTH, DUBS QUARRY, Innominate Tarn, Blackbeck Tarn, perched boulder, Great Round How, stile, HONISTER PASS, ENNERDALE, GREEN GABLES, BRANDRETH, contour lines 1800, 1700, 2000, 2100, 2200, 2300, 1900, with N arrow and ONE MILE scale)

To BRANDRETH, 2344': 2 miles
Depression at 1540':
850 feet of ascent
ESE, E, S and SE

The first mile is excellent.

On a clear day a route of one's own choice may be taken over the top of Haystacks, aiming for the corner of the Brandreth fence. But the regular path off Haystacks, by way of Innominate and Blackbeck Tarns, passes through the finest scenery and should certainly be preferred by those to whom it is new, in which case the indefinite junction of the Brandreth path below Great Round How should be watched for carefully — it occurs just before the main path swings left and starts to descend towards Dubs Quarry.

From the corner of the fence there is no cause for further deviation, the fence leading most of the way to the summit of Brandreth up an easy grass slope and crossing two well-known paths in the course of doing so.

To HIGH CRAG, 2443'
1¼ miles : W, then NW
Depression at 1425' (Scarth Gap)
1100 feet of ascent

A fine walk in spite of scree

Follow faithfully the well-made path to the west from the summit, a delightful game of ins and outs and ups and downs. An alternative path south of the summit encounters an area of loose stones and should be avoided. From Scarth Gap a beautiful path climbs through the heather to

(map showing HIGH CRAG, BUTTERMERE, Seat, tarn, Scarth Gap, HAYSTACKS, contour lines 2300, 2100, 2000, 1900, 1800, 1700, 1600, 1500, with N arrow)

High Crag, from Scarth Gap

Seat; then a good ridge follows to the final tower of High Crag: this deteriorates badly into slippery scree on the later stages of the ascent.

HALF A MILE

from Black Sail via the High Level Traverse

The last time we filmed on Pillar was for a programme called *The Wasdale Round*. At Pillar Rock we met a remarkable chap called Ken Ledward. Already in his seventies, he went up it like a mountain goat, despite the fact he had two pot hips. Ken's day job is testing mountain equipment to destruction – tents, waterproofs, walking poles, boots. When we got round to filming the Granada series *Wainwright Country*, one of the things we wanted to do was reflect the dedications Wainwright added to each volume of the Pictorial Guides. The early books were easy – the men of the Ordnance Survey, the men who built the stone walls and so on. But by the time A.W. got to volume six he was dedicating it to 'my right leg and my left leg'.

Having heard somewhere that, to make best use of time, Ken Ledward sometimes tested two sets of boots at the same time – one left and one right – he seemed the ideal candidate. Mind you, what Wainwright would have made of the fancy fell-walking equipment Ken tested is anybody's guess. The thought of A.W. in lycra, sporting a titanium cooking stove and carbon fibre walking poles, doesn't bear thinking about.

A.W. wasn't wearing anything fancy, reflective or high tech the day we took him to the Youth Hostel at Black Sail, nestling under Haystacks at the head of Ennerdale. That was the nearest we managed to get him to Pillar during those months of filming. We'd come up with ever more crafty ways of revisiting places in the mountains he'd thought for years that he'd never see again, but Pillar itself was beyond us.

Yet it didn't matter. That day at Black Sail was a real delight (apart from the little filming difficulties mentioned earlier). The hut was A.W.'s sort of place. A shrine to proper, down-to-earth fell walkers. We sat him on a bench in a sunny window and the spirits of the hills settled on him. There was no rationing that day. He reminisced about every route that led away from the hut. In memory he walked over Scarth Gap into Buttermere, over Black Sail Pass into Mosedale, over Windy Gap to Styhead Tarn. Mountain storms came and went, pin-sharp horizons faded into the blue greys of late afternoon. He remembered great days in the hills from which came his strength and his creative imagination.

Of course, he asked if there was fish and chips on the menu but happily settled for a sandwich and a cup of tea. And then he walked out onto the patch of scrubby grass by the hut and breathed in the summits soaring around him. He spent time with each one in turn so that none would be missed, none offended. I suspect he was slightly nervous about coming back. Didn't want a brief, stumbling visit in old age to take the edge off earlier, more capable, more vibrant memories. But when he finished the roll call he was smiling and his long-drawn-out sigh was as contented as a sigh can be. It was a very special day.

Practical bits

Map: OL4.

Ascent: For *Wainwright Walks*, BBC4 chose the ascent from Ennerdale shown on Pillar 10 in *The Western Fells*; additional summit detail is on Pillar 11. Start at Black Sail Youth Hostel (NY195124). This route skirts Looking Stead but, as AW says, a diversion to the summit is worth it for the views of the high level route ahead. 2000 feet and 2¾ miles.

Descent: Depending on your transport arrangements, there are a number of good descents. If you need to make it a reasonably circular walk – at least ending up in the same valley – take the sharp, direct descent to the memorial bridge in Ennerdale, the reverse of Pillar 13. Alternatively, you can drop in from Black Sail Pass to Wasdale Head, the reverse of the route shown on Pillar 9.

Pillar 2927´

from Brin Crag, Brandreth

NATURAL FEATURES

Great Gable, Pillar and Steeple are the three mountain names on Lakeland maps most likely to fire the imagination of youthful adventurers planning a first tour of the district, inspiring exciting visions of slim, near-vertical pinnacles towering grandly into the sky.

Great Gable lives up to its name, especially if climbed from Wasdale; Pillar has a fine bold outline but is nothing like a pillar; Steeple is closely overlooked by a higher flat-topped fell and not effectively seen.

Pillar, in fact, far from being a spire of slender proportions, is a rugged mass broadly based on half the length of Ennerdale, a series of craggy buttresses supporting the ridge high above this wild north face; and the summit itself, far from being pointed, is wide and flat. The name of the fell therefore clearly derives from a conspicuous feature on the north face directly below the top, the most handsome crag in Lakeland, originally known as the Pillar Stone and now as Pillar Rock. The Rock, despite a remote and lonely situation, had a well-established local notoriety and fame long before tourists called wider attention to it, and an object of such unique appearance simply had to be given a descriptive name, although, at the time, one was not yet needed to identify the mountain of which it formed part. The Pillar was an inspiration of shepherds. Men of letters could not have chosen better.

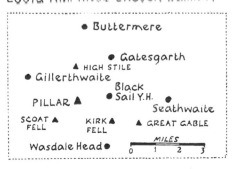

- ● Buttermere
- ● Gatesgarth
- ▲ HIGH STILE
- ● Gillerthwaite
- Black ● Sail Y.H.
- PILLAR ▲
- ●
- Seathwaite
- SCOAT ▲ FELL
- KIRK ▲ FELL
- ▲ GREAT GABLE
- Wasdale Head ●

MILES
0 1 2 3

The north face of the fell has a formidable aspect. Crags and shadowed hollows, scree and tumbled boulders, form a wild, chaotic scene, a setting worthy of a fine mountain.

continued

NATURAL FEATURES

continued

Pillar is the highest mountain west of Great Gable, from which it is sufficiently removed in distance to exhibit distinctive slopes on all sides. It dominates the sunset area of Lakeland superbly, springing out of the valleys of Mosedale and Ennerdale, steeply on the one side and dramatically on the other, as befits the overlord of the western scene. A narrow neck of land connects with a chain of other grand fells to the south, and a depression forms the east boundary and is crossed by Black Sail Pass at 1800', but elsewhere the full height of the fell from valley level is displayed. Some of the streams flow west via Ennerdale Water and some south via Wast Water, but their fate, discharge into the Irish Sea from the coast near Seascale, is the same, only a few miles separating the two outlets.

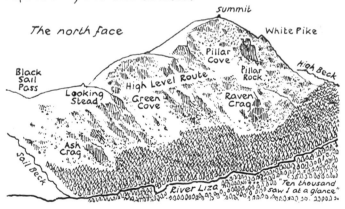

The north face

summit

White Pike

Black Sail Pass

Looking Stead

Green Cove

High Level Route

Pillar Cove

Pillar Rock

Raven Crag

High Beck

Ash Crag

Sail Beck

River Liza

"ten thousand saw I at a glance"

Afforestation in Ennerdale has cloaked the lower slopes on this side in a dark and funereal shroud of foreign trees, an intrusion that nobody who knew Ennerdale of old can ever forgive, the former charm of the valley having been destroyed thereby. We condemn vandalism and sanction this mess! Far better the old desolation of boulder and bog when a man could see the sky, than this new desolation of regimented timber shutting out the light of day. It is an offence to the eyes to see Pillar's once-colourful fellside now hobbled in such a dowdy and ill-suited skirt, just as it is to see a noble animal caught in a trap. Yet, such is the majesty and power of this fine mountain that it can shrug off the insults and indignities, and its summit soars no less proudly above. It is the admirers of this grand pile who feel the hurt.

A Pillar Rock
portfolio

from the east

Pillar 5

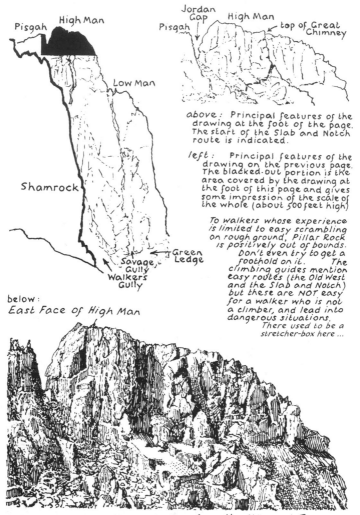

Pisgah High Man

Low Man

Shamrock

below:
East Face of High Man

Savage
Gully
Walkers
Gully

← Green
Ledge

Jordan
Gap
Pisgah High Man   top of Great
Chimney

above: Principal features of the
drawing at the foot of the page.
The start of the Slab and Notch
route is indicated.

left: Principal features of the
drawing on the previous page.
The blacked-out portion is the
area covered by the drawing at
the foot of this page and gives
some impression of the scale of
the whole (about 500 feet high)

To walkers whose experience
is limited to easy scrambling
on rough ground, Pillar Rock
is positively out of bounds.
Don't even try to get a
foothold on it.   The
climbing guides mention
easy routes (the Old West
and the Slab and Notch)
but these are NOT easy
for a walker who is not
a climber, and lead into
dangerous situations.
          There used to be a
stretcher-box here ...

as seen from the Shamrock Traverse.

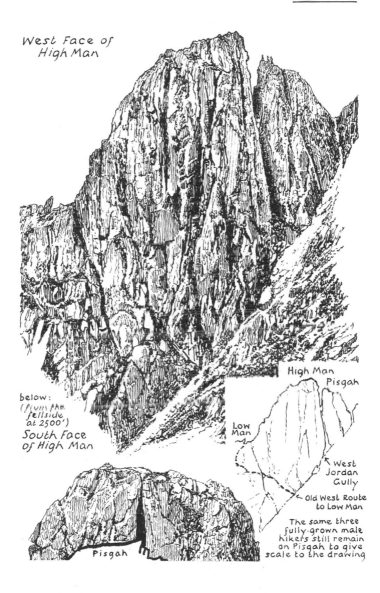

West Face of
High Man

below:
(from the
fellside
at 2500')
South Face
of High Man

Pisgah

High Man
Pisgah

Low
Man

← West
Jordan
Gully

← Old West Route
to Low Man

The same three
fully-grown male
hikers still remain
on Pisgah to give
scale to the drawing

MAP

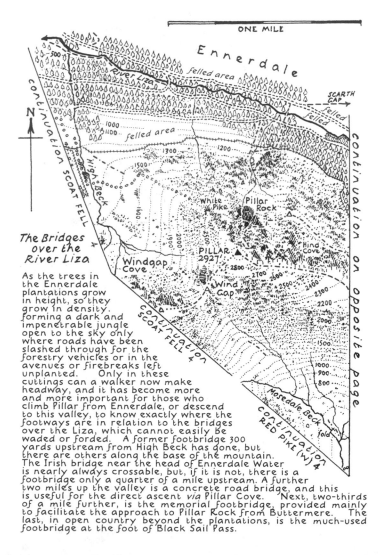

ONE MILE

E n n e r d a l e

SCARTH GAP →

felled area

felled

felled

River Liza

500

1000

1100

felled area

1300

1200

continuation SCOAT FELL →

N ↑

High Beck

White Pike

Pillar Rock

1500

1900

2000

2500

PILLAR 2927

2800

Hind Cove

2700

2600

2500

2400

2300

2200

2000

1500

1000

900

800

Windgap Cove

Wind Gap

continuation on opposite page

continuation SCOAT FELL →

Moredale Beck

continuation RED PIKE (W) →

fold

The Bridges over the River Liza

As the trees in the Ennerdale plantations grow in height, so they grow in density, forming a dark and impenetrable jungle open to the sky only where roads have been slashed through for the forestry vehicles or in the avenues or firebreaks left unplanted.   Only in these cuttings can a walker now make headway, and it has become more and more important for those who climb Pillar from Ennerdale, or descend to this valley, to know exactly where the footways are in relation to the bridges over the Liza, which cannot easily be waded or forded.   A former footbridge 300 yards upstream from High Beck has gone, but there are others along the base of the mountain. The Irish bridge near the head of Ennerdale Water is nearly always crossable, but, if it is not, there is a footbridge only a quarter of a mile upstream. A further two miles up the valley is a concrete road bridge, and this is useful for the direct ascent via Pillar Cove.   Next, two-thirds of a mile further, is the memorial footbridge, provided mainly to facilitate the approach to Pillar Rock from Buttermere.   The last, in open country beyond the plantations, is the much-used footbridge at the foot of Black Sail Pass.

MAP

Black Sail is the most remote youth hostel in the Lake District, being 6 miles along the valley from the public car park at Bowness Point. The hostel is open to all but it is advisable to book well in advance.

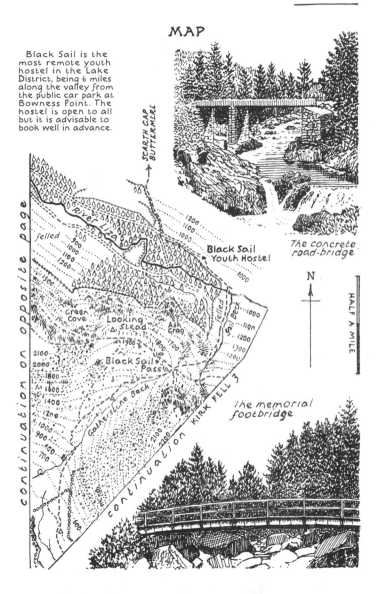

The concrete road-bridge

The memorial footbridge

SCARTH GAP BUTTERMERE

River Liza

felled

Black Sail Youth Hostel

Green Cove

Looking Stead

Ash Crag

Sail Beck

felled

Black Sail Pass

Gatherstone Beck

continuation on opposite page

continuation KIRK FELL 3

N

HALF A MILE

ASCENT FROM WASDALE HEAD

2700 feet of ascent
4½ miles via Black Sail Pass
3¼ miles via Wind Gap

The short cut is not really a time-saver in ascent, the better plan being to go on to the top of the pass and do the whole ridge.

looking north

PILLAR

Wind Gap
2500

2600
2500
2400
2300
2200
2100
2000
1900
1800
1700
1600
1500
1400
1300
1200
1100
1000
900
800
700

Wistow Crags

grass

At this point the High Level route goes off to the right (see next page)

Looking Stead
Black Sail Pass

grass

tarn

short cut

paved

1800
1500

last water on the ascent

Gatherstone Beck

Indistinct track on a rising tongue of grass

old bield

grass

Wind Gap

scree shoot

fold

Mosedale Beck

bracken

pen

800

700

Wind Gap

scree shoot

If using the Wind Gap route, be careful to identify the Gap correctly from the valley. It is clearly in sight and identifiable by its long scree-run. But note that the Gap is not the true head of the valley, this being Blackem Head away to the left, where Mosedale Beck has its source.

The usual route (via Black Sail Pass and the ridge) is an excellent walk and the easiest way to any of the Wasdale summits. A good walker will do it nonstop.
The more direct Wind Gap route is out of favour, being more confined, less attractive in its views, and damned by an unpleasant and unavoidable scree-run.

Mosedale

The Wind Gap route turns (indistinctly) from the Black Sail path at the cairn at 500'.

600
500
400
300

Don't go wrong at the very start! The way lies NOT over the bridge but along the bank of the stream, passing behind the farmhouse of Row Head.

Wasdale Head
Row Head
Inn

ASCENT FROM ENNERDALE
(BLACK SAIL YOUTH HOSTEL)
2000 feet of ascent : 2¾ miles
(2100 feet, 3 miles
by High Level Route)

The main ridge, from Black Sail Pass to the summit, is a pleasant walk without difficulty, three stony rises being succeeded by splendid turf. A line of iron posts accompanies the ridge but the path, in many places, deviates to the left. The High Level route is a traverse across the fellside (aiming for Pillar Rock), not a way to the summit, although the two can be connected (see next page). This is a fine pedestrian way, highly recommended, rough but not difficult.

Originally the High Level Route had an awkward start. A new variation avoids the difficulty.

PILLAR

Great Doup

Hind Cove

Green Cove

grass

Pillar Rock

Robinson's Cairn

High Level Route

← detail →

2700
2600
2500
2400
2300
2100

Looking Stead

WASDALE HEAD
direct route

1900

tarn

1800

WASDALE HEAD

1700

Black Sail Pass

1600

There is a gate at the top of the pass but only a fanatical purist would think of using it.

The path avoids the actual top of Looking Stead, but walkers should not. It is an excellent viewpoint for a survey, both of the High Level route and of Ennerdale.

Main ridge :
1 : zigzag path
2 : direct path
High Level route :
3 : original start
4 : new variation
Main ridge :
5 : from Black Sail

Ash Crag

1500
1400
1300
1200
1100

River Liza

Sojourners at the hostel are fortunate in having Pillar on their doorstep, and can enjoy one of the best days of their young lives by climbing it.

felled
Sail Beck
1100

1100

1000

Black Sail Y.H.

moraines

looking west

Robinson's Cairn to the summit

The end of the Traverse with stretcher box (now gone)

Pisgah

summit

2800
2700
Great Doup
2600
2500
steep loose scree slope
Pisgah
High Man
Pillar Rock
Shamrock Traverse
2400
2300
Low Man
start of Traverse
2200
scree slope
Shamrock
2100
low rock ridge
slight descent across a bouldery hollow
High Level Route
△ Robinson's Cairn

There are no difficulties or dangers on this route *provided the path is kept underfoot*. There ARE difficulties and dangers if exploratory deviations are attempted, especially on the Traverse. The walking is rough, but not steep; the track is loose and stony, but safe. The rock-scenery is magnificent.

The start of the Traverse (a wide, tilted shelf or rake)

Robinson's Cairn

—a memorial to JOHN WILSON ROBINSON, a pioneer fellwalker and rock-climber; a man sincerely devoted to the fells. A tablet, beautifully worded, is affixed to a nearby rock.

ASCENT FROM ENNERDALE
(HIGH GILLERTHWAITE)

2500 feet of ascent
3¼ miles (A) : 2¾ miles (B)

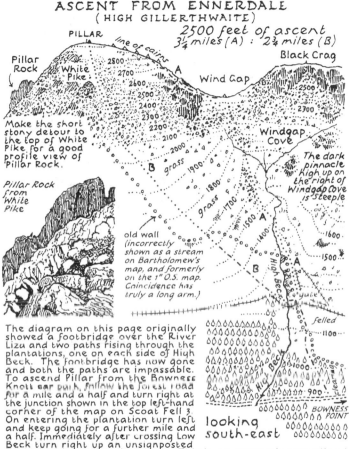

PILLAR

line of cairns

Pillar Rock

White Pike

Black Crag

Wind Gap

2800
2700
2600
2500
2400
2300
2200
2100
2000
1900
1800
1700
1600
1500
1400

2500
2300

A

B

Windgap Cove

The dark pinnacle high up on the right of Windgap Cove is Steeple

Make the short stony detour to the top of White Pike for a good profile view of Pillar Rock.

Pillar Rock from White Pike

old wall (incorrectly shown as a stream on Bartholomew's map, and formerly on the 1" O.S. map. Coincidence has truly a long arm.)

grass

grass

High Beck

gate

felled

1600
1500
1100
1000
900

BOWNESS POINT

looking south-east

The diagram on this page originally showed a footbridge over the River Liza and two paths rising through the plantations, one on each side of High Beck. The footbridge has now gone and both the paths are impassable. To ascend Pillar from the Bowness Knott car park, follow the forest road for a mile and a half and turn right at the junction shown in the top left-hand corner of the map on Scoat Fell 3. On entering the plantation turn left and keep going for a further mile and a half. Immediately after crossing Low Beck turn right up an unsignposted path that is easily missed. This is an attractive woodland path alongside a steep-sided ravine and comes as a surprise. A hundred yards up the hill there is a signpost to Pillar. The route is obvious here, but it is reassuring to know that you have come the right way. When you come to a forest road turn left. From here onwards the route is shown on the diagram on this page. Thirty yards past a cleared strip take a path on the right, again unsignposted, and continue through a felled area to a gate. Above the gate, two routes are given. Route A is the more usual, and a recognised pass between Ennerdale and Wasdale, but Route B is an obvious alternative up the north-west ridge, easy to 2000' and then very stony.

ASCENT FROM ENNERDALE
(direct from THE MEMORIAL FOOTBRIDGE)

2250 feet of ascent
1¼ miles

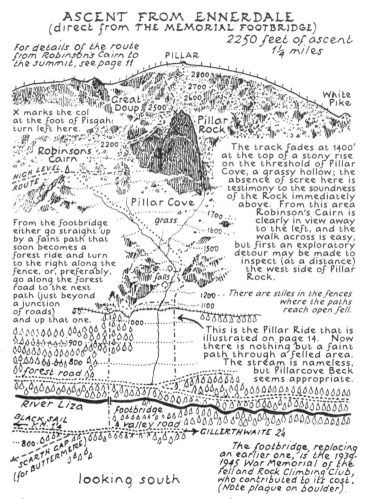

For details of the route from Robinson's Cairn to the summit, see page 11

X marks the col at the foot of Pisgah: turn left here.

The track fades at 1400' at the top of a stony rise on the threshold of Pillar Cove, a grassy hollow; the absence of scree here is testimony to the soundness of the Rock immediately above. From this area Robinson's Cairn is clearly in view away to the left, and the walk across is easy, but first an exploratory detour may be made to inspect (at a distance) the west side of Pillar Rock.

From the footbridge either go straight up by a faint path that soon becomes a forest ride and turn to the right along the fence, or, preferably, go along the forest road to the next path (just beyond a junction of roads) and up that one.

There are stiles in the fences where the paths reach open fell.

This is the Pillar Ride that is illustrated on page 14. Now there is nothing but a faint path through a felled area. The stream is nameless, but Pillarcove Beck seems appropriate.

The footbridge, replacing an earlier one, is the 1939-1945 War Memorial of the Fell and Rock Climbing Club, who contributed to its cost. (Note plaque on boulder).

looking south

A steep and rough, but romantic and adventurous climb in magnificent surroundings: the finest way up the mountain. Pillar Rock grips the attention throughout. Unfortunately the route is somewhat remote from tourist centres, but strong walkers can do it from Buttermere via Scarth Gap.

ASCENT FROM BUTTERMERE

Most walkers when planning to climb a mountain aim to avoid any downhill section between their starting-point and the summit, and if the intermediate descent is considerable the extra effort of regaining lost height may rule out the attempt altogether. A good example is Great Gable from Langdale, where the descent from Esk Hause to Sty Head is a loss of height of 700 feet and a double loss of this amount if returning to Langdale. Plus the 3000' of effective ascent this is too much for the average walker. Distance is of less consequence. The same applies to ascent of Pillar from Buttermere. This is a glorious walk, full of interest, but it cannot be done without first climbing the High Stile range (at Scarth Gap) and then descending into Ennerdale before setting foot on Pillar. If returning to Buttermere, Ennerdale and the High Stile range will have to be crossed again towards the end of an exhausting day. There is no sadder sight than a Buttermere-bound pedestrian crossing Scarth Gap on his hands and knees as the shadows of evening steal o'er the scene. *The route is therefore recommended for strong walkers only.*

The most thrilling line of ascent of Pillar is by way of the memorial footbridge, this being very conveniently situated for the Buttermere approach (the bridge was, in fact, provided to give access to Pillar from this direction). A slanting route down to the footbridge leaves the Scarth Gap path some 150 yards on the Ennerdale side of the pass. The bifurcation is not clear, but the track goes off to the right above the plantation, becoming distinct and crossing the fences by three stiles. The climb from the bridge is described on the opposite page. A less arduous route of ascent is to keep to the Scarth Gap path into Ennerdale and climb out of the valley by Black Sail Pass to its top, where follow the ridge on the right — but this easier way had better be reserved for the return when energy is flagging.

To find the slanting path from Scarth Gap look for the rocky knoll, with tree (illustrated) and turn right on grass above it

Via the footbridge : 3550 feet of ascent · 5¼ miles
Via Black Sail Pass : 3250 feet of ascent · 6¼ miles

Pillar Rock, from the north

The Pillar Ride

THE SUMMIT

shelter   north shelter

As in the case of many fells of rugged appearance, the summit is one of the smoothest places on Pillar, and one may perambulate within a 50-yard radius of the cairn without being aware of the declivities on all sides. There are stones, but grass predominates. The number of erections, including two wind-shelters and a survey column, testifies to the importance of the summit in the esteem of fellwalkers and map-makers.

DESCENTS

To Wasdale Head : In fair weather or foul, there is one royal road down to Wasdale Head, and that is by the eastern ridge to join Black Sail Pass on its journey thereto. The views are superb, and the walking is so easy for the most part that they can be enjoyed while on the move. There should be no difficulty in following the path in mist — only in one cairned section is it indistinct — but the fence-posts are there in any event as a guide to the top of the Pass. The improved path from Black Sail Pass is preferable to the short cut from Looking Stead. The route into Mosedale *via* Wind Gap is much less satisfactory, and no quicker although shorter. Another way into Mosedale sometimes used is the obvious scree-gully opening off the ridge opposite the head of Great Doup, but why suffer the torture of a half-mile of loose stones when the ridge is so much easier and pleasanter?

To Ennerdale : If bound for Black Sail Hostel, follow the eastern ridge to the pass, and there turn left on a clear path. If bound for Ennerdale Youth Hostel (High Gillerthwaite) or places west, head northwest to White Pike and its ridge, which has a rough section of boulders below the Pike; but in stormy weather prefer the route joining High Beck from Wind Gap.

To Buttermere : In clear weather, the direct route climbing up out of Ennerdale may be reversed; at the forest road beyond the memorial footbridge walk up the valley for 120 yards, then taking a slanting path through the plantation on the left to Scarth Gap. In bad conditions, it is safer to go round by Black Sail Pass.

To any of the above destinations via Robinson's Cairn

Leave the summit at the north wind-shelter. Pillar Rock comes into view at once, and a path with many bends leads down to the point where the first of its buttresses (Pisgah) rises from the fellside. Here turn right (where there was once a stretcher box) and along the Traverse to easy ground and the Cairn. On no account descend the hollow to the right of Pisgah: this narrows to a dangerous funnel of stones and a sheer drop into a gully. (This is known as Walker's Gully, NOT because it is a gully for walkers, but because a man of this name fell to his death here).

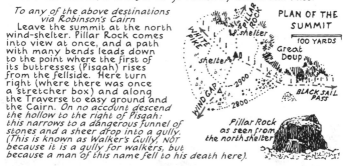

PLAN OF THE SUMMIT

PILLAR ROCK

WHITE PIKE

W. shelter

Great Doup

shelter

WIND GAP — 2900

2800

BLACK SAIL PASS

100 YARDS

Pillar Rock as seen from the north shelter

RIDGE ROUTES

To SCOAT FELL, 2760': 1¼ miles: WSW
Depression at 2480' (Wind Gap): 300 feet of ascent
A fine little journey in spectacular scenery.

After an indefinite start, a line of cairns leads down to Wind Gap, the last stage of the descent being steep and rough, but not difficult. Beyond the Gap a clear path goes up the facing slope into the boulders preceding the easy grassy promenade along the top above Black Crag. Then follows a slight loss of height before the final rise to Scoat Fell, the summit wall of which is joined in a chaotic pile of boulders.

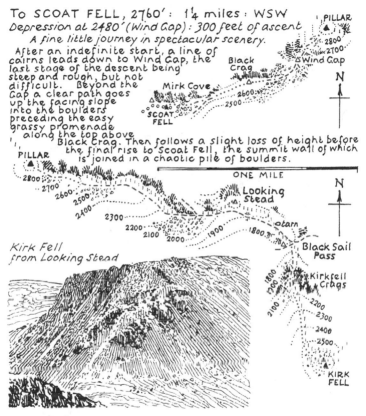

Kirk Fell from Looking Stead

To KIRK FELL, 2630': 2½ miles: ESE, then S
Depression at 1800' (Black Sail Pass): 850 feet of ascent
Excellent views, both near and far; a good walk

The Ennerdale fence (what is left of it) links the two tops, and the route never ventures far from it. The eastern ridge of Pillar offers a speedy descent, the path being clear except on one grassy section, which is, however, well cairned. At the Pass, the crags of Kirk Fell look ferocious and hostile, but a thin track goes off bravely to tackle them and can be relied upon to lead to the dull top of Kirk Fell after providing a minor excitement where a high rock step needs to be surmounted.

THE VIEW

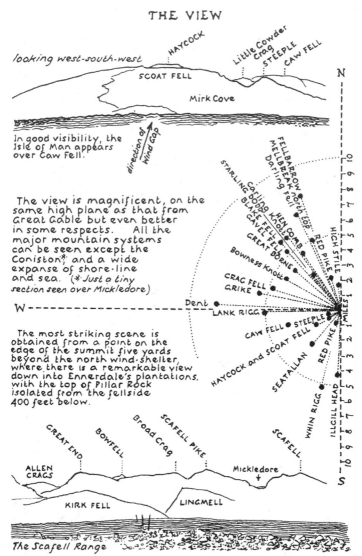

looking west-south-west

HAYCOCK

Little Cowder Crag

STEEPLE

CAW FELL

SCOAT FELL

Mirk Cove

N

In good visibility, the Isle of Man appears over Caw Fell.

direction of wind gap

The view is magnificent, on the same high plane as that from Great Gable but even better in some respects. All the major mountain systems can be seen except the Coniston*, and a wide expanse of shore-line and sea. (*Just a tiny section seen over Mickledore*)

FELLBARROW
MELLBREAK North Top
Darling Fell
STARLING DODD
CARLING KNOTT
HEN COMB
BLAKE FELL
GAVEL FELL
GREAT BORNE
Bowness Knott
CRAG FELL
GRIKE

HIGH STILE

RED PIKE

W - - - - - - - - - - - - - - Dent

LANK RIGG

CAW FELL   STEEPLE

HAYCOCK and SCOAT FELL

SEATALLAN

WHIN RIGG

RED PIKE

ILLGILL HEAD

The most striking scene is obtained from a point on the edge of the summit five yards beyond the north wind-shelter, where there is a remarkable view down into Ennerdale's plantations, with the top of Pillar Rock isolated from the fellside 400 feet below.

S

GREAT END

BOWFELL

Broad Crag

SCAFELL PIKE

SCAFELL

ALLEN CRAGS

Mickledore

KIRK FELL

LINGMELL

The Scafell Range

THE VIEW

Principal Fells

Lakes and Tarns

SSE : *Eel Tarn*
SSE : *Burnmoor Tarn*
WNW : *Ennerdale Water*
NNW : *Loweswater*

Innominate Tarn on Haystacks, ENE, is brought in the view by walking 10 yards from the column eastwards

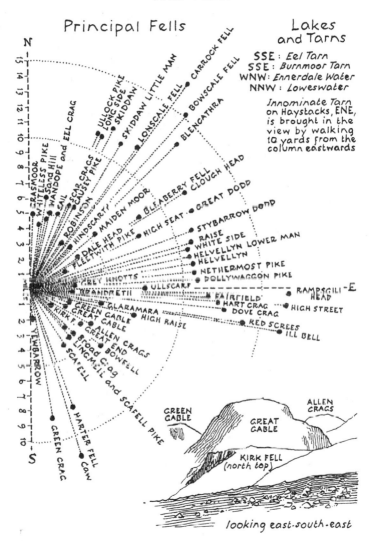

looking east-south-east

17 Yewbarrow
from Overbeck Bridge

You'd be hard pushed to find another mile and a half of this quality anywhere in Britain. Now, there may be a certain bias in that remark, given that the Wasdale Valley is my favourite place on earth. I've lived there for the best part of twenty-five years and have no intention of leaving while still vertical.

Wainwright loved it almost as much. 'The road along the side of Wast Water emerges from the trees into a naked and savage landscape that stuns the senses … ahead, in a blinding revelation, is a scene almost brutal in its wildness and desolation.' So there you are. If you're of a nervous disposition stay away. The place can have the strangest effect on people. I know of bold young climbers who came to work in the valley because they'd be close to the big mountains but who couldn't hack the sunless solitude of a Wasdale winter and ran away. I once met a couple who'd taken their caravan to Wasdale Head. The wife insisted it was sold there because she refused to let her husband take it back down the valley past the glowering lake.

It can be a fearsome place but it has a whimsical side too. The lake shore is a favourite haunt of amateur divers and it's said they've created an underwater community of garden gnomes on the lake bed. That's certainly a tale that would have tickled the fancy of old Will Ritson who once owned the Wasdale Head Inn and was, by reputation, the world's biggest liar.

We've filmed time and again in Wasdale, often in conditions that tested men and electronics to the limit, but the soakings and freezings were more than compensated for by the scenes of glory that we were able to capture between the squalls and flurries. One afternoon, high on the Yewbarrow side of the valley. we watched a great storm approach from the Isle of Man. It drenched us as it passed and then squabbled with the mountains at the valley head, blackening and thundering around the peaks. Then out of the blackness rose a double rainbow spanning the lake.

The valley's dominated by the 1800 ft high wall of shifting rock that's the Wastwater Screes. It captures the light like a multi-facetted mirror changing, extraordinarily, from grey to mauve, from orange to red depending on the conditions. From Yewbarrow we'll get great views of them.

There was another phenomenon in Wasdale that fascinated Wainwright, a strand of fence wire on legs called Joss Naylor. He was once one of the greatest fell runners in the world and A.W., the self-confessed plodder, marvelled at the stamina of a man who ran all 214 Pictorial Guides summits in a week. If he'd still been around to see it, he would have marvelled even more when Joss ran the sixty highest peaks in Lakeland to celebrate his sixtieth birthday and ticked off seventy peaks to mark his seventieth. For many years Joss farmed at Bowderdale by Overbeck Bridge where we start our ascent of Yewbarrow. When Fred Talbot set off to film the walk for *Wainwright Country* I didn't tell him that Joss would sometimes train on Yewbarrow and go up and down our route in twenty-four minutes. I thought it might be dispiriting.

Practical bits
Map: OL6.
Ascent: Start at Overbeck Bridge on the main Wasdale Valley road (NY168069). The route we're taking is on Yewbarrow 5 in *The Western Fells*: 1½ miles and 1900 feet.
Descent: Wainwright's Yewbarrow 6, which is a slog to the summit in reverse, makes a spectacular descent with grand views of the best valley head in Lakeland (2½ miles and 1900 feet of descent).

A great time to do this walk is the second Saturday in October when, on the way down, you can call into the beer tent at the Wasdale Head Show. It's a fine valley tradition, a reminder of the shepherds' meets held in every Lakeland valley, where shepherds would get together once a year to gather up stray sheep that had wandered from their hefts on the mountain tops.

Yewbarrow

2058′

RED PIKE ▲

YEWBARROW ▲   ● Wasdale Head

▲ MIDDLE FELL
● Bowderdale

MILES
0 1 2 3 4

from Netherbeck Bridge

NATURAL FEATURES

Many mountains have been described as having the shape of the inverted hull of a boat, but none of them more fittingly than Yewbarrow, which extends along the west side of Wasdale for two miles as a high and narrow ridge, the prow and the stern coming sharply down to valley level with many barnacled incrustations. These latter roughnesses make the long summit rather difficult of attainment from either end, while the steep sides also deter ascent, so that Yewbarrow is not often climbed although it is a centre-piece of magnificent fell country and commands thrilling views. Nor is the ridge itself without incident, one feature in particular, Great Door, being a remarkable cleft where the crest narrows at the top of the craggy declivity above Wastwater.

Yewbarrow's western side is well defined by Over Beck, which comes down from Dore Head, the col linking the fell with Red Pike and the Pillar group. At one time, Dore Head had the reputation of providing the best scree-run in the district on its northern side, descending to Mosedale, but generations of booted scree-runners have scraped the passage clean in places and left it dangerously slippery.

left : Dropping Crag

below : Dropping Crag and Bell Rib, on the approach up the south ridge.

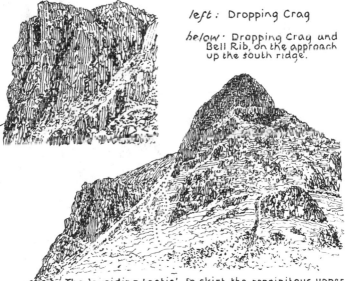

The 'avoiding tactic', to skirt the precipitous upper rocks of Bell Rib, is indicated by a dotted line.

above:

Great Door, as it is seen on the descent of the south ridge. The line of escape from this *impasse* is indicated (→)

The South Ridge

right: Just before reaching Great Door on the descent, a similar cleft is met which might be mistaken for it; this, however, is rounded without difficulty.

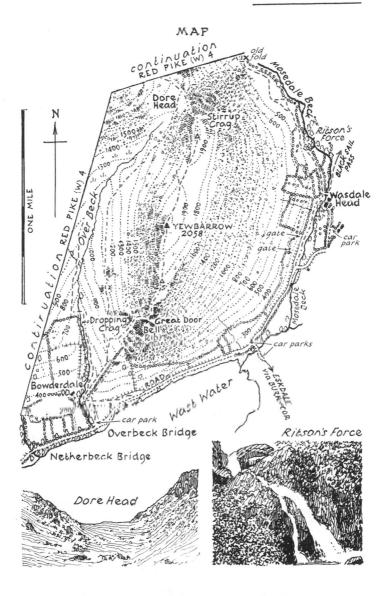

MAP

continuation
RED PIKE (W) 4

old fold

Mosedale Beck

Dore Head

Stirrup Crag

Ritson's Force

BLACK SAIL PASS

ONE MILE

N

Over Beck

1500
1400
1300

1900
1800

YEWBARROW
2058

1900 1800

1700

1600

1500

1400

1300 1200

1100
1000
900
800

700
600
500

gate
gate

Wasdale Head

car park

continuation RED PIKE (W) 4

1000

800

700
600
500

400
300

Dropping Crag

Great Door

Bell

Rib

car parks

ESKDALE VIA BURN MOOR

Bowderdale

700
600
500
400

ROAD

West Water

Mosedale Beck

car park

Overbeck Bridge

Netherbeck Bridge

Dore Head

Ritson's Force

ASCENT FROM WASDALE
(OVERBECK BRIDGE)
1900 feet of ascent : 1½ miles

Very prominent in the early stages of the ascent is the towering pinnacle of Bell Rib, directly astride the ridge. Bell Rib cannot be climbed by a non-expert, and maps that show a path straight up it are telling fibs.

From the wall take the slanting track towards Dropping Crag and scramble up the steep but easy grass to the right of it, entering higher a constricted gully full of loose stones, where progress is better on the simple rocks to the left. At the top of the gully, on an open slope, climb half-right to reach the ridge exactly, suddenly and dramatically at Great Door: a thrilling moment. The top of Bell Rib is here only a few rocky yards away on the right.

Turn left, now on a path, following the ridge to the summit.

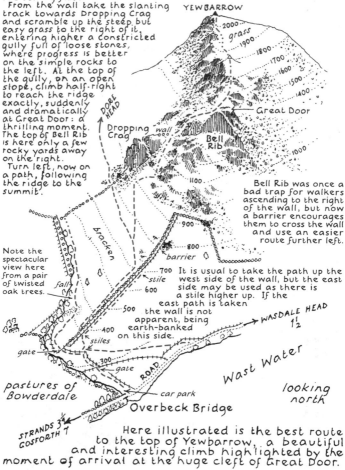

Bell Rib was once a bad trap for walkers ascending to the right of the wall, but now a barrier encourages them to cross the wall and use an easier route further left.

Note the spectacular view here from a pair of twisted oak trees.

It is usual to take the path up the west side of the wall, but the east side may be used as there is a stile higher up. If the east path is taken the wall is not apparent, being earth-banked on this side.

Here illustrated is the best route to the top of Yewbarrow, a beautiful and interesting climb highlighted by the moment of arrival at the huge cleft of Great Door.

ASCENT FROM WASDALE HEAD
1900 feet of ascent : 2½ miles

Start the climb to Dore Head from the path at the foot of the slope below it; short cuts across the boulders are not rewarding. Keep to the grass on the right of the scree-run.

From Dore Head, Stirrup Crag looks very formidable, and the upper band of rock unassailable, but getting up it is nothing more than a strenuous exercise in elementary gymnastics and unusual postures. The way lies within the confines of rocky cracks and chimneys, and there is no sense of danger or indecent exposure.

Follow the trail of blood left by the author, or, if the elements have removed this evidence of his sufferings, the debris of dentures, bootsoles, etc., left by other pilgrims, and step happily onto the pleasant top. Between this point and the summit of the fell is a wide depression.

Those of faint heart may avoid Stirrup Crag entirely by proceeding from Dore Head towards Over Beck, turning up a grass slope to the depression when the boulders cease.

For such, the author bled in vain.

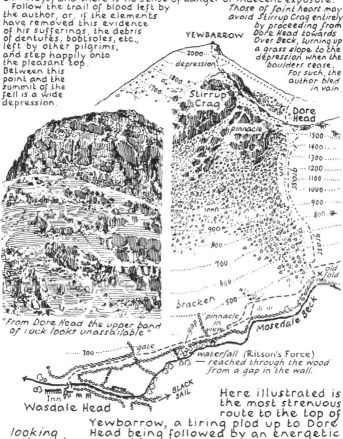

YEWBARROW

2000 .... depression

1800

1700

Stirrup Crag

Dore Head

pinnacle

1500
1400
1300
1200
1100
1000
900
800

grass

1000

900

800

700

grass

600

old fold

bracken 500

pinnacle in view

gap

Mosedale Beck

300 .... gate

waterfall (Ritson's Force) — reached through the wood from a gap in the wall.

Inn
Wasdale Head

BLACK SAIL

looking south-west

"From Dore Head the upper band of rock looks unassailable"

Here illustrated is the most strenuous route to the top of Yewbarrow, a tiring plod up to Dore Head being followed by an energetic scramble up a rocky rampart.

THE SUMMIT

KIRK FELL   GREAT GABLE   HELVELLYN   GLARAMARA

After the agonies and perils of the ascent it is an anticlimax to find the summit a peaceful and placid sheep pasture, an elevated field, with the cairn crowning a rocky outcrop.

DESCENTS: The usual descents by way of the ridge, north or south, encounter rock and need care. The south ridge, at first easy, narrows to the width of the path at Great Door in exciting surroundings. The natural continuation of the ridge lies up the facing rocks onto the top of Bell Rib, *but do NOT venture into this bad trap*; instead, at this point, turn down the slope ON THE RIGHT into a short rocky gully where loose stones are a menace and skirt the lower buttresses of Bell Rib to regain the ridge at a wall, whence an easy slope leads down to Overbeck Bridge. The north ridge route crosses a depression, rises to the cairned top of Stirrup Crag, and then drops steeply and sharply down a series of rocky cracks in the crag for a few desperate minutes: a bad passage, but neither dangerous nor difficult if care is taken. If all goes well, Dore Head, immediately below, is then soon reached at the top of the scree-run into Mosedale. Those who do not fancy steep rocks can avoid Stirrup Crag entirely by slanting down left from the depression; *in bad conditions, this is the best way off the fell.* A descent may be made direct to Wasdale Head from the summit cairn, but note that the only gate in the intake wall is that shown on page 4.

RED PIKE

2600
2500
2400

The Chair

2625

2300
2200
2100
2000

1600

Dore Head   Stirrup Crag

1500
1600
1700

1900   1800

YEWBARROW

The use of the Bottom in Mountaineering.

A fellwalker's best asset is a pair of strong legs; next best is a tough and rubbery bottom. In ascent this appendage is, of course, useless, but when descending steep grass or rocks such as are met on the ridge of Yewbarrow the posterior is a valuable agent of friction, a sheet-anchor with superb resistance to the pull of gravity.

RIDGE ROUTE
TO RED PIKE, 2707'

1¼ miles: NNE, NW and N
*Depression at 1520'
1350 feet of ascent*

Reach Dore Head over Stirrup Crag or by the variation, as described above; then follow the fair track up the opposite slope. An excellent journey.

N

HALF A MILE

THE VIEW

1: RED PIKE
2: Black Crag
3: Wind Gap
4: PILLAR

Principal Fells

N

ROBINSON
HINDSCARTH

12½ miles
10 miles

SKIDDAW
SKIDDAW LITTLE MAN

HELVELLYN

PILLAR
Black Crag
RED PIKE
SCOAT FELL
(Summit)
HAYCOCK
CAW FELL
Dent

KIRK FELL
GREAT GABLE
CLARAMARA
SEATHWAITE FELL

W — SEATALLAN
GREAT END
LINGMELL
Broad Crag
SCAFELL PIKE
— E

MIDDLE FELL
2½
5 miles
WHIN RIGG
ILLGILL HEAD
7½ miles

SCAFELL
SLIGHT SIDE

HARTER FELL
Cow
GREEN CRAG
Stickle Pike

CONISTON OLD MAN
DOW CRAG

S

Lakes and Tarns
SSE: Burnmoor Tarn
SW: Wast Water
NW: Low Tarn

It is a feather in Yewbarrow's cap that all four of the Lakeland 3,000-footers can be seen from its modest summit, but this is a freak of its position and not an indication that the view is everywhere extensive: in fact it is severely restricted by the neighbouring loftier fells around Wasdale. However, most visitors to the cairn will be content to study this nearby array of noble peaks.

1: ROBINSON   2: SKIDDAW
3: SKIDDAW LITTLE MAN
4: HINDSCARTH   5: Black Sail
Pass 6: Top of Stirrup Crag

from Gatherstone Head

Yewbarrow is one of only two fells in the
Pictorial Guides with an odd number of pages.
So this page is blank.

18 Stickle Pike
from Broughton Mills

When the Wainwright Society decided to mark the fiftieth anniversary of the publication of the first Pictorial Guide by organising ascents of all 214 Wainwright summits plus the fifty-six in his book *The Outlying Fells of Lakeland*, I stuck out for chairman's perks. I snaffled Stickle Pike. Ever since Wainwright introduced me to it, describing it as his mini Matterhorn, it's been my favourite little summit in all of Lakeland.

We filmed it on a truly, madly, deeply, glorious day for *Wainwright's Remote Lakeland*. The crew had a spring in their step, so good was the weather. Even your old, bearded presenter was less grumpy than normal, so the cameraman said. If fact the only person who wasn't happy with the proceedings was the lady fell runner we found fast asleep by the summit. She jumped awake. She saw the camera. She was horrified. We were going to defile her favourite, secret place. She'd never be able to have it to herself again once it had been on the telly.

I suggested, gently, that Stickle Pike was hardly a secret. Weren't those people having a picnic in the layby below us?

'But they never come up here,' says she. 'You'll encourage people who can walk.' She looked me up and down as if to suggest that I might just stumble into that category. 'Then where will we be?'

'Still on Stickle Pike,' said Terry the sound recordist, trying to be helpful.

'Precisely,' said the lady fell runner, gathering her bits and pieces and bounding away down the fell.

'But hang on a minute,' I said to the departing figure. 'It's a bit unreasonable to expect to have a whole mountain to yourself. Even a little one like Stickle Pike.'

But she'd gone and answer was there none.

For my part I hope that lots of people walk up from

Broughton Mills over Little Stickle and Great Stickle (which isn't) and Tarn Crags to the perfect, pointed, rocky summit. If they did there would be less trouble in the world. Standing on top of the Dunnerdale Fells with the mighty Caw ahead, and in the far distance Pillar and Scafell, and to the right the Coniston range, is a fine place to find perspective. Look over your shoulder to the sun sparkling on the Duddon Estuary and I defy you not to have peaceful thoughts. Look down to the little gem of Stickle Tarn, with its reflections of the sky, and even if the next person up from Broughton Mills happened to be a lady tax inspector married to a man from the VAT, you'd smile and shake her hand and say, 'Happy to be able to share my mountain with you.' It's that good.

Practical bits
Map: OL6.

Ascent and descent: Wainwright describes it as a circular walk starting and finishing in Broughton Mills (SD223906). 5¼ miles and 1700 feet of ascent. The route can be found on page 126 of *The Outlying Fells of Lakeland*.

If you have an amenable driver, a more challenging second half of the walk would be to cross the road below Stickle Tarn and walk out to Caw by way of Stainton Ground quarries and the Park Head Road. The ascent of Caw and descent to the Duddon Valley is described in *Outlying Fells*, pages 122–3. Mind you, if you do all that you'll be ready for a pint at the Newfield Inn at Seathwaite.

Stickle Pike

visiting
Great Stickle, 1001'
Tarn Hill, 1020'
Stickle Pike, 1231'
a nameless summit, 1183'
The Knott, 925'

1700 feet of ascent

from BROUGHTON MILLS

5¼ miles

5 hours

This walk may be described as "The Dunnerdale Horseshoe" (bearing in mind the note below)

from the south

Dunnerdale, to most Lakeland visitors, is the valley of the River Duddon, this being the name of the parish, but the true Dunnerdale is, geographically, a side-valley of the River Lickle two miles in length and watered by Dunnerdale Beck, quite independent of the Duddon. Nor should Stickle Pike and Stickle Tarn, referred to in this chapter, be confused with places of like name in Langdale — they are a day's march away.

The Dunnerdale Fells are low in stature, small in extent and insignificant on the map, yet they assert themselves on the local landscape in a bristly defiance of accepted mountain standards. Of course they are not worthy of comparison with Scafell or Great Gable, but they refuse to admit it. Where else in Lakeland is there so rugged a skyline? Where else, outside Skye, is there an array of peaks so crowded? Well, there is something in their claim. Here, certainly, is an upland tormented by a confusion of crags and peaked outcrops: all in miniature, amounting to nothing, really, in the general lie of the land, but with a magnetism that compels the eye and challenges the feet. Picnic parties by the lower Duddon notice the pugnacious, rather impudent beginning of the group in the sharp rocky turrets rising out of steep bracken slopes; walkers in the valley of the Lickle see their eastern aspect as a serrated skyline of abrupt upsurges and downfalls, a chaotic jumble of mini-summits.

The kingpin of this area is Stickle Pike, a mere 1231 feet above the sea yet a budding Matterhorn with many juvenile satellites.... But it is all make-believe, really, all pretence. To do the round of the ridges is actually quite simple. The aggressive appearance from below is belied on acquaintance ..... there are no dragons on these tops, no menace in their rocks. Instead there are lovely tarns where asphodel and cotton grass and bogbean colour the shallow waters, adding gaiety to the scene and scenting the air, lichened boulders bright with parsley fern, soft carpets of turf and bracken, innumerable pleasant couches where one can lie in comfort and think of real fells like Scafell and Great Gable. But do not voice these thoughts: Stickle Pike is proud and easily hurt.

Stickle Pike
from
Great Stickle

Some walks have obvious beginnings and follow so natural a line that directions are not really necessary. This one is not in that category. It is not easy to see, at Broughton Mills, how to get a footing on either of the two ridges that rise from the maze of woodlands and walled fields above the hamlet, nor at this distance to identify precisely the fells peeping over the trees. Only the Knott is clearly in view.

However, the thing to do is to get started correctly, and, over the bridge across the Lickle, a tarmac lane with a NO THROUGH ROAD sign points the way to go. There is no further guidance by signs, here or beyond. At the first farm, Green Bank, do not enter the farmyard, but take a lane uphill as far as a cottage, opposite which a thin and stony track winds up into a wood with a wall on the left. Escape at a gate from the clutches of foliage and continue ahead, passing a picnic table with a beautiful view, and bearing left into a lane, which contours the slope, rising and falling slightly, and reaches the open fell at the second of two gates, above a barn. The shapely Hovel Knott appears ahead : contour around its base, still on a path, and ascend its far slope of bracken, where walls are left behind. Bear right at the first fork, right at the second fork and left at the third fork. Little Stickle is now close on the right. At the end of a marshy area bear right to the ridge, where a detour to the right leads to the Ordnance column (S.5453) on the abrupt summit of Great Stickle. The main objective, Stickle Pike, is now in view to the north. Reach it by keeping to the indefinite ridge over the well-named Tarn Hill to the depression below the sharp rise to the Pike. After passing a fenced marsh the path heads in the wrong direction; cut across to a clear path, bearing right to avoid the bracken if necessary. Don't tackle Stickle Pike directly up its steep front but follow the clear path to a col on its east side, from which an indistinct path climbs steeply left and joins the main path to the summit, which is a fine vantage point. Having got your wind back, go down by the main path, joining a wide grass path that passes near to Stickle Tarn on its gentle descent to the top of the road now in sight ahead. (This path is obviously the tourist route to the Pike from cars parked on the verge). The road links Broughton Mills and the Duddon Valley, and provides a quick way back to the starting point (right not left) if your legs are buckling. Those who are damned if they will give in should cross the tarmac to a path going forward to the extensive Stainton Ground Quarries and ascend amongst the spoil heaps to the topmost hole. A slanting course half-right now climbs easily to the second of the walk's two ridges (and the least interesting). Go along this to the right, over point 1183' but skirting Raven's Crag to the left and descend to a depression beyond which is a simple walk to the big cairn on the Knott. Take a last look round (most of the route is visible from here), then descend due south, keeping to grass rather than bracken, and, with the farm of Knott End well to your right, reach a gate at the foot of the slope giving access to a tarmac road, which follow downhill, joining the valley road, passing the church and so returning to Broughton Mills pleased with yourself. A very good performance, considering your age.

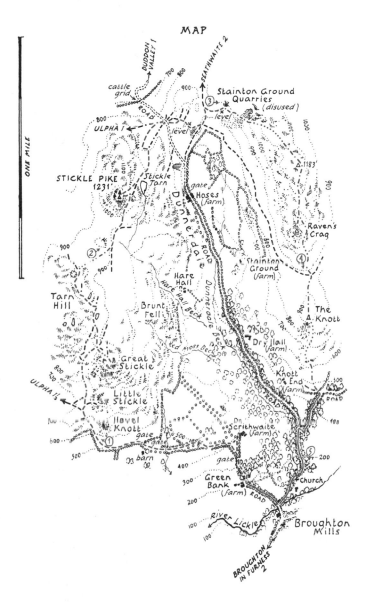

MAP

DUDDON VALLEY 1

SLATHWAITE 2

cattle grid

700 800

900

Stainton Ground
Quarries
(disused)

③

ROAD

level

level

ULPHA 1

800

level

STICKLE PIKE
1231

1000

Stickle
Tarn

gate

Hoses
(farm)

△.1183

900

1020

1000

1100

Dunnerdale ROAD

Raven's
Crag

②

900

900

Stainton
Ground
(farm)

④

900

Tarn
Hill

Hare
Hall

Hare Hall Beck

Brunt
Fell

Dunnerdale Beck

The
Knott
△

ULPHA 1½

800

900

800

Great
Stickle

Red Moss Beck

Dr Hall
(farm)

800

600

Little
Stickle

Knott
End
Farm

500

ROAD

ROAD

100

700

Hovel
Knott

①

gate

Scrithwaite
(farm)

⑤

200

600

500

barn

400

gate

300

Green
Bank
(farm)

ROAD

Church

300

200

100

100

River Lickle

Broughton
Mills

100

BROUGHTON
IN FURNESS 2

ONE MILE

Stickle Pike

Mountain summits are
especially attractive
when they are rocky,
abrupt on all sides,
small in extent and
exciting. These are
attributes in which
Stickle Pike's top
scores over those
of many a higher
and better-known
fell. It has also
the added appeal
of a shapely
cairn on a
natural
plinth:
a rock
outcrop
on the
highest
point.

A second cairn occupies the south end of the short and
undulating ridge forming the summit, but this is very
inferior to the main cairn.

The view is good within the limitations imposed by the
modest altitude. The high skyline of the Pillar, Scafell,
Bowfell and Coniston groups forms an effective horizon
to the north but much of the detail of these mountains
is obstructed by the nearer Harter Fell and Caw, which
stand like sentinels above the lovely Duddon Valley. In
other directions the scenes are mainly coastal with the
estuary and lower reaches of the Duddon, backed by a
full-length Black Combe range, intimately prominent.

Further left is a glimpse of Morecambe Bay.

Near the beginning
of the walk —
Hovel Knott

Near the end of the walk —
Cairn on The Knott,
looking to Raven's Crag and Caw

.... So this is farewell to the present series of books.

The fleeting hours of life of those who love the hills is quickly spent, but the hills are eternal. Always there will be the lonely ridge, the dancing beck, the silent forest; always there will be the exhilaration of the summits. These are for the seeking, and those who seek and find while there is yet time will be blessed both in mind and body.

I wish you all many happy days on the fells in the years ahead.

There will be fair winds and foul, days of sun and days of rain. But enjoy them all.

Good walking! And don't forget — watch where you are putting your feet.

AW.

Christmas, 1965.

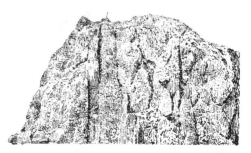

The Pictorial Guides to the Lakeland Fells
by the one and only Alfred Wainwright
are all still in print
and available from Frances Lincoln
www.franceslincoln.com
unrevised and uncut, just as A.W. wrote them.

All seven Pictorial Guides are also available as Second Editions
revised and updated by Chris Jesty (with paths and routes
shown in red, as they are on the fell pages in this anthology).
Further Second Editions are in preparation.
See www.franceslincoln.com for further details.

Watson's Dodd 3

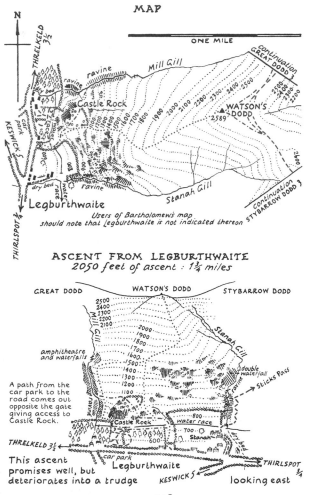

MAP

ONE MILE

N

THRELKELD 3½

KESWICK 5

THIRLSPOT ¾

ravine

Mill Gill

ravine

dry bed

Castle Rock

car park

water race

dry bed

ravine

Legburthwaite

Stanah Gill

WATSON'S DODD
▲ 2589

Continuation GREAT DODD 3

Continuation STYBARROW DODD 3

Users of Bartholomew's map
should note that Legburthwaite is not indicated thereon

ASCENT FROM LEGBURTHWAITE
2050 feet of ascent : 1¼ miles

GREAT DODD   WATSON'S DODD   STYBARROW DODD

amphitheatre
and waterfalls

Mill Gill

Stanah Gill

double
waterfall

Sticks Pass

A path from the
car park to the
road comes out
opposite the gate
giving access to
Castle Rock.

water race

Castle Rock

Stanah

THRELKELD 3½ ←

car park

This ascent
promises well, but
deteriorates into a trudge

Legburthwaite

KESWICK 5

→ THIRLSPOT ¾

looking east

338

Mardale Ill Bell 5

ASCENT FROM MARDALE
1700 feet of ascent : 2 miles from the road end

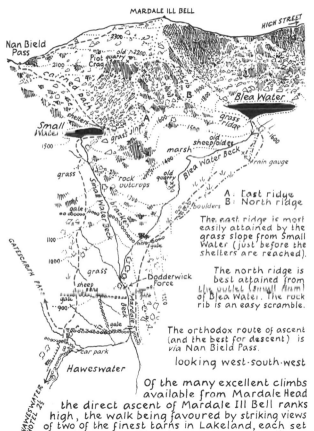

A: East ridge
B: North ridge

The east ridge is most easily attained by the grass slope from Small Water (just before the shelters are reached).

The north ridge is best attained from the outlet (small dam) of Blea Water. The rock rib is an easy scramble.

The orthodox route of ascent (and the best for descent) is via Nan Bield Pass.

looking west-south-west

Of the many excellent climbs available from Mardale Head the direct ascent of Mardale Ill Bell ranks high, the walk being favoured by striking views of two of the finest tarns in Lakeland, each set amongst crags in wild and romantic surroundings.